Inside West Nile

World Anthropology

Series Editors Wendy James & N. J. Allen

Inside West Nile

Violence, History & Representation on an African Frontier

Mark Leopold

Senior Associate Member
St Antony's College, Oxford

James Currey
OXFORD

School of American Research Press
SANTA FE

Fountain Publishers
KAMPALA

James Currey
73 Botley Road
Oxford OX2 OBS

School of American Research Press
Post Office Box 2188
Santa Fe, New Mexico 87504-2188

Fountain Publishers
P.O. Box 488
Kampala

British Library Cataloguing in Publication Data
Leopold, Mark
  Inside West Nile : violence, history & representation on an
  African frontier. - (World anthropology)
  1. West Nile District (Uganda) - History
  I. Title
  967.6'1

                          ISBN 0-85255-941-0 (James Currey cloth)
                          ISBN 0-85255-940-2 (James Currey paper)
                      ISBN 9970-02-496-5 (Fountain Publishers paper)

Library of Congress Cataloging-in-Publication Data
Leopold, Mark (Mark Anthony)
  Inside West Nile : violence, history & representation on an African frontier / Mark Leopold
    p. cm. -- (World anthropology)
  Includes bibliographical references and index.
  ISBN 1-930618-64-6 (alk. paper)
      1. Violence--Uganda--Arua District. 2. Violence--Uganda--Arua District--History. 3.
  Ethnic conflict--Uganda--Arua District. 4. Ethnic conflict--Uganda--Arua
  District--History I. Title II. World anthropology (Santa Fe, N.M.)
  HN794.Z9V57 2005
  303.6'096761--dc22   2004065382

                    ISBN 1-930618-64-6 (School of American Research Press cloth)
                    ISBN 1-930618-65-4 (School of American Research Press paper)

Typeset in 10/12 pt Monotype Photina
by Long House Publishing Services, Cumbria, UK
Printed and bound in Great Britain
by Woolnough, Irthlingborough

Contents

Illustrations

MAPS

PHOTOGRAPHS

FIGURES

Acknowledgements

The research on which this book is based was originally undertaken for my doctorate, but the present book differs somewhat from my thesis, 'The roots of violence and the reconstruction of society in North Western Uganda' (University of Oxford, Institute of Social and Cultural Anthropology, 2001). It has been considerably restructured and rewritten, with additional material and some omissions. Since the inception of the research, a number of personal, intellectual and financial obligations and debts have been built up, and I would like to acknowledge them here.

A brief preliminary visit to Arua district, Uganda, in 1995, was partially funded by the Institute's Godfrey Lienhardt Memorial Fund. The main research was funded from October 1995 to March 1999 by the UK Economic and Social Research Council under research studentship award R00429534198, and the initial writing up was supported from October 1998 to September 2000 by St Anne's College, Oxford, where I held the post of Ioma Evans-Pritchard Junior Research Fellow. I am very grateful to all these institutions, and also to my colleagues at Goldsmiths College's Department of Anthropology, for giving me enough time to finish writing this book.

My research benefited considerably from the wise, knowledgeable and supportive supervision of Professor Wendy James, and also from the encouragement and advice of Dr Tim Allen and Dr Douglas Johnson. Professor Elizabeth Colson first inspired me to study social anthropology, and Dr Paul Dresch first taught it to me, in an equally inspiring way. Other early influences on the research were Professor Terence Ranger (who tried to persuade me to become a historian), and Dr Barbara Harrell-Bond, who first introduced me to the West Nile and some West Nilers, as well as to much else.

Thanks for archival assistance are due, in the UK, to the staff of Rhodes House library and the library of the Refugee Studies Centre at Queen Elizabeth House, both in Oxford; of Cambridge University Library; and of the Public Records Office. In Uganda, thanks are due to the staff of the Uganda National Archives in Entebbe, and of the libraries of Makerere University, Makerere Institute of Social Research and the Uganda Society in Kampala. Mr Patrick Madaya and others at the Makerere Institute for Social Research and the Uganda National Council for Science and Technology facilitated my research permission, and I am particularly grateful to the authorities in Arua for tolerating my presence. In Kampala, Dr

Maryinez Lyons and Professor A.G. Gingyera-Pinycwa gave me friendly and useful advice, and the former, together with my fellow social anthropology doctoral students (now Drs) Tania Kaiser and Jo DeBerry, helped keep me more or less sane during my long wait for research clearance.

I am sad that many of the West Nilers who helped me cannot be named and thanked here, but I can mention, in Kampala, Mrs Grace Yumah and Mr Antony Uzzi for help, advice and hospitality, and, in Arua, Mr Kitami Ali Garawan and Mr Simon Vigga for occasional research assistance, the staff at the De l'Ambience hotel and the Continental Bar for looking after me, and especially Mr Nathan Droti for his patient, daily attempts to teach me Lugbara. I am very grateful to all the local historians, elders and teachers who shared their knowledge and insights with me, including Mr John Alokore, Mr Doka Ali Kujo and Mr Samson Geria, also to the officers of the Arua Council of Elders and the Lugbara Literature Association, especially Mr Nahor Oyaa Awua and Mr Jason Avutia. Above all, I owe particular thanks to Mr Lulua Odu, a thoughtful and painstaking historian of the Lugbara, and a good colleague and friend throughout my fieldwork.

There are, however, two people without whom this book would have been completely impossible. One is my wife, Dr JoAnn McGregor, with whom I have discussed every aspect of the work, from the initial conception of the research to the final manuscript of this book, and on whose intellectual, emotional and practical support I have relied throughout. The other is the late Mr Justin Vusi Koma of Dufile, whom I first met in Oxford and who went on to introduce me to Arua life and to the initial contacts so vital to the fieldworker. With refugee status in the UK, a degree and professional accountancy qualifications, he nevertheless chose to work for a local NGO in Arua town (where he also helped form a Madi Cultural Association). He sustained my fieldwork with ideas, conversation and good company on many occasions, and his unselfish and unsectarian devotion to the West Nile and its people remains an inspiration. Sadly, shortly after I left the district in 1998, he died of cancer. This book is dedicated to his memory.

Acronyms & Abbreviations

ADC	Assistant District Commissioner
ADFL(C-Z)	Allied Democratic Front for the Liberation of Congo-Zaïre
BAT	British–American Tobacco Co.
CAO	Chief Administrative Officer
CAP	Community Action Programme
CPSAD	Committee for Peace and Stability in Arua District
CSM	Cerebro-spinal meningitis
DCWN	District Commissioner, West Nile
DISO	District Internal Security Officer
ESRC	(UK) Economic and Social Research Council
FAO	(UN) Food and Agriculture Organisation
FUNA	Former Ugandan National Army
HSM	Holy Spirit Movement
IBEAC	Imperial British East Africa Company
JMAS	*Journal of Modern African Studies*
JRAI	*Journal of the Royal Anthropological Institute*
KAR	King's African Rifles
LC (1–5)	Local Council (formerly RC – Resistance Council), Levels 1 (Parish) to 5 (District)
LRA	Lord's Resistance Army
LULA	Lugbara Literature Association
LWF	Lutheran World Federation
MISR	Makerere University Institute of Social Research
MSF	Médecins Sans Frontières
NRA/M	National Resistance Army/Movement
PCNP	Provincial Commissioner, Northern Province
PRO	(UK) Public Records Office
RDC	Resident District Commissioner
RH	Rhodes House Library (University of Oxford
RSC	Refugee Studies Centre (University of Oxford)
SIR	Sudan Intelligence Reports
SNV	Dutch government assistance organisation
SPLA/M	Sudan Peoples' Liberation Army/Movement
UA	Ugandan Army
UNA	Uganda National Archives

UNHCR	Office of the United Nations High Commissioner for Refugees
UNLA	Uganda National Liberation Army
UNRF II	Uganda National Rescue Front Part Two
UPC	Uganda Peoples' Congress
UPDF	Uganda Peoples' Defence Forces
USAID	United States Agency for International Development
WEP	Women's Empowerment Programme
WNBF	West Nile Bank Front

1

'Why are we Cursed?'
An introduction

Many of us sons and daughters of West Nile, who have seen terrible things happen to them or their relatives and friends, often ask ourselves quietly, 'Why are we cursed?' or 'What have we done to deserve this?' It is often our easy way out to avoid self assessment and self-criticism, and sometimes hide our ignorance about the evil things that we Ugandans, and for that matter we the West Nilers, are capable of doing to each other. (Report of the Committee for Peace and Stability in Arua District, 1995)

The area of Uganda to the west of the River Nile, as it rises from Lake Albert and heads north towards Sudan, was known for most of the twentieth century as West Nile district. Today the largest part of it is a district named after its major town, Arua (see Map 1.1 for the district boundaries in the late 1990s), on Uganda's borders with Sudan and the Democratic Republic of Congo (formerly Zaïre). In the twenty-first century, for most people outside Uganda, West Nile means a sometimes lethal disease, West Nile Fever, first discovered in the district. But in the past this area has been renowned for other reasons; most recently as the home district of Uganda's notorious dictator, Idi Amin.

In 1995, a group of five eminent local men (a couple of former senior army officers, a retired senior civil servant, a local businessman and a prominent politician), who were concerned about the security situation in the area, formed themselves into a Committee for Peace and Stability in Arua District (CPSAD) and produced a report, which was sent to the President of Uganda, Yoweri K. Museveni. After a brief introduction, the report begins with a section headed 'Historical background', which is quoted at the head of this chapter. It sketches the colonial and postcolonial history of the district, from the Berlin Conference of 1884–5 to the seizure of national power, on 25 January 1971, by the district's most famous, or infamous, son, General Idi Amin Dada. 'Since that day', the report states:

[T]he history and image of West Nile have been read and seen upside down by everybody, Ugandan and non-Ugandan alike. The rest of Uganda has convinced the entire world of this negative imagery.... [R]ecognition is continually denied to the region. Bad blood and victimisation is the only notable reward. Reducing West Nilers to perpetually think with their feet since 1980, running up and down for their lives.... It would therefore appear to us that the roots of our lack of 'Peace and Stability', hence the lack of sustainable development in West Nile until now, must be looked at in the light of the foregoing [history].[1]

---

[1] Report of the Committee for Peace and Stability in Arua District, unpublished document in the possession of the author.

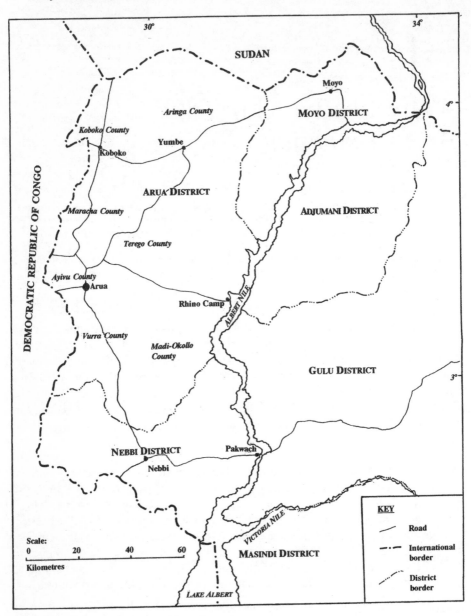

Map 1.1 Arua & neighbouring districts in 1998

It is unsurprising that the people of Arua wanted to dissociate themselves from Amin's discredited regime. But in fact the 'negative image' of the district, as a marginal place populated by inherently violent people, long predated the former dictator. It began before British colonial rule, or even that of its Belgian and Ottoman predecessors. For a century and a half, Arua (formerly West Nile, formerly the Lado Enclave, formerly southern Equatoria) has been a liminal frontier zone, a border area in much more than the purely politico-juridical sense, and its people continue to experience the violent and marginalised history that has characterised their experience since they first encountered outsiders from a radically different culture, in the form of Arab slave raiders in the mid-nineteenth century.

The politics of beginning

At the start of his second book, *Beginnings* (1997 [1975]), Edward Said cites the eighteenth-century Italian philosopher Giambattista Vico's axiom, that 'doctrines must take their beginning from that of the matters of which they treat' (Vico 1984: 92). For Vico, as another of his twentieth-century admirers, the philosopher R.G. Collingwood, put it, history 'is not concerned with the past as past. It is concerned, in the first instance, with the actual structure of the society in which we live; the manners and customs which we share with the people around us' (Collingwood 1993 [1946]: 66). In this spirit, I begin, conventionally enough for an anthropologist, with my arrival for the first time in Arua town, in September 1995, a month or so after the report of the CPSAD was sent to President Museveni. But my 'arrival narrative' does not quite fit the conventional anthropological model, caricatured by James as 'the scholar virgin's first encounters' (2000: 89). Although I was just beginning my doctoral research, I was in my late thirties and had some prior experience of fieldwork, albeit non-anthropological, in refugee camps in the Middle East and Southern Africa. I had also known some people from Arua district for several years and, before getting to Arua, I had spent three weeks in the Ugandan capital, Kampala, staying with a family from the town of Koboko in the north west of the district (see Map 1.1).

In Kampala, I learned that close human networks linked Arua with the capital. Packed buses made the ten-hour journey two or three times per week, and a small shop near Kampala's long-distance bus station acted as an information exchange and meeting place for people from my hosts' home area. People moved to and fro for a variety of reasons, usually to trade or for family occasions. Traditional authority structures were, to an extent, transferred to the capital; on one occasion while I was there, a group of elders from Koboko came to the city to deal with the circumstances that had led to the suicide there of a young man from the district. But, although my hosts thus kept in touch with events in Koboko, like most of the other West Nilers I met in Kampala, they seemed afraid to go back to the district.

After making the bus trip to Arua myself, I realised that very close links also existed between the town and its rural hinterland, including cross-border connections into Sudan and Zaïre. But much wider networks also operated. Back in Britain I had been introduced to a man from the district who had, like most of the population, become a refugee after Amin's overthrow in 1980. As a youth, he had been 'resettled' in Canada and, when I met him, he was working with Canadian peace-keeping forces in the former Yugoslavia, monitoring sanctions against Serbia. He gave me a business card for his private import-export business, with postal addresses in Toronto, Arua and Belgrade. This is not wholly unrepresentative of the links that tie this apparently obscure and marginal part of central Africa into the wider world. There is a sense in which small towns can be more 'cosmopolitan' than big cities; in the latter, sheer size allows social groups to separate out, whereas in the former they may have to mix to a far greater extent. Arua town struck me from the start as a very cosmopolitan place (Chapter Two considers the town in more detail).

When I first arrived in Arua, though, my overwhelming visual impression seemed a highly inappropriate one for an anthropologist, but in fact represented something true about both the place itself, and European perceptions of it (two things which will, in the course of this book, become increasingly intertwined). It all looked strangely familiar: the sun, the dust, the low verandahed buildings lining the wide main street, the men standing around with guns, or bows and arrows ... surely this was the Wild West of a thousand cowboy movies from my childhood? This superficial reaction quickly faded, but a sense of incongruity about my presence and position remained. My first trip was a brief, unofficial, visit and I did no formal research. I was, however, somewhat frightened to be told by a number of people about a previous graduate student doing research in the area, a Canadian agronomist, who had been shot dead in mysterious circumstances two years earlier. Some hinted at a political motive for the killing, others suggested that he had become involved with gold smugglers, or some other form of the 'informal economic activity' rife in the district. In either case, it was clearly a warning to be careful of something, though I was never quite sure what it was.

Another initial impression, which was vastly reinforced by my later work, was the power of the international aid agencies and NGOs, most of which were concerned with the large numbers of Sudanese refugees in the district, rather than with the West Nilers themselves. But their influence extended far beyond their intended beneficiaries; they funded major local government projects and determined much of the local economy, and their senior staff were obviously and visibly better paid, dressed, equipped and housed than virtually anyone else in the district (they were also among the very few people with cars – invariably new white Landcruisers). In Arua town, they tended to live in the area formerly inhabited by colonial officers. On my first brief visit, a somewhat cynical local man who had worked for international NGOs for several years told me the district had only two cash crops: tobacco and refugees.[2]

My initial impressions of Arua, then, were the characteristic ones of violence and marginality. Today, the frontier status of West Nile derives from its position on international boundaries. The area is bordered to the west by the watershed of

---

[2] Chapter Two explores these issues in greater detail, see also Leopold (2001).

the Nile and Congo rivers, which forms the international frontier with Congo/ Zaïre. The northern boundary of the district is the Sudan border. But long before colonial powers defined the borders, this small area (around a hundred miles long by fifty wide) was successively in an ethnolinguistic 'frontier zone' (Kopytoff 1989 [1987]),[3] in a marginal 'tribal zone' at the edge of expanding states (Ferguson and Whitehead 2000 [1992]), and in the 'contact zone' (Pratt 1992) in relation to incursions from more powerful groups of people with very different cultures (Europeans and Arabs). Most Ugandan districts are defined on ethnic lines, with one or two dominant 'tribes' (the term is still widely used in Uganda), but the former West Nile was, and Arua is, home to people from several different ethnic groups. As the CPSAD Report quoted at the head of this chapter puts it, the district 'stands out as a multi-national region... carved through an accident of history and geography, yet representing a living evidence of ethnic coexistence through diversity'.[4]

The largest ethnic group, as conventionally defined, is the Lugbara people; others recognised in Uganda's 1995 Constitution[5] are the Alur, principally in today's Nebbi district, the Madi in Moyo district (and Adjumani across the river), the Kakwa in the north-west of Arua district, the Jonam between the Alur and the Lugbara, and smaller groups of Lendu and Kuku people by the Congo and Sudan borders (see Map 1.1). These names represent supposedly discrete languages which, in traditional anthropological linguistics, fall into two families; the Sudanic group (which includes Lugbara and Madi) and the Nilotic group (including Alur, Jonam and Kakwa). More recent ('post-Greenbergian') linguistics classifies all these groups as part of the same 'phylum', termed the Nilo-Saharan languages.[6] In practice, the boundaries between the various West Nile languages are fluid, vague or non-existent, while many, probably most, people are multi-lingual (see below; also Allen 1994). Moreover, within Arua town especially, but also elsewhere in the district, live people from many other backgrounds: other Ugandans, refugees and traders from neighbouring countries and a wider international community were all part of the society I encountered in 1995.

All the ethnic categories associated with local languages could reasonably be placed in scare quotes, and the ethnogenesis, de facto flexibility and linguistic complexity that lie behind such apparently discrete groups will be discussed at various points in this book. Here it is important to emphasise that local people share a common history and, notwithstanding linguistic distinctions, are part of a regional culture zone, which extends deep into southern Sudan and north-east Congo. Unlike the Bantu language-speaking kingdoms of southern Uganda, the traditional social units throughout this region were small-scale, kinship-based 'segmentary' societies, of the kind represented for generations of social anthro-

---

[3] See also D.H. Johnson (2002 [1986]) on 'the Nilotic frontier', and other contributors to D. Donham and W. James (eds) (2002 [1986]).

[4] Report of the CPSAD.

[5] Article 10a of the 1995 Constitution of the Republic of Uganda defines Ugandan citizenship in terms of (i) birth in Uganda and (ii) parental or grandparental membership of 'any of the indigenous communities existing and residing within the borders of Uganda as at the first day of February 1926 and set out in the Third Schedule to this Constitution'. The colonial-era list in the schedule names fifty-six 'indigenous communities'.

pologists by the work of E.E. Evans-Pritchard on the Sudanese Nuer (especially his earlier work on the subject, 1940).

I returned to Arua in September 1996 to begin my substantive research. After several months waiting in Kampala for research permission, I was at last properly equipped, with an affiliation to Makerere University's Institute of Social Research (MISR) and an official government Research Pass, approved by the Ugandan security services, with my photograph and the title of my project, 'The roots of violence and the reconstruction of society in North Western Uganda'. After a couple of weeks, I was beginning to settle in and meet people, when a senior local government/military officer, the District Internal Security Officer (DISO), himself a West Niler, came up to me in a bar, grinning broadly, 'I've just had instructions from Kampala about you,' he said. 'They say I have to give you every assistance. They don't understand the violence here, and they think you're going to explain it to them.' This had not occurred to me as one of my aims, nor did I find it as amusing as the DISO did. It was an early reminder, had I needed one, of the political dimensions of the research.

Beginnings also, as Said stressed, have political as well as intellectual implications. Any account of the violent history of Arua/West Nile district runs the risk of being teleologically determined by its choice of starting-point. Begin in the postcolonial era, and the account will be dominated by the hulking figure of Idi Amin. However, Amin was at least as much a creation of West Nile's past as he was a shaper of its future. If one begins with the colonial era, then both Amin's rule and the subsequent misfortunes of the district appear to be the product of systematic colonial underdevelopment combined with British imperial fantasies about inherently 'martial races', and there is some truth in this picture. But it, too, was determined, perhaps over-determined, by an earlier period, which in fact lasted rather longer than effective colonial rule. From around the middle of the nineteenth century to its incorporation into the Uganda Protectorate in 1914, the area saw incursions by successive groups of Arab slave-traders, remnants of the Egyptian army escaping from the Mahdi's rebellion in Sudan, the forces of King Leopold's notorious Congo Free State and European ivory hunters. All contributed to the image of the area as a Conradian 'heart of darkness'. However, any historical account which seeks to begin any earlier than this, 'before contact', faces not only the problem of a lack of hard evidence, but also the risk of implying that something innate in the society or culture of the local 'tribes' produces an ineluctable violence.[7]

In these circumstances, the narrative structure of a chronological account contains its own agenda; as Hayden White put it, 'narrativizing discourse serves

---

[6] The classical linguistic/anthropological accounts of these distinctions are in Nalder (1937), Tucker (1940), Crazzolara (1950–54, 1960), Huntingford (1953) and Baxter and Butt (1953). The earliest versions, based on the notorious 'Hamitic hypothesis', further distinguish between 'true Nilotes' such as the Alur and other Luo speakers, and 'Nilo-Hamitic' peoples, including the Kakwa (these distinctions are also maintained in popular Ugandan accounts, such as Nzita and Mbaga-Niwampa 1995). The recent linguistic debates are summarised in Bender (2000); some of the historical implications are explored in Ehret (1998).

[7] All these historical explanations, especially the latter, occur in (amongst other places) Ugandan media accounts of West Nile in the 1990s. See Leopold (1999).

the purpose of moralizing judgements' (White 1987 [1980]: 24). In the case of West Nile history, the legacy of the past is inevitably traced to the point of departure of the account, while the language of violence attached to the district has functioned as a performative rather than a purely descriptive language, in J.L. Austin's sense that 'if a person is making an utterance of this sort we should say that he is *doing* rather than merely *saying* something' (1970: 235). A comparable (if in many ways dissimilar) process can be found in Lisa Malkki's account of the 'mythico-history' of Hutu refugees, in which their historical narratives serve to reinscribe and reinforce the structures of violence between Hutu and Tutsi in Rwanda and Burundi. She compares the process with Bible morality tales, 'stories which classify the world according to certain principles, thereby simultaneously creating it' (Malkki 1995: 54). This is a process as well known in vernacular English as in academic discourse, in the form of the popular idea of the 'self-fulfilling prophecy', and of phrases such as 'give a dog a bad name' or 'throw enough mud and it will stick'. Successive outside powers, as they exerted themselves in the district, always already 'knew' the local reputation for violence and responded accordingly.[8]

History, anthropology & representation

In this context, I have taken the unusual step of writing the historical chapters of this book 'backwards', in a series of 'layers' or temporal strata, from the present day[9] into the distant past. Despite all the recent interest among anthropologists, historians and others in the relationship between violence, history (or memory) and modes of representation or narrative form,[10] there has been little attempt to actually experiment with new narrative forms, rather than simply theorising about them. Having attempted to 'write history backwards', I can see why. Writing about Laurence Sterne's *Tristram Shandy* (a novel I read during field-work), Horace Walpole noted that 'the whole narration [was] always going backwards', and added, 'I can conceive of a man saying it would be droll to write a book in that manner but have no notion of his persevering in executing it.'[11] As David Hume argued, conjunction implies causation; remove the causal implications by moving backwards through time, and it is very difficult to avoid narrative incoherence, causing problems for both writer and reader.

The advantage of moving backwards, however (which is both intellectual and political or ethical), is precisely to disrupt the causal implications, in order to throw into question the repetitive association of the people of West Nile with

---

[8] Cf. the reputation of the Nuer (Johnson 1981, 1994).

[9] To be precise, from the standpoint of an 'ethnographic present', which refers to the late 1990s.

[10] The interest in narrative can probably be traced in history to White's work (e.g. 1987) and in anthropology to the influence of Clifford and Marcus (1986).

[11] Quoted by literary critic Carol Watts, in the *Guardian Saturday Review*, 23 August 2003, p. 28. More recent fictional reversals of chronology include Harold Pinter's play *Betrayal* (1978) and Martin Amis's novel *Time's Arrow* (1991), which used the device of backwards narration to explore the nature of the Nazi Holocaust. Amis's approach to writing reverse chronology is very close to that of J.G. Ballard's (much earlier) short story 'Time of Passage', first published in *Science Fantasy* magazine in 1964 (reprinted in his *Complete Short Stories*, 2001).

violence and the consequent implication that they are the source of their own marginality and misfortunes. Whether or not the approach of backwards narration entirely succeeds in avoiding the teleological pull which traces the violence and marginality of the area to a predetermined origin, it does have the advantage of allowing history and anthropology to question and criticise each other in what I hope are fruitful ways (just as, in the course of the research, fieldwork and archival work, each affected my understanding of the other).

In adopting this structure, I was in part thinking of Lévi-Strauss's famous passage in *Tristes Tropiques* in which he speaks of geology (along with Marxism and psychoanalysis) as an inspiration for his anthropology, and of Foucault's notion of 'archaeologies' of knowledge. Like archaeological and geological strata, the historical 'layers' I isolate each contain traces from earlier periods and leave their own traces in the later temporal strata, (including those encapsulated in the present). Another idea in the back of my mind was the approach to time adopted in psychoanalytic techniques, where the present is confronted (perhaps sometimes even 'explained') by events that happened in the past (especially in childhood), while the analysand's past is reinterpreted in terms of present unhappiness. One of the techniques of the analyst is to shift the topic of discussion between past and present, in a way that aims to uncover repressed memories or projected fantasies, and to understand silences as well as speech, all of which became relevant to my research.

However, the main inspiration for this reverse-chronological approach lies in the work of R.G. Collingwood, for whom history begins, inevitably, with questions asked from the standpoint of the present. These form the evidence that can allow the 're-enactment' of the past by the historian (Collingwood 1993 [1946]: 231–334). We can only understand the past through encountering traces of it 'incapsulated' in the present day (Collingwood 1970 [1939]: 140). In an interesting conjunction in the history of ideas, the anthropologist of the Lugbara people of West Nile, John Middleton, under the influence of his supervisor, Evans-Pritchard, read Collingwood's *The Idea of History* at the end of his fieldwork, while trying to understand Lugbara ritual (Middleton 1970a: 3). Although Evans-Pritchard himself may fairly be said never to have put his ideas about the relationship between history and anthropology fully into practice in his ethnographic writing,[12] he foreshadowed the reverse-chronological approach in his famous 1961 lecture on anthropology and history, where he wrote that the two disciplines have:

> [A] difference of orientation, due largely to the emphasis we [social anthropologists] place on fieldwork as part of our training. Historians write history, as it were, forwards and we would tend to write it backwards. The historian of the British Parliament ... begins with the Witenagemot or thereabouts and then traces its development to the present day.... In doing this he might not feel the need to go near Westminster, and he might even feel that it would be a disadvantage to do so.... We, on the other hand, would be inclined to proceed in the reverse direction, to make a study of Parliament today... and then in the light of what we have learnt about the present to interpret phases of its development in the past. (Evans-Pritchard 1962: 60)

[12] But see James's introduction to Evans-Pritchard (1990 [1951]), where 'descent' is cast as a mode of historical understanding.

There are other precedents, too. W.N. Fenton, an 'ethnohistorian' of Native Americans in the 1950s and 1960s, developed a technique he called 'upstreaming': '[T]he method utilizes patterns of culture existing in the living culture for reinterpreting the earlier sources, and proceeds by linking these to earlier patterns in a direct sequence, but against the tide of history, going from the known present to the unknown past' (Fenton 1962: 12). In the present context, 'upstreaming' has another connotation: it is a commonplace of North-East African studies that persisting racial stereotypes show 'tribes' becoming more 'primitive' as one moves up the River Nile from the Mediterranean, through Egypt and Sudan, towards its sources (see, for example, O'Fahey 2002: 56; cf. Leopold 2003). In Uganda itself, however, the geographical trajectory of the stereotype is reversed, with northerners (whether West Nilers, the Acholi people of the central north or the Karamojong of the north-east) being seen as culturally 'backward' in relation to the Bantu-speaking southerners (Gingyera-Pinycwa 1989, 1992; Leopold 1999). Either way, the peoples of the Uganda/Sudan border areas become seen as the epitome of 'primitiveness'.

The present book, after this introductory chapter, continues with an ethnographic account of Arua town during the period of my fieldwork in the late 1990s (Chapter Two). Chapter Three uncovers the first historical layer; the postcolonial period (1995–1962), when the fate of West Nile was so closely linked with that of Idi Amin. Successive chapters, four to six, then proceed, using different kinds of sources, to discuss the marginalisation of the district under colonial rule (1961–1925), the initial establishment of British rule under the Uganda Protectorate (1924–1914) and the period before the area's incorporation into Uganda but after the first incursions by outsiders with radically different technologies and cultures (1913–c. 1850). In Chapter Seven, I consider West Nile's 'pre-contact' societies, before returning to the (ethnographic) present to focus on local accounts of, and responses to, the burden of this history. Chapter Eight is an afterword, which revisits the fundamental questions of violence, history and representation raised in this introduction, in the light of the analysis in the intervening chapters. The segmentation of the historical 'layers' is for narrative convenience rather than to affirm any intellectually necessary or useful separation between the selected 'periods'. On the contrary, in discussing each 'layer', i.e. in writing each chapter, I point to themes that have echoes in both chronologically earlier and later periods, focusing in particular on those past events which have left traces in the present, which may help in understanding the situation the people of Arua found themselves in at the end of the twentieth century.

Violence & history

Turning from the modes of historical representation adopted in the present book to those deployed by West Nilers and other Ugandans, it is clear that the problematic picture of the West Nile past presented by conventional histories was very much an issue for local people themselves at the time of my fieldwork.

Several of them, all relatively educated male elders,[13] wrote histories in the attempt to explain themselves to both outsiders and other West Nilers. My work, and this book, would not have been the same without the writings of, and conversations with, these men, many of whom were associated with the Lugbara Literature Association (LULA), a local cultural association discussed in Chapter Seven. They included Mr Nahor Oyaa Awua, a retired senior local government officer who is Coordinator of LULA; Mr Lulua Odu, lawyer and author of *A Short History of the Lugbara (Madi)*, a school textbook published by LULA; Mr Samson Geria, Principal of Arua Teacher Training College and author of a 1973 Makerere University undergraduate dissertation entitled 'A traditional history of the Northwestern Lugbara of Uganda'; and Mr Doka Ali Kujo, former District Education Officer, who wrote an unpublished history of 'The coming of Islam in Uganda'.

According to all accounts, the first contacts between the people of what was to become West Nile and outsiders from a radically different culture came in the form of raiding by Arab slavers from (Turco-Egyptian) Sudan, around the middle of the nineteenth century. Children and adults were either taken off to the north to join the slave armies or be sold on, or they were ransomed for ivory. The first Europeans to reach the area came in with the slavers after 1860, and in the late 1880s the area came dramatically to the notice of the European imperial metropolises, due to the presence of a German Muslim convert known as Emin Pasha, who in 1888 was 'rescued' from the area by Henry Morton Stanley, in what was perhaps one of the first international media events. Thanks to Emin, as a later European participant in the area's history put it, 'this little territory has perhaps passed through more vicissitudes and has at one time had more interest centred around it, than any part of central Africa' (Stigand 1923: 4).

Emin's legacy was both material and ideological; he left behind him an enduring place for the region in European fantasies of Africa, and he also left a considerable number of troops, former slave-soldiers who settled in the area forming the core of what became a new 'ethnic' category, the 'Nubis' or 'Nubians', whose numbers later included Emin's namesake,[14] Idi Amin himself. It was Emin's troops, believed by the British to be 'the best material for soldiery in Africa' (Moyse-Bartlett 1956: 50), who were used by Captain Frederick Lugard of the Imperial British East Africa Company to enable the Buganda kingdom to overcome the neighbouring polities and form what in 1900 became the Uganda Protectorate. The 'Nubis' were supposedly their descendants, but under colonial rule 'Nubian' identity became open to a variety of local people who converted to Islam, took up a military career and spoke 'KiNubi', a variety of trade Arabic.

At the beginning of the twentieth century, the future West Nile was simply the southern part of 'the Lado Enclave' (named after the town of Lado in southern Sudan), an anomalous region that changed imperial hands three times between 1894 and 1914 (see Map 1.2). At the beginning of this period, it was recognised

---

[13] Female education in the district has always been poor. See Chapter Two.
[14] 'Emin' is the Turkish version, and 'Amin' a transliteration of the Arabic form, of a fairly widespread Muslim name meaning 'Faithful'. Those who considered themselves 'Nubi' quite often named their children after their leaders of the 1880s. 'Pasha' was an Ottoman military/diplomatic rank.

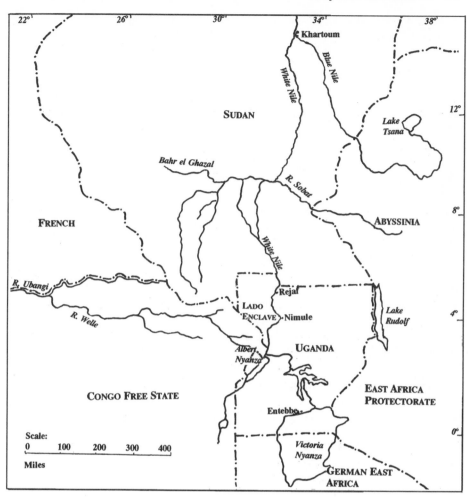

Map 1.2 The Lado Enclave in relation to surrounding countries, *c.* 1909 (based on Stigand 1923)

as the personal property of King Leopold of the Belgians and administered as part of the Congo Free State; this was a time which left particularly bitter memories among some of the people I spoke to. A complex deal in the European scramble for Africa ensured that, on Leopold's death, the Enclave would come under British control as part of the Sudan condominium, and Belgian interest in the place accordingly faded over the first decade of the twentieth century. The Lado became a playground, and a killing ground, for white adventurers, the last place in Africa in which unrestricted, unregulated elephant hunting was possible.

Leopold died in late 1909, and a few months later the Lado Enclave was duly transferred to the Anglo-Egyptian condominium of Sudan, as part of its southernmost province, Mongalla. The Congo–Sudan border in this section was defined as the watershed of the rivers Nile and Congo. Four years later, just before the outbreak of the First World War, the southern tip of the Enclave was transferred to the Protectorate of Uganda in a territorial swap between these neighbouring components of the British Empire. This complex imperial history explains why the area appears in the *Cambridge History of Africa* as part of Western Equatorial Africa in volume six (Oliver and Sanderson 1985) and as part of East Africa in volume seven (Roberts 1986). Its brief period as part of North Africa goes unmentioned.

Under the Uganda Protectorate, once effective colonial rule was established in West Nile (an occasionally violent process which took several years and in which the Nubi played a central role), the district was used as a labour reserve, gazetted as a 'closed area' from which outsiders were excluded and systematically under-developed in favour of the cash-crop agriculture of southern Uganda. The British established the definitions and boundaries of the varied 'tribes' of the district: primarily the Alur in the south, the Kakwa in the north-west, the Madi on both sides of the river, and the Lugbara in the centre and west (all these groups also existed over the international borders). Many local people worked in the southern plantations, others joined the army, as Idi Amin did, or took up other coercive trades of the state, as police officers, prison warders or informers. The very marginality of the district was attractive to social anthropologists of the postwar British school and, in the 1950s and 1960s, John Middleton and Aidan Southall produced classic ethnographies in different parts of the district. Independence at first changed little or nothing for local people, and even under Amin's rule the district remained poor and lacking in basic infrastructure. After his overthrow by the Tanzanian army in 1979, the 'liberation' forces and successive Ugandan regimes (notably the second Obote government) devastated West Nile, and most of the population was forced over the international borders into Sudan and Zaire in the first half of the 1980s. Once again they became the subjects of Western anthropological knowledge, being studied as refugees (notably by Barbara Harrell-Bond) and as returnees (notably by Tim Allen).[15]

From the mid-1980s, and especially after the victory of Yoweri Museveni's National Resistance Army in 1986, most of the remaining West Nile refugees returned to the district, but sporadic conflict continued between the Ugandan army and rebel groups led by former associates of Amin, while the economic, social and political marginality of Arua has persisted, as has the violent reputation of its people. During the period of my research, as the struggle between Ugandan government forces and local rebel groups flowed into, and combined with, civil wars in Sudan and Zaïre, the fragility and permeability of the international borders increased considerably, and the efforts of local people to reinvent and rebuild the society they had lost with exile in the 1980s, and to redefine their relationship with the rest of Uganda, were impeded and frustrated by transnational forces and events well beyond their control.

---

[15] Relevant works by Middleton, Southall, Harrell-Bond and Allen are listed in the bibliography.

Images & histories

This skeletal account of the political history of an apparently obscure part of central Africa (which will be fleshed out later) can only hint at the interplay between 'image' and 'history', to use the terms of the CPSAD, in the construction of a space of violence and of marginality, cultural, political and economic. Unfortunately, people have had to live in this space. This book explores some of the answers to the CPSAD's question 'Why are we cursed?', by tracing the interrelationships between discourse and reality, and between past and present, in creating the conditions in which the people of Arua found themselves towards the end of the twentieth century. The ways in which the district has been imagined by more powerful and wealthy people from elsewhere (both Europeans and other Africans) have had concrete, material effects on local people's lives and livelihoods. Trying to understand their history therefore entails an understanding of their 'image', that is, the discourse of West Nile as it was elaborated over time by such hegemonic outsiders.

Looked at in this way, the history sketched above, far from being obscure, links two of the most influential negative images of Africa in contemporary Western culture. It was probably the story of Emin Pasha's enclave, surrounded by hostile African forces, which inspired Joseph Conrad to begin writing his *Heart of Darkness* (according, for example, to Lindqvist 1997 [1992]: 43). It was also Emin's material legacy, in the form of his troops who founded the ethno-religious occupational group known as the Nubi, which produced the phenomenon of Idi Amin, perhaps the pre-eminent modern exemplar of Africa as a heart of darkness (the only living person, for example, to appear in the 2002 UK Channel Five TV series 'The Most Evil Men and Women in History'; see Chapter Three). The images of inherent violence and marginality conjured up both by Amin and by Conrad's book are intimately linked with the history of West Nile, both as causes and as effects; however, the processes involved in this also tell us a good deal about Euro-pean domination in its material and ideological, colonial and postcolonial forms.

It is all too easy to create a false opposition between 'discourse theory' and 'real history'. In West Nile, the image and the reality have had an intimate (once, one might have said dialectical) relationship. The reality of the violence and marginality that have characterised the history of the district is intricately bound up with the discourse of marginality and violence attached to the area by outsiders whose power to influence the world with their performative utterances was much greater than that of local people. The discourse of West Nile violence, as we shall see, involves not only Lugard, Conrad and the vast literature on Amin, but also such influential contributors as Theodore Roosevelt and Carl Gustav Jung.

Anthropologists, too, have contributed to the image. As early as 1911 and as far away as Paris, Arnold van Gennep used the region as an exemplar of primitiveness and violence in his satire on contemporary anthropology, *Les Demi-Savants*. His spoof ethnographer, Désiré Pépin, is sent to, 'the Enclave of Lado, which belonged to neither France nor to Belgium, and the inhabitants of which were content to be natural Negroes, civilised according to their notions, not yet according to ours' (van Gennep 1967 [1911]: 28). Frustrated by the natives' lack of cooperation, 'Désiré Pépin was seized with rage, a stick was in reach and with this he delivered some sound blows. The Negroes fled, and did not reappear for some days' (ibid.: 31). Eventually, he comes to a deal with the 'Negroes' and supplies them with 'several gifts' in return for which they answer his question-naires. Returning to Paris, he wins prizes and eventually becomes 'the renovator in France of scientific ethnography' (ibid.). More recently, and in a more serious vein, John Middleton was open in describing the motivations behind his own choice of the Lugbara as his ethnographic subject, primarily in terms of margin-ality and an association with violence:

> I chose the Lugbara mainly for the simple reason that no anthropologist had ever worked among them and I was romantic enough to want to find a relatively 'untouched' society.... The Lugbara live in a remote part of Uganda, a country that I had visited during the war and which held a great fascination for me.... In addition, I knew that the Lugbara actually existed because I had met Lugbara troops during the war in various parts of East Africa and the islands. But other than their being tall, very dark skinned and apparently both cheerful and somewhat easily quarrelsome people, I knew nothing about them. (Middleton 1970a: 2–3)

For Harrell-Bond and Allen in the 1980s, it was the effects of war and displacement that drew them to research on West Nile people, and my own initial focus was also the aftermath of conflict and exile. In West Nile, it seems, the story has always been one of violence and marginality.

Moreover, this story, the historical 'curse', has repeated themes, which have recurred over long stretches of time. But they do not precisely repeat themselves: this is not a case of the 'myth of the eternal return' which Eliade (1955) saw as characteristic of 'traditional' societies' notions of the past. As Collingwood says of Vico's 'cyclical' view of history, 'it is not a circle but a spiral; for history never repeats itself, but comes round to each new phase in a form differentiated by what has gone before' (1993 [1946]: 68). The raids by rebel groups during the period of my fieldwork had many similarities with much earlier patterns of raiding – armed Muslim groups coming from the north, abducting children as recruits, servants or 'wives'; despite many differences (particularly the fact that the events of the 1990s occurred in the context of inter-state and intra-state conflict), this was a pattern familiar to local people from oral traditions of the mid-nineteenth-century slave raiders (see Chapter Six).

A striking visual image of violence inscribed on the body dates from the same period, and was also to be repeated in different forms in a Vicovian historical 'spiral'. Some of the nineteenth-century slavers had engraved the mark of three parallel lines on the cheeks of their captives as an identification sign. As the descendants of the slave armies formed the basis of the British colonial army in the region, the markings came to denote 'Nubi' identity. When the Uganda Protectorate took over West Nile, Nubian officers were used to impose British administration and taxation, and came to dominate long-distance trading and much of urban life. The three facial marks, as a colonial officer noted in 1925, were increasingly adopted by the Lugbara (and other local groups), and were said to 'convey some social distinction'[16] amongst them. As West Nilers became

[16] R.E. McConnell, 1925: 447.

disproportionately involved in the colonial armed forces over the twentieth century, 'Nubi' identity provided an elective, strategic, potential alternative ethnicity for many of them, and this was the background from which Idi Amin sprang. During the Amin era, Ugandans referred to his Nubian supporters as 'the One-Elevens', because so many of them had the three vertical lines scarred on their cheeks as a token of loyalty to the regime. Even Amin's British assistant, 'Major' Bob Astles, had the marks scored on his face as a sign of his devotion to the President.[17] The One-Eleven facial markings and their evolving meanings crystallise in a single image the complex legacy of the past in West Nile. On the one hand, they can be seen as a 'floating signifier' with no fixed meaning, connoting different things at different times; on the other hand, the association with violence (precolonial, colonial, postcolonial) is always, seemingly inevitably, there in the foreground of the significance of the marks.

The notion of history repeating itself may also fit with some local idioms used to refer to aspects of Uganda's postcolonial history. Social movements and organisations, for example, are frequently named after their predecessors: Ugandans refer to Milton Obote's two regimes as 'Obote I' and 'Obote II'; southern Sudanese speak of local rebellions against the Khartoum government as Anya Nya I and II; former officers of Amin's army formed a rebel group named the West Nile Bank Front (WNBF) and later the Uganda National Rescue Front Part Two (UNRF II). Like the 'post-' prefix in Euro-American academic discourse, the 'II' suffix serves both to associate the present with and to dissociate it from the past. It suggests repetition, but at a different level the second time from the first.

Although I stress the importance of the interrelationship between discourse and reality in understanding the history of West Nile, this book is not primarily an exercise in critical discourse theory, any more than it is intended as a work of historical scholarship, even one written backwards. It is a historical anthropology, based largely on ethnographic fieldwork, together with some (non-exhaustive) archival work. It was by 'being there' and winning a degree of trust from some West Nilers that I was able to get access to such documents as the CPSAD Report, local history writings and other unpublished material. More than this, it was only through interviews and conversations with people over an extended period that I could begin to understand the written materials. For example, while the 'curse' mentioned in the Report is obviously intended, at one level, as a straightforward metaphor for the violence of West Nile history, it also refers, for at least some local people, to an actual, literal curse, dating from the period of Belgian occupation and laid on anyone collaborating with successive governments. This curse was only lifted in 1992, through a ritual conducted by some of the elders, which can be seen as part of the same peacemaking process as the CPSAD Report (see Chapter Seven). Cursing and the removal of curses are quintessentially performative utterances, just like the associations between violence and history in the story of West Nile. Moreover, some of the same people who were involved in the curse-lifting rituals were also involved in the production of the written histories I have mentioned. In this context, there is no room for the conventional

---

[17] See photo in *Drum* magazine, January 1979.

binary distinctions between 'traditional' and 'modern', 'oral' and 'written' or, in Connerton's (1989) terms, 'incorporated' and 'inscribed' histories.

Violence & ethnography

My initial intention in devising the research in West Nile had been to look at social reconstruction after conflict but, by the time I arrived in the area, any prospect of 'reconstruction' seemed extremely remote. Throughout my fieldwork, I experienced a society in flux, caught up in international political and economic forces beyond its control, deeply alienated from much of the rest of Uganda and mired in poverty and insecurity, but struggling to assert itself and improve its situation. At a personal level, it was an experience about which I remain profoundly ambivalent; I was often very frightened, depressed and lonely, it was difficult to 'do fieldwork' in the ways I wanted and intended, and I was frequently faced with the difficulties of trying to justify - to myself and others - the value of doing this kind of work in a low-intensity war zone at all. In the course of an attack on 'the revered social-anthropological method of participant observation', Alex de Waal observed that: 'It is one thing to convince oneself that it is morally justifiable to do anthropological field work during a famine, but it is another thing actually to do it. Observing a famine is possible; participating in it is more difficult. Consider a comparison: how would a social anthropologist participate in a war? By shooting people, by being shot?' (de Waal 1989:3). The answer that I discovered (there may be others) was to 'participate' by doing what most other people around, including the fighters, do during a war; that is, trying *not* to be shot. I succeeded in this, but what the NGOs euphemistically termed the 'security situation' was to have a powerful effect on my fieldwork, especially during my first extended research stint, from September 1996 to April 1997.

When I arrived, a conflict between Ugandan army (the Ugandan People's Defence Forces UPDF) and local rebels belonging to the West Nile Bank Front (WNBF) was reaching its peak; the countryside was being ravaged by rebel attacks while the town was virtually under siege and packed with people trying to escape the violence. One international NGO situation report in my possession lists thirty-three 'security events' over the month, ranging from land-mines on the roads to rebel attacks on hospitals and trading centres. In all, it lists thirty-one killings, together with innumerable injuries and burned homesteads, and this is a very partial picture, listing only those incidents that affected the (medical) work of the NGO.

The whole atmosphere was one of fear, suspicion and tension. Arua (especially its more salubrious hillside suburbs) was full of refugee workers, including many whites, who had evacuated from the camps, while local staff were being laid off. Unsurprisingly, I spent rather a lot of my first couple of months in the company of other Europeans. For the contemporary anthropologist of Africa, the international NGOs present much the same kind of problem as a previous generation of social anthropologists faced in the missionaries (not, of course, by any means the only resemblance between NGOs and missionaries). While I tried not to spend too much time 'sitting on the mission verandah', as it were, it seemed to me important not to repeat the old mistake of affecting to ignore these actors on the local scene, as an earlier generation of anthropologists did with the missionaries. Many local people's attitudes towards me were based on their automatic association of *bazungu* (white people; sing. *muzungu*) with the international agencies, whose Euro-American staff (since the Africanisation of the churches) formed most people's sole or main experience of white people.

The 'identity' (gender, age, ethnicity) of the fieldworker is, of course, an important factor in anthropological research, but perhaps not as important as what is going on in the field site. In my own case, as a thirty-eight-year-old white male, if I was not an NGO worker I must be some kind of spy.[18] Clearly I could not be a 'student', which in Uganda usually refers to someone in primary school. My difficulties in explaining what my research was about (a problem which must be familiar to most anthropologists) did not help matters. Having spent some months at Makerere University in Kampala before returning to Arua, I had found that social anthropology still had a distinctly colonialist reputation in Uganda, so I tended to tell people that I was researching the history of the district. Although this was true, it did not fit in very well with my obvious interest in current events and contemporary life in the town. In the end, I gave up trying to convince people that I was not engaged in espionage, and accepted whatever they wanted to believe about my motives for being in Arua. Whatever I was, I was not, considering all the other problems the West Nilers had, a significant threat to anyone. While Kirsten Hastrup may be right to assert that 'the drama of fieldwork, as played out on the stage established between ethnographer and informant, implies a degree of violence on the ethnographer's part' (Hastrup 1992: 122), this symbolic 'violence' was nothing compared to the *real* violence of everyday life in Arua in 1996–7.

In the circumstances, it was not possible for me to live with a local family, as I had planned. Everyone, except those who lived in gated compounds with armed guards, was scared that my presence would attract unwelcome attention, whether from criminals (I was assumed to be rich), rebels or the state. I instead stayed in a small hotel near the centre of town, the De l'Ambience, run by a Kakwa man from Koboko and staffed mostly by Zaïrean women (many of whom spoke French). The other guests were usually all Ugandans, including army officers, government officials and agency workers (expatriate agency staff normally stayed at the White Rhino Hotel, above the golf-course near the Office of the United Nations High Commission for Refugees (UNHCR) headquarters). The hotel seldom provided food, and I usually ate elsewhere in town. It felt fairly safe; at night the gates of the compound were locked and the place was patrolled by guards, who preferred to arm themselves with bows and arrows rather than the ancient semi-automatic rifles carried by other local security staff. The arrows were lethally barbed (I spoke to an Italian doctor who had operated on such wounds), and West Nile children, girls as well as boys, grow up learning to shoot

---

[18] Paul Dresch (2000) has written persuasively of the parallels between anthropological fieldwork and espionage. As it happens, I was accustomed to being mistaken for a spy, having written on security and intelligence issues in the past (e.g. Fitzgerald and Leopold 1987).

Photo 1.1 The anthropologist's hotel room

them very accurately. They also have the advantage over firearms of making no spark or noise to attract return fire.

Much of my work was carried out from the verandah of a nearby café bar, the Continental Club, run by a Sudanese woman (when she was not away trading). This became known as my 'office', and people came to expect me to be there every morning. I met an extraordinary range of people there, from ragged street people, who came to beg cigarettes,[19] to senior military officers (who may have come to find out whether I was indeed a spy). One day, I calculated that I had spoken to people of eight different nationalities that morning. I also overheard many conversations (perhaps I *was* a spy!). One such, which occurred early in my research, was revealing of local attitudes towards the dominant south of Uganda. Two local men were speaking in English, which was not unusual. One said that the rebels had killed a soldier the previous night. 'Black or brown?' was the query in response. The questioner was asking whether the dead man was from one of the (darker-skinned) northern Ugandan groups or a (lighter-coloured, Bantu language-speaking) aouthern Ugandan. The first man replied 'brown' and the other simply shrugged. Ethnicity and racism, albeit operating in categories unknown to Euro-American theories, were not merely issues for the fieldworker, but aspects of the field.

In the circumstances in which I found myself, conventional ('ethnographic',

---

[19] One of these was a woman with extraordinarily intense eyes, dressed in shredded rags, who on most days would stand a couple of feet away and stare at me for hours, occasionally barking out unanswerable questions in English (one was 'why do men hate women?') I was told she had been a teacher who had been driven insane by unspecified 'family problems'. Only once did she ask me for money.

'participant observation') fieldwork: – living with a family, observing a complete annual agricultural cycle, learning to converse in the local language, etc., – was completely impossible. While anthropologists have discarded much (some would say too much) of the traditional model, the linguistic issue remains important to the discipline. In Arua, however, most people speak several languages fluently, while (not being codified or taught) the local languages vary so much that two 'Lugbara' villages more than a dozen miles apart are likely to speak mutually incomprehensible dialects. Many people therefore customarily speak to each other in a 'trading' language such as Kiswahili or English.[20] Despite regular lessons in the Lugbara language, I never progressed beyond a few words and phrases, partly because of the way I had to work, and partly because of the complexity of Sudanic languages, which are 'tonal', in that the meaning of a word varies with the intonation with which it is pronounced (Lugbara has, depending on the dialect, up to seven basic tones).[21]

The ethnographic constraints under which I was operating also adversely affected my approach to another 'identity' issue for the fieldworker, that of gender. I was seldom able to conduct any extended conversations with West Nile women, and this is consequently a very male view of West Nile history. Nor, without the experience of living with a family, did I feel able to focus very directly on the construction of masculinity, which had been one of my initial research issues. I am conscious, then, of a gap in my work concerning a range of questions involving gender (which, on the other hand, might be seen as presenting potential opportunities for future, female, fieldworkers).

This book, then, is based on an unusual kind of fieldwork, but it is, I hope, nevertheless a contribution to what a recent edited collection calls 'ethnography ... as a methodology for exploring the zones (literally and figuratively) where people are entangled, abandoned, engaged and altered by the reconfiguration of states' (Greenhouse et al. (eds) 2002: 4). 'The matters of which I speak', in Vico's terms, are based to a large extent on my experiences during this fieldwork and, although this book is by no means an exercise in 'reflexive anthropology', the circumstances under which the research was produced are central to my understanding of life in the district. I shall therefore end this introductory chapter with an account of these circumstances 'inside West Nile'.

Inside West Nile

Shortly after I arrived in town, the rebels of the WNBF moved from Sudan to a base less than twenty miles from Arua, in the Zaïrean border town of Aru, where

[20] My Kakwa hostess in Kampala was consciously bringing up her children to be multilingual and spoke to them all from birth in a mixture of English, Kiswahili, Kiganda and Kakwa. What qualifies as a 'mother tongue' in such circumstances?

[21] I was told several times that no *muzungu* had ever spoken Lugbara well. Catholic missionaries tried, but it was said that they often made hilarious mistakes in their sermons. Tim Allen (personal communication) confirms that previous anthropologists in the area have had problems with the language, even where more conventional fieldwork was possible. I also failed to learn to play the *adungu*, a stringed instrument.

President Mobuto's forces were also massing. There were several 'cross-border incidents', and the international agencies were beginning to evacuate from town. One evening in November 1996, I was drinking tea with an Irish road engineer named Mike and his local assistant, Moses. They had been attempting to get their last bulldozer out of the refugee camp at Yumbe, some fifteen miles from Arua town, but had encountered the WNBF. The day after our conversation, they tried again, and were ambushed. This time Moses was shot dead, while Mike ran off into the bush, to turn up that evening, very shaken, at an Oxfam base. Later, I heard from Moses's brother that the rebels had warned Mike, in writing, not to return to the camp, having accused him of helping government soldiers.

Almost all the agencies had stopped working in the camps, and some had left the district altogether. Throughout Arua district an estimated 26,000 refugees and West Nilers were displaced, while some 15,000 Sudanese went back over the border, fearing the war there less than the one now going on around their places of refuge. UNHCR's declaration of a 'stage four' emergency entailed the evacuation of families and non-essential staff from all the international NGOs, the closure of all programmes except essential services to the refugee camps and the preparation of an evacuation plan for all expatriates (including, for some reason, me). The Ugandan authorities restricted road travel within the district to between 10 a.m. and 3 p.m.

The last agency working in the refugee camps on anything other than essential food and water supply was the Jesuit Refugee Service (JRS) whose nuns ran the primary schools, which they were forced to close as soon as the Primary Leaving Examinations were over, due to the abductions and mass rapes of schoolgirls by the rebels. Some two months after the JRS closed the settlement schools, Oxfam issued an extraordinary job advertisement in the national and international press for teachers to re-establish these schools under Oxfam auspices. These adverts gave no hint of the security situation (which had worsened since the JRS pull-out), instead concentrating on the need for a gender-aware, participatory approach and the ultimate aim of integration with the Ugandan national school system. Only one throw-away line suggested that experience working in difficult situations would be 'an advantage'.[22]

I have analysed elsewhere (Leopold 2001) the results of the NGOs' strategy of withdrawal, first from the camps, then from the centre of town into their compounds up the hill, and ultimately from the district altogether. From my point of view, it had its advantages. By December 1996 I was the only *muzungu* living in the centre of town (as opposed to the agency compounds up the hill), while the expatriate agency staff were avoiding the place as much as possible during the day and largely obeying self-imposed curfews at night. Local attitudes to the agencies around this time were summed up by some graffiti that appeared on a wall in town, which read, 'Oxfam/Oxfat/Oxfi'. *Fi* is a Lugbara word meaning stomach or intestines, and such anatomical terms, in Arua as elsewhere in Africa, imply not only wealth, but also corruption (Bayart 1993).

The district authorities were also furious with the NGOs, for what they saw as

[22] See Leopold (2001). Payne (1998) gives an alternative (Oxfam-based) view of events over this period.

a retreat from their responsibilities, and my own relationships with the former improved accordingly. I could now easily deflect the (fairly frequent) attentions of police and soldiers, by telling them to consult senior officers about my presence in the district, as well as deploying my cherished government Research Identity Card. Sitting around in bars talking to the military proved to be a more useful fieldwork technique than I had initially thought, but it had its problems: local distrust of the army was growing, largely due to an ill-timed counter-insurgency exercise which involved reregistering every ex-soldier (i.e. most adult males) in the district. All kinds of rumours spread about the 'real purpose' of the exercise, and it consider-ably weakened support for the army, especially as the latter appeared unable to deal with the rebels, other than to contain their activities to specific areas of the district.

Fortunately, it was not just the soldiers but other West Nilers, too, who appreciated my sticking it out in town, and gradually I had to spend less time justifying my presence and my work against hostile questioning from local intellectuals and elders; in fact, some of those who initially challenged me ended up introducing me to some of my most interesting sources. Gradually I began to extend my network of contacts within the district. Sometimes, people heard about me and came to find me to tell their stories; on other occasions, I would meet someone by accident. In a bar I got talking to a middle-aged teacher who, it transpired, had been a young boy in Middleton's main fieldwork site in Vurra County while he was doing his research. On another occasion I spent a fasci-nating afternoon listening to an argument about traditional medicine between a couple of its supporters and a vehemently opposed local doctor.

By January 1997, the conflict seemed to be moving into another phase. More and more troops were moving into the district, and rebel operations were increas-ingly constrained. The head of UNHCR strongly advised NGO staff to avoid the centre of Arua at night, after the assassination in town of a prominent local politician and one of his relatives. At the end of the month, the first attacks by a new rebel group, the 'Aminist' Uganda National Rescue Front Part Two (UNRF II), began, with raids into Aringa County from government-controlled Sudan. One night, I was lying in bed reading *War and Peace*, when I heard an explosion, followed by automatic weapons fire: a local security official had been assassinated in the middle of town. More attacks followed, and I became relatively used to the sound of AK47s after dark. More frightening was the Sudanese government's Antonov bomber, which began to circle over Arua town from time to time. In the event, we were never bombed, though Koboko and Moyo towns were. The only deaths in Arua were those of two children killed by inefficient anti-aircraft fire aimed at the bomber from the local army base, but the drone of the Antonov scared everyone in town. To this day, the sound of a large turboprop aircraft sends a shiver of fear through me.

In February, rumours of an impending advance by the Sudan Peoples' Liberation Army (SPLA) and the UPDF began to grow, but such rumours had ebbed and flowed over the previous three years, and many now disbelieved them on principle. As trucks full of soldiers passed through town, locals would point some out as 'SPLA', though I could see no difference from the UPDF men. Increasingly, the rumbles and crunching of tanks and heavy artillery moving in convoy joined the regular funeral drumming and occasional gunfire among the night sounds of Arua. Would-be 'experts' knowledgeably identified 'Stalin organs' (Russian-built multiple rocket-launchers) and (British) Challenger tanks. As well as the support of the Ugandan government, the SPLA also had the more or less overt allegiance of many expatriates working for the international organisations, including those whose official position was one of studied neutrality. These were usually people with previous experience in southern Sudan, a category that included a high proportion of the expatriates. On one occasion, talking to an Icelander working for a neutral international humanitarian organisation, I made the mistake of beginning a sentence with 'If the SPLA take Juba'. He hissed at me vehemently '*When* Juba is *liberated*!'

By this time, I was increasingly meeting local elders, from both Arua town and elsewhere in the district, particularly Maracha and Aringa Counties where the refugee camps were the main focus of much of the violence in the district. From these men, I was to gather many of the historical narratives I draw upon in this book. I also started my Lugbara language lessons with a young secondary school teacher. I opened an account with the local branch of the (Catholic Church supported) Centenary Rural Development Bank, whose motto, 'Unite, love and serve', did not sound like any financial institution I was familiar with (nor did its occasional habit of running out of cash). However, one of the managers was a young Alur man who was a great admirer of the anthropological work of Aidan Southall, which made for interesting conversations during the lengthy process of gaining access to one's money.

However, the pervading violence continued to impinge on my work, as it did on the lives of everyone. On St Valentine's Day, I was visited by a man who had been helping me to find and interview Nubi and Aringa elders. He told me that his brother, a senior commander in the WNBF (and an ambassador under Amin), had been shot a couple of days earlier by the UPDF during a massive attack on the rebels' base in Ariwara (some fifteen miles inside Zaïre). The brother had been a big man in Arua, the head of an important Muslim family and one-time owner of considerable property in town, much of which had been given to the mosque. In view of his status, the army had brought his body back to town and exhibited it in the taxi park for several hours as a trophy, before allowing his family to take it away for burial. Within hours of the UPDF assault, anti-government Zaïrean rebels of the ADFL (C-Z) took Ariwara, and the WNBF fled north to the Zaïre/Sudan border, followed by the ADFL. A couple of days later, the ADFL had taken over the border area with Uganda, up to its junction with the Sudan border, and spread along the latter frontier, a move that was to prove an essential preliminary to subsequent events.

Throughout early 1997, Arua social life had a particular intensity. This puzzled me at first. Parties, parades, meetings and concerts became more frequent and the numbers attending social gatherings of all kinds, from church services to all-night discos, seemed greater than usual. The all-night dances (convenient at a time of curfew, since participants could stay until dawn) were especially popular, celebrating every possible occasion, from Eid Ul-Fitr (which I had never before seen celebrated with an all-night disco) to International Women's Day. The music was invariably a genre of Zaïrean pop music called *Lingala* (the name of the trade language in which the lyrics are sung), whose dance tunes go on for up to twenty minutes or so. Sometimes these occasions were raucous. On Women's Day, in a classic carnival of inversion, husbands stayed at home and looked after the children, while their wives went out on the town. By 2 a.m., the disco in the yard of the White Rhino Hotel was packed with unmarried young men and married or single women who had been celebrating their gender with more enthusiasm than sobriety for most of the day. The atmosphere was wild, and (as tabloid journalists used to say) I made my excuses and left.

There were practical reasons for this intense social activity. Both the assistance agencies and the local authorities were explicitly trying to keep their people amused during a time of forced inactivity. This also happened to coincide with the hot, dry season, described by an early colonial officer as the traditional time for 'killing ... dancing and drinking' among the Lugbara (McConnell 1925: 443). But these considerations did not account for all the increase in social activity. I came across a more persuasive sociological explanation while reading in my room. In the chapter in *War and Peace* on Moscow in 1812, Tolstoy writes:

> At the advent of danger there are always two voices that speak with equal force in the human heart: one very reasonably tells a man to consider the nature of the peril and the means of escaping it; the other, with a still greater show of reason, argues that it is too depressing and painful to think of the danger since it is not in man's power to foresee everything and avert the general march of events, and it is better therefore to shut one's eyes to the disagreeable until it actually comes, and to think instead of what is pleasant. When a man is alone he generally listens to the first voice; in the company of his fellow men to the second. So it now was with the inhabitants of Moscow. It was a long time since Moscow had seen so much gaiety as there was that year. (Tolstoy 1957 [1869]: 887)

The long-awaited SPLA advance began in the early hours of Sunday, 9 March, by which time it was clear to even the most sceptical that something was about to happen. Conveniently, during the last week in February the main road through Arua town had been resurfaced with tarmac, paid for by UNHCR, and no sooner was it laid than it was chewed to pieces by tank tracks. Artillery weapons began to move through even in broad daylight. Rumours grew wilder, though they were seldom entirely implausible: Sudan was shelling Koboko; Ethiopian military planes were landing at Arua airport at night; tanks were being driven by black Americans; the President's brother, a controversial army commander and businessman named Salim Saleh, was in town (this was true; I saw him); the President himself was here (not, so far as I know, true). In the event, the SPLA operation, when it finally occurred, was a classically executed pincer movement, moving into Sudan through north-east Zaïre as well as north-west Uganda, the ADFL advance in mid-February having paved the way. The Sudanese government-held border towns quickly fell and the SPLA forces headed for the key local centre of Yei.

Fortuitously, I had previously arranged to go to the border town of Koboko with a group of expatriate agency staff on 10 March, for a party to celebrate the building of a supposedly bombproof bunker in the heavily guarded compound of one of the international agencies. It says something about life at the time that such a concept seemed to the humanitarians who attended, including myself, more a good excuse for a party than an unacceptably sick joke. On the way we were stopped several times by UPDF soldiers, who seemed anxious above all to check that we were not journalists. Koboko was full of soldiers and of refugees waiting to return to Sudan in the wake of the ongoing SPLA advance. From the compound we could hear distant shellfire, and see the tiny shape of a Sudanese Antonov bomber circling above the front line. As night fell, we drank and danced, staying up late to watch the tracer fire against the dark sky, while an Australian doctor played the saxophone, until the agency's security guards, fearing trouble from the authorities, told us to shut up and go to bed. Woken at 5 a.m. by the sounds of a cat killing a chicken, we listened to radio reports of the SPLA advance on short wave. Three days later, Yei fell and the rebel forces headed towards the major district capital of Juba. When I returned to Arua from Koboko, a garage proprietor who claimed to have refuelled some of the SPLA tanks told me they had only enough fuel for eleven days. In the event, many vehicles returned a week or so later, with the regional Sudanese capital, Juba, surrounded but still unconquered.

The effects of the SPLA advance on life in Arua district were immediate. Most of the WNBF and UNRF II rebels had been wiped out in the assault, while Juma Oris himself was reported (inaccurately, it later transpired) to be either dead or badly injured, and most of the high command were captured or killed. Official Ugandan figures say that more than 500 WNBF and UNRF II fighters were captured by the SPLA during the offensive, while a further 400 surrendered to the UPDF.[23] The West Nile rebel groups based in Zaïre and Sudan seem to have been more or less wiped out as an organised force and their bases captured or destroyed. Meanwhile, the Sudanese refugees largely repatriated themselves, 'encouraged' in some cases by attacks (by whom is not clear) on the temporary displaced-persons camps where many of them were living. Some 13,500 of those that remained were later regrouped in Oxfam's small settlement at Imvepi (Payne 1998: 36). By the time I left Arua for Kampala and England, in April 1997, it was apparent that the circumstances which had dominated my first main fieldwork stint had changed dramatically.

I returned to West Nile in December. On the plane from Entebbe, I ran into a group of timber loggers, a British man and a couple of Indonesians employed by a Vietnamese-based company, who were working near Yei, in what was now SPLA-controlled 'New Sudan'. In the few months I had been away, Arua town had experienced rapid changes. In the centre of town now stood a shiny silver shipping container with a satellite dish on its roof, from which (for a price well beyond the means of most) one could phone or fax internationally. I was able to use this to copy-edit a paper for publication (Leopold 1999) while 'in the field', a feat unimaginable a year earlier. The world of the international agencies had changed, too. The refugee assistance programme was much smaller than it had been, but the international agencies were still very much in evidence, many engaged in cross-border operations in New Sudan. One new development-oriented agency was the Women's Empowerment Programme (WEP). An offshoot of the Dutch-supported

23 Reported in the *Guardian*, 11 April 1998.

local NGO, the Community Action Programme (CAP; see Chapter Two), it employed a far greater number of expatriates than its parent organisation, mostly on literacy projects. The NGO staff, however, were no longer the only *bazungu* in town; a couple of weeks after my arrival, Arua's first backpacker arrived: a somewhat reckless New Zealander, he claimed to be heading for Chad, but developed a bad case of malaria and had to return to Kampala.

Some strange people were now operating over the Sudanese border. Several groups of American fundamentalist Christians passed through town in luxurious four-wheel drives, heading for the border to show support for what they believed to be their persecuted co-religionists. A group of Israelis, who said they were ex-military officers, arrived in the district as 'tourists', became involved in gold-mining and trading in New Sudan, and then decided that supplying trucking services to the NGOs was a more profitable business. Koboko in particular was full of competing cross-border organisations, and suitable vehicles for the rough New Sudanese countryside were at a premium. One of the first acts of the SPLA/Sudan People's Liberation Movement (SPLM) government had been to institute a system of vehicle registration and 'NS' (New Sudan) number-plates, which ensured a small but steady supply of foreign exchange for the new authorities.

My own work went well at this time. Having been away and returned, I was regarded with greater trust by many people, who were used to *bazungu* disappearing for ever. The security situation was much improved, though sporadic bandit attacks continued in the countryside. While I was back in the UK, the District Council Secretary for Security had been arrested; a number of mines and other arms and ammunition had been found hidden in his compound, and he was accused of working with the WNBF. Things seemed to have quietened down still further after his disappearance. But now my research hit a new snag. To move into a rural field site, as I intended, would require permission from Local Council (LC) officers, and the LCs were all suspended, pending local elections. I was told that, in the circumstances, government permission would not be forthcoming for my proposed move until after the elections.

The electoral process took a long time, and campaigning was fierce. I knew several candidates for the various levels of local government (both pro- and anti-National Resistance Movement (NRM)) and most agreed that, in general, the election passed off peacefully and reasonably fairly, although political parties, in accordance with Ugandan law, were not allowed to campaign, while government officials openly canvassed for 'Movementist' candidates. District-level (LC5) elections were not held until the end of April, and the process was further extended by a rerun for the women's post on the council.[24] Day after day, parades supporting one or another candidate would pass down the main street of town. In the event, broadly pro-Movement candidates won most of the important positions;

---

[24] The District Secretary for Women post was the only one voted on, not by secret ballot, but by the voters openly lining up behind the candidate of their choice. This was because of the very low rates of literacy among women, but it caused problems. The post was hotly contested, with candidates buying soft drinks and similar petty inducements for voters. Many, however, found themselves in the uncomfortable position of having promised their support to more than one candidate, and simply avoided turning up to be counted. As a result, the women's turnout was unconstitutionally low, and the whole process had to be rerun. The Movementist candidate eventually won.

in contrast to the presidential elections of a couple of years earlier, a mass popular vote in West Nile was now supporting the government. The new alignment was sealed on 21 May, with a state visit to Arua town by President Museveni, bringing with him President Moi of Kenya to 'witness' his promise to tarmac the Karuma–Pakwach road, which links the West Nile area to the rest of Uganda.[25]

It was somewhat frustrating to still be restricted to Arua town and its surroundings, but I was now working well with the elders of LULA, as well as making new contacts in the worlds of the market and the informal economy. I had become a well-known figure in town, and people simply turned up to talk to me, rather than my having to track them down for interview. Whenever possible, I attended whatever local events were going on: political meetings, opening ceremonies, parades, sports matches. Not everybody was happy to speak to me (I wasted ages trying to interview a former Cabinet Minister, who prevaricated but after many months decided he did not wish to talk), but at least most people now knew who I was, and I no longer had to explain myself to suspicious soldiers or policemen, or to justify my presence in town to critical local intellectuals. I felt pretty much part of the furniture.

In April, the townspeople were surprised by the sudden decision of Arua's most eminent Asian family to sell up and leave. The Chawdas had run their various businesses in town for sixty-five years. The family stayed throughout the Amin period, despite his notorious expulsion of Asians elsewhere in the country, and went into exile in the Congo with other locals in 1980, returning to re-establish their garage, shops and nightclub. The Chawdas were well-known and popular figures in Arua, especially among traders and the market people, many of whom they employed from time to time. Some interpreted their departure as a bad omen but, in financial terms, it was probably a reasonably good time to sell up.

By the time the electoral process was over in May, just when it might have been possible for me to move to a rural area, the violence in the countryside began to flare up again, with all the seeming inevitability of a Vicovian historical cycle. In May and June, there were a number of attacks, supposedly by UNRF II rebels, based in government-held Sudan, and some ex-WNBF elements in Aringa and Koboko counties. Dozens of people were said to have been taken from villages, removed from a bus at gunpoint, and even (in the case of a reported fifty people) abducted from a mosque in Aringa, to swell the ranks of the rebels. Once again, roads and bridges were being blown up, houses were burned, cattle abducted, people displaced. A couple of small grenade attacks in Arua town (including one on the electricity generator) were followed by an extensive military 'stop and search' operation. The Koboko–Yumbe–Moyo road was closed again (making it impossible, as I had planned, to spend some time with my friend Justin in Moyo district). It was all at a rather lower level than 1996–97, but it seemed depressingly familiar. In July 1998, I left Arua for Kampala and England. I have not yet been able to return.

---

[25] See reports in the *New Vision*, 23 May 1998, and the *Monitor*, 22 May 1998.

2

'Arua Means Prison'
Violence & ethnography
at the end of the twentieth century

Over my time in Arua town I came to see it as three different, if overlapping, towns (see Map 2.1). The first is the busy, cosmopolitan heart of the place, containing the extensive, packed market area; the government buildings, shops and bars of the main streets; and the lodging places and lorry parks used by truckers and traders. This inner town is surrounded by the second town, which merges into the surrounding villages and homesteads. This is where most of the local people live, in traditionally built tukuls or small tin-roofed bungalows; predominantly they are Lugbara-speakers, but there are also patches of other north-western and northern Ugandans, some of whom have lived in Arua for generations, as well as others from neighbouring parts of Sudan and Congo.[1]

The third town is up the lower slopes of Arua Hill, largely separated from the town centre by the golf-course (built in 1916–17). This is where the colonial élite used to live and it is where the postcolonial élite live now. The people who live on the hill, in fenced and guarded compounds, are comparatively wealthy and powerful local families, the senior staff of international assistance agencies and important men from other parts of Uganda stationed in Arua for official or commercial reasons. The area also holds Arua's smartest hotel, the White Rhino, as well as the offices of most of the international agencies. The pattern, common to many Ugandan towns, is an imperial one: the European quarters were separated from the 'African town' by the open expanse of a golf-course. Some Arua elders still refer to the area up the hill by the colonial military term 'senior lines'. This town-planning model was laid down in Lugard's political memoranda and is characterised by the anthropologist of imperialism, Helen Callaway, as 'imperial ideology in spatial form' (Callaway 1987: 65). She outlines the model as it was elaborated in Nigeria:

> Lugard set out ... the precise details for a new township consisting of a European Reservation, to be surrounded by a non-residential area 440 yards across. He gives three reasons for this segregation of Europeans, of first importance being 'that they shall not be exposed to the attacks of mosquitoes which have become infected with the germs of malaria or yellow fever, by preying on Natives'. Next, this served as a valuable

---

[1] For example, near Arua Hill is a village or suburb of Alur people (from present-day Nebbi district) who are descendants of the losing brother in a succession dispute, which was 'resolved' by the first British District Commissioner of West Nile (DCWN) in 1914. A.E. Weatherhead took Omwech (or, as Aidan Southall transliterates the name, Unwec) to Arua town, as 'one of his agents' (Southall 1953: 283).

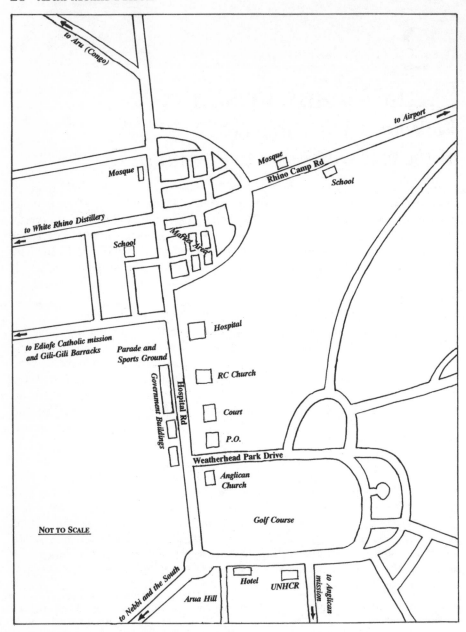

Map 2.1 Sketch plan of Arua town in 1998

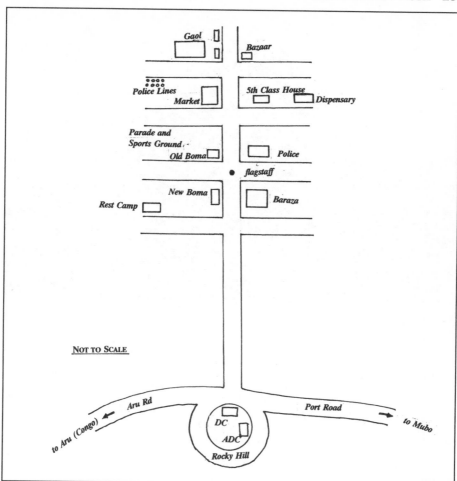

Taken from a plan in the Uganda National Archives (UNA A/46/1275, Secretarial Minute Papers SW 4102, headed 'West Nile District, Opening Up Of') drawn by H.G. Knight, Overseer in Charge, Public Works, Northern Province. His accompanying report, dated 6 December 1916, reads: 'Station is built on flat tableland in short grass countty. Mosquitos are very few. Station has been well laid out and has named roads, plenty of room being allowed each house, 100 yards house to house which are:

DC's.	Stone walls, grass roof
ADC's.	do.
5th Class House for collectorate clerk.	Wattle and daub
Dispensary:	do.
Police Office:	do.
Collectorate.	New building nearly completed. Stone walls
Collectorate store:	Wattle and daub
Police Lines.	do
Gaol	Stone walls
Baraza Hall.	do.
Rest House	Wattle and daub

Native population large, food plentiful, small Indian bazaar (5 traders), good water from spring ... probably the best temporary houses in the Protectorate.'

Map 2.2 Sketch plan of Arua town in 1916

Plate 2.1 Arua hill

> safeguard against the bush fires common in the 'Native quarters'. And finally, it
> removed the inconvenience felt by Europeans 'whose rest is disturbed by drumming
> and other noises dear to the Native'. These were eminently practical reasons as befitted
> a pragmatic administrator, but they left unstated certain assumptions at a different
> level. Physical separation helped to ensure the social distance necessary to maintain
> imperial authority. It was not racism as such which dictated segregation, though
> clearly there is ample evidence of assumed racial superiority. (Callaway 1987: 65)

This was the plan implemented by Arua's colonial founder, A.E. Weatherhead,
who gave his name to the road that separates the golf-course from the town. The
power structures expressed in the model persist in the postcolonial era, much as
the West Nile Golf Club itself does.

But this is not the only way in which Arua's colonial past is inscribed on the
townscape. Above the arch of the vegetable market and on the façades of the
main street shops, are etched colonial dates of foundation. Outside the local
government headquarters are painted the colonial-sounding titles of the political
élite (Resident District Commissioner, Chief Administrative Officer, etc.). The
largest local beer-brewing and drinking place, known as the Enyau-Kabiri Kpete
Club (*kpete* is the Lugbara name for a local beer), spreads out round the trees that
surround and grow up through the ruins of an imperial court-house. Similarly
the town itself has grown around the skeleton of the town Weatherhead built, as
a comparison between Maps 2.1 and 2.2 demonstrates. Aside from the small
airport, which was Amin's sole significant contribution to the infrastructural
development of his home district, little has been added to the basic structure of
Arua town since independence.

Arua was founded in 1914, the site chosen by Weatherhead apparently on the advice of the experienced Sudan administrator C.H. Stigand (see Chapters Five and Six). It had not previously been a place of any significant settlement, but there were local stories about its precolonial past, and it seems to have been close to the site of a small Belgian base (some people spoke of an occasion when the Belgians had captured and held a group of people on Arua Hill). Several local elders told me the story of how Weatherhead, on his arrival, met a blacksmith[2] sitting under a fig-tree[3] near the bottom of the hill and asked him the local name of the place. The blacksmith replied 'Arua', which is a diminutive form of the name of the local Belgian headquarters, Aru,[4] a word which means 'prison' or 'place of confinement' in Lugbara; 'Arua' therefore means, roughly, 'little prison', a name which reflected pretty accurately contemporary local perceptions of European rule. One elder I interviewed explained the meaning of 'Arua' as follows:

> Yes, Arua means prison. When the Belgians were here, they used to collect people and bring them here for imprisonment. It was the first time people knew about a prison where you would be brought from your home and brought here, to have punitive actions against you, lock you up, give you fatigues, and so on. So they refer to it, as this is a place to manage people; to manage people, that's it. Arua means to manage you, if you think you are big-headed. But Arua is also prison. Arua means prison and that you will be managed in prison.[5]

A Nubi account of the founding of the town is slightly different, raising the possibility of an earlier, Nubian place of imprisonment on the site, before the Belgians came:

> Of course, formerly, the name of the town was not Arua town. This was called Boma.[6] When the Nubians came here, they called this area Boma [which] means a military camp for them. So, where they used to go and stop, resting, for one year or six months, they called that area Boma. So it was now Captain Lugard who came and asked the ethnic original of this area 'What is that hill's name?' It was a man called Audele, a Lugbara. He said, 'The hill is called Aru'. Aru means a place of prisoning people in. Of course, how it came to that, it came when the Nubians came here, most of the people whom they have arrested, captured, of course on the way, they prisoned them down there. To that hill. So in Lugbara the word prison is called 'aru'. Then the European man says, 'OK, I think this town should be called Arua.' 'I'm going to Arua' means, 'I'm going to prison'. Now there is a town, the name is Arua, a nickname by an old man, an ethnic tribesman, a Lugbara man called Audele who nicknamed the name of Arua after the Nubians had departed to Buganda.[7]

---

[2] As elsewhere in Africa, blacksmiths are special people with spiritual powers. They are not associated with any particular clan or area. Middleton says (e.g. 1962: 578; 1971b) that blacksmiths were all Ndu (Lendu) people (who now live over the border in the Congo), but this was specifically denied by several of my informants, though they said some smiths may have been Ndu, especially in the south of the district (these informants were from Maracha and Aringa counties, and from Moyo). Middleton's main fieldwork site was in Vurra County, south of Arua town.

[3] The particular tree (a descendant of the original) was pointed out to me. *Ficus* trees are frequently planted to mark the burial places of important men (see Middleton 1982: 151), but no grave was apparently associated with this one.

[4] Aru, just over the Congo border, is a connecting point between Arua and the Congo hinterland, including towns deeper inside the country, such as Ariwara – see Meagher (1990: 73).

[5] Interview, Mr Nahor Oya, 4 February 1997. Transcribed from tape.

[6] I have been told that 'Boma', a common place-name in East and Central Africa, stands for 'British Overseas Military Administration.' The British had not, of course, arrived at this time.

[7] Interview, Mr Kitami Ali Garawan, 25 January 1997. Transcribed from tape.

The speaker, it should be noted, habitually refers to Weatherhead as 'Captain Lugard', sometimes distinguishing between 'Lugard I' (the historical Lugard who encountered the Nubi by Lake Albert in 1891 and took them to Buganda) and 'Lugard II' (who founded Arua and was the first District Commissioner (DC) West Nile, that is, A.E. Weatherhead).

Perhaps the blacksmith could foresee the future. The town was the centre from which imperial rule was extended over the district slowly, unevenly and against sporadic opposition. In January 1916 Arua was gazetted as a township and frontier post, and its 'lock-up' as a prison.[8] Its *baraza* (meeting hall) was used to bring in representatives of every part of the district for instruction and entertainment, as the Provincial Monthly Report for January 1916 demonstrates: '[A] large Baraza at Arua ... was attended by representatives of the Whole District, even from the as yet unorganised Madi Aiivu and was thus instrumental in bringing together all the three Tribes of the District. Police sports open to all comers followed, many of the quite unsophisticated natives entering for the events.'[9]

Map 2.2 shows the town in December 1916, demonstrating the prominence of buildings designed to discipline and punish, alongside the sports grounds. They were, naturally, built largely by the forced labour of the West Nilers, which became more widely available as taxation, and its alternative of unpaid work, was gradually imposed on people with little or no cash. In 1918, for example, Weatherhead wrote to the Provincial Commissioner (PC), 'I propose to bring in to Arua non tax-payers for work on the station, and that such men be marked-up by the chiefs in the tax registers as having worked in lieu of tax.' The proposal involved bringing in up to 1,000 non-taxpayers 'to be employed on station clearing and planting, and repairs to houses'.[10]

Perhaps of even greater social impact on the district than the prisons and barracks were the roads that radiated out of Arua town into every sub-county, also built by forced labour, which brought British rule into the rural areas. Unsurprisingly, this work was contested. In July 1915, Weatherhead wrote to the PC, 'it is essential that my roadmen should be armed. I am reluctant at present to put men out without rifles, where good work could be done, if the natives are aware that the foreman carries a rifle and live ammunition.' The request was approved in principle, but rifles and ammunition were 'not available at present'.[11] There was, after all, a world war going on.

Another important factor in this imperial penetration, still highly visible on the ground in Arua town, was the establishment of churches (encouraged by the administration as a means of providing English-speakers who could be used as clerks) and mosques (not encouraged by the British, but spreading as a conse-quence of British rule and the role of Islam in the army). 'Native clerks' were essential to the working of administration and the implementation of the judicial

---

[8] Uganda National Archives (UNA) A46/1275 (SMP 4102) West Nile District, Opening Up Of. Minute, Acting Governor to Acting Chief Secretary, Uganda Protectorate, 17 January 1916.

[9] UNA A46/793, Northern Province (NP) Monthly Reports 1916, para 13.

[10] UNA A46/248, Poll Tax in the West Nile District, 7 June 1918, DCWN (Weatherhead) to PCNP.

[11] UNA A46/919, Northern Province, Administration of. Item 218, 12 July 1915.

system, and in this respect Catholic missions could be as useful as Protestant ones. Despite sharing the widespread British suspicion of Catholic missions, Weatherhead in 1916 'Placed on record his gratitude to Father Vignatio, the Superior, and others of that mission ... for the prompt way in which his request for Alur native clerks have been met. The material supplied is proving satisfactory.'[12]

The town was always a centre of trade as well as administration, and (like the administration) was mostly out of the hands of local people during the colonial period. Trade goods spread out of town along the new roads, which also brought traders and peasants into town to sell and buy. Already by 1916 there was a 'small Indian bazaar' with five traders (see note to Map 2.2). In the early 1950s there were 'around 40' shops run by 'Indian and Arab traders' (Middleton 1962: 569), while the town as a whole, in John Middleton's account (e.g. in 1962, 1971b), was less of a Lugbara place than a Nubi one, though the categories, as Middleton himself says, overlapped considerably:

> Arua town is a town of almost 8,000 inhabitants, most of whom are Moslem.... These Moslems are known as Nubi and maintain that they are the descendants of Emin Pasha's troops.... In fact, there are very few of these men left, and most Nubi are Lugbara, Alur, Kakwa and other tribesmen who have converted to Islam or whose fathers were so converted.... The Nubis form a markedly distinct population; besides being Muslim and having their own schools, they deal in hides and skins or follow other urban occupations. (Middleton 1971b: 44–5)[13]

However, even in the 1950s, a majority of Middleton's sample of African shop-keepers and traders in Arua town were Christian Lugbara, 'members of the class known as 'Ba odiru ("the new people"), a class composed of government officials, school teachers and so on' (Middleton 1962: 571).

Middleton says that Lugbara markets, including the large one in Arua, are always enclosed, surrounded by a hedge or fence, though he concedes that 'there are usually several women [trading] outside the market fence' (ibid.: 572). The vast majority of sellers and buyers were women trading in foodstuffs and domestic items such as pots, with a much smaller number of male shopkeepers and pedlars selling 'knives, razor blades, salt, tea, soap and other cheap consumer goods' (ibid.). In all, perhaps 500 people were trading in Arua market in the 1950s.[14]

Some years before the time of my fieldwork, two things (apart from the end of the colonial regime) had dramatically changed the size and character of Arua market, and thereby the nature of the town itself and indeed of the district. Both were caused by Idi Amin: the first was the expulsion of Uganda's Asian popula-tion in 1973 and the subsequent 'Africanisation' of trade. The second was the refugee experience, which turned the rural majority of the district upside down, and emptied many of them out into a more urbanised lifestyle, if not into Arua town itself. By the time of Kate Meagher's study in 1988, only two years after the beginning of the mass return to the district, the market had spilt over its colonial-

---

[12] UNA A46/810, 'Northern Province Annual Report for 1916–1917.
[13] Many of Arua's suburbs bear names attesting to their Nubi origins – names of places where their Nubi founders had served during their army days, such as 'Kenya Village' and 'Tanganyika Village'.
[14] Middleton's figure for 'a large market' is 500 (Middleton 1962:572).

era boundaries of the central walled square to dominate the town, and things were much as I found them eight years later:

> The market consists of a large walled, open-air structure, a taxi park ... and a large open area of stalls some 150 metres beyond the market building. Arua market operates seven days a week, with 'big markets' on Mondays and Thursdays. Retail traders from the surrounding areas and villages and wholesalers from more distant areas bring their goods to Arua on these days, transforming the market from a local centre of exchange to a major distributive centre.... The turnover in food crops alone ... is far in excess of the consumption needs of the area, and suggests a substantial proportion of what is bought in Arua market is for trade across the border[s]... A section of particular interest in the market are the hawkers stalls, located beyond the taxi park to the left of the market building. Here, half an acre of neatly arranged stalls made of sticks function as the main outlet for the shops which line the three main streets of Arua.... In addition to being the distributive outlet for imported goods from Kampala, the hawkers' stalls are also distributive outlets for goods purchased on the parallel market in Zaire. (Meagher 1990: 68).

Even all this abundance of commerce, she concludes, was to a large extent just a front for an even more extensive 'informal' or (the preferred term in MacGaffey 1991) 'secondary' economy involving trade across the international borders. In the next section, I discuss both formal and informal economies (which together form what MacGaffey terms the 'real economy') in the context of Arua's social and economic life in the late 1990s.

Economies & societies

If the physical environment of Arua town is structured predominantly by the brief colonial period, its social and economic dynamics bear the traces of earlier times, as well as the more recent past. As Meagher recognises (1990: 65-7), Arua's international trade networks, formal and informal, follow patterns laid down before British rule, particularly in the post-contact period but also earlier (see Chapter Seven). Both economically and socially, Arua town is closely linked into its rural hinterland: through trade, migration (forced and unforced, in so far as the distinction makes any sense in this context) and family and other social ties. Similar networks also link the town into the wider world: for the researcher trying to track down individuals to talk to, the second most frequent disheartening phrase to hear, after 'Mr X has gone to the village', is 'Mrs Y has gone to Kampala/Yei/Congo'.

A study of Arua, therefore, cannot adopt the hard dichotomy between the urban and the rural, the modern and the traditional, found in much recent anthropological and historical writing on provincial towns in Africa. Whereas the ethnographer in John Middleton's day was expected to portray 'the Lugbara' as an unchanging, traditional, bounded group, the pressure today is to emphasise the globalised, modern (or post-modern) nature of an unbounded cultural 'reservoir' (Amselle 1998). But Arua is simultaneously traditional and modern, both cosmopolitan and a backwater. The town is by no means, as Thomas Spear says of Arusha, 'a town of strangers ... alienated from its rural hinterland' (Spear

Plate 2.2 Arua town in 1996

2000: 109), nor were its people, like those in James Ferguson's recent study of a copper-belt mining town, divided absolutely between 'two contrasting cultural modes', which he terms 'localist' and 'cosmopolitan':

> On the one hand were the cosmopolitan workers, relaxing in bars and clubs, drinking bottled beer or liquor, listening to Western or 'international' music, speaking English and mixing languages with ease, dressing smartly (and even ostentatiously) and adopting an air of easy familiarity with whites like me. On the other hand were the localists, drinking in private homes or taverns, preferring 'African' or home-brewed beer, speaking the local languages of their home region, dressing in drab or even ragged clothes, listening to 'local' music, and presenting to a white foreigner like me an impression of intimidation and sometimes even servility. (Ferguson 1999: 91–2)

In Arua, on the contrary, I found a spectrum of blended or hybridised variations on these 'cultural modes' (which are surely as economic as they are cultural). Arua town was much more like Hortense Powdermaker's earlier, but to my mind much richer, description of the copper belt in the early 1950s:

> Now traditional and modern orders exist side by side. Men who participated in a tribal dance on Saturday afternoon might be dancing on Saturday night to jazz music in the Welfare Hall. Witchcraft thinking did not prevent people from using the services of the clinic and hospital. They listened to modern songs and to current news and stories over the radio, and used their traditional proverbs and folk tales to make a point in colloquial conversation.... The goal of individual careers was new, but it had not eliminated traditional duties to kindred. Many people went to church, but they also followed some traditional customs at birth, puberty, marriage and death.... Some people tended to be more traditional and others more modern in their general orientation, with many gradations between the extremes. The traditional and modern were found not only in disparate groups, but within the same individual. (Powder-maker 1962:7)

Part of the reason for such a mixture, in the case of Arua, is precisely its relationship with its rural hinterland. This is linked not only to the social disruption caused by the refugee experience (and earlier migrations), but also to the continuing poverty of the district and the sporadic violence in the countryside. The town represents a place to trade, to seek refuge, to pass through in search of work elsewhere or to hang around in to find out what is happening. For town-dwellers, the 'village' is often both a source of anxiety (What is happening to the . family out there? Shall I be able to take them enough gifts when I go back?) and of comfort and social reproduction (a place of weddings and family celebrations, a theatre for the prodigal to exhibit his or her sophistication and wealth, and somewhere to catch up on the local news while resting from the pressures of working life). The traffic between urban and rural lives is both ways.

A further factor uniting the country and the city is the small size of both the district and the town. Many people who stay most of the time in town have an alternative base: a family farm, or at least a small plot of land (a *shamba* as they are known throughout Uganda) in the nearby countryside. Even many professional men and women, traders or government workers, will get an important part of their livelihood from farming for their own consumption, with most of the labour carried out by other family members. Such plots are likely to be within an easy bicycle ride from the town.

This pattern of interaction between the urban and the rural is also true for the broader processes of migration from the district. Aidan Southall has given a sad portrayal of the effects of migration on the Alur of Nebbi district, the southern part of West Nile, using the metaphor of an 'hour-glass', in which the Alur and their knowledge have been 'propelled' in a series of 'pulses' from their rural homeland into the alien urban world of Kampala:

Alur society and culture are posed at either end of the hour-glass. One end holds the impoverished peasantry, with a few brave teachers, symbol managers (such as pastors, catechists, learned men, healers), administrators and entrepreneurs. This is the land of irredeemable Alur culture and speech, for the cultural elite leaves as soon as it is produced. Around the capital are the ambitious and the enterprising, their children educated in English and unwilling to contemplate going home. (Southall 1995:51)

While much of this is true for Arua as well as Nebbi, the sand in the hour-glass does not always flow in the same direction. West Nilers in southern Uganda do often go back home to visit (sometimes for extended periods) and they frequently keep rights over a plot of land there. As Chapter One indicated, most stay in touch with events in 'the village', and many will call out the elders if problems occur in Kampala. Moreover, Arua, like other provincial centres near areas of out-migration, functions as an intermediary point, both literally, as a stopover on the way from the village to Kampala, and figuratively, as offering the chance of a lifestyle midway between that of the village and that of Kampala, which allows closer contacts with both than either provides with the other.

This of course depends on the ability of the formal and informal economies of Arua to provide the economic opportunities to support the diverse population of the town. By the time of my first visit in 1995, Arua municipality (an area of some 20 km^2) had an official population of around 30,000, out of a district of some 707,680 inhabitants.[15] In fact, at points during the fieldwork period, local officials estimated that the town had swollen to perhaps twice its official size, as people from the rebel-affected areas of the countryside and others moved into Arua for safety. Moreover, these figures do not include non-nationals, such as the Sudanese refugees. According to Payne (1998: 7) there were more than 100,000 Sudanese refugees in the district in 1994. By 1995, some 55,000 of these were living in the rebel-affected refugee settlements in Aringa County, and over the next couple of years many moved into Arua town in search of safety (Payne 1998: 23, Leopold 2001: 66).

Different groups of temporary and permanent townspeople have varying reasons for being in the town, different sources of economic support and livelihood strategies, and contrasting 'bundle[s] of beliefs, usages and forms' (Thompson 1991: 338) associated with the socio-economic aspects of their life. Loosely speaking, one may discern four main groups of 'social institutions' (Berry 1989) or arenas of socio-economic activity, which operate as competing but overlapping fields of attraction for the people of the town. These are the worlds of the land, the market, the state and the assistance regime. However, individuals usually operate in more than one of these fields, or move between them, in the attempt to survive and to live the lives they want.

Anthropologists and historians have used various phrases to express the embeddedness of economic behaviour in social and cultural norms and values. I was tempted here to use Edward Thompson's term 'moral economy' (Thompson 1991: Chs IV and V; see also Scott 1976). The advantage of this phrase is that it emphasises the cultural and moral aspects of exchange, the tensions between reciprocity and contestation in socio-economic relations and the rootedness of 'the economic' in specific and changing historical circumstances. However, as used by Thompson, Scott and others, 'moral economy' has a specific context in disputes over the supply of food staples in times of dearth, and expresses a binary, Marxist opposition between (to oversimplify somewhat) a weak peasantry appealing to 'tradition' and a ruling class asserting the claims of the free market (see Thompson 1991: 336–51). In Arua, it seems to me, things are more complicated than this, and I have therefore resorted to the somewhat vaguer metaphors of 'worlds', 'fields' or 'spheres' of socio-economic activity.

What I term the 'world of the land' is the sphere of the local peasant farmers whose land happens to be near enough to the administrative capital of the district for them to be drawn into the orbit of Arua town. Many of them grow a few cash crops, such as vegetables for sale in the market or tobacco, which is by far the main cash crop, grown by small farmers on plots of 0.5 to 3.0 acres, and bought mostly by the British–American Tobacco Co. (BAT), which until 1996 had a monopsony. Similar producers include the fishermen and women of the riverine area. The world of the land also includes the role of the elders (predominantly from near the town, but also including a few from further afield in the district, who have chosen to live in or near the town and are regarded with similar respect by local people to that accorded their own clan leaders). They represent

---

[15] Figures based on projections from the 1991 Census in Community Action Programme (CAP 1993: Chapter 3.1 and Appendix 2. The CAP report is in Refugee Studies Centre RSC LU-65.1 OLO.

the link I have stressed between the town and its agricultural hinterland: their reason for being in Arua is that it is their family land, their place of birth, and the social and economic relationships they enter into with others are predicated on this sense of belonging and ownership.

The 'world of the state' involves a pyramid of 'state's men' and women (Davis 1992b), from the Resident District Commissioner (RDC) at the top, through MPs, army officers, civil servants and policemen, down to people such as the ragged market boy who proudly showed me his army (UPDF) identification, a laminated photocard which showed his number, name and rank, of 'Informer' (his ambition was to be promoted to the rank of enlisted private, but he lacked the necessary educational qualifications). The state's men, who include both locals and other Ugandans, receive an income from the state, but in many cases this is inadequate or infrequently paid, and (to varying degrees) other sources of income are necessary, many of which involve exercising the power of the state in the patrimonial interests of themselves or their clients (see Berry 1989; Bayart 1993; Allen 1998). However, to an extent at least, their relationship with the state gives them a particular set of economic 'beliefs, usages and forms'.

An encounter between the values of the state and the market, trivial in itself but demonstrating a perverse kind of 'moral economy', occurred while I was talking to a UPDF colonel in the Continental bar one afternoon. A young market boy came up selling newspapers but, that day, the government daily, the *New Vision*, was giving away a large colourful map of the country and copies had been snapped up quickly. The paper-boy tried to sell me a copy for twice the going rate (in Arua, the latter is 100 shillings over the cover price) and was upbraided by the colonel, who forced him to kneel and listen to a lecture: 'How dare you try to cheat the *muzungu*? What will the *muzungu* think of Uganda if you do this? You are giving Africans a bad name' and so on. I reflected that most *bazungu* would think that such entrepreneurial spirit was exactly what Africa needed. Eventually I persuaded him to let the boy go.

I do not, however, want to suggest that the various kinds of 'state's men' and women form a monolithic group. I use Davis's term to cover a variety of forms and sites of state power. Most discussion of Ugandan politics under the National Resistance Movement (NRM) has concentrated on the bottom-up system of Local Councils (LCs, formerly Resistance Councils, RCs), which range from village or urban ward level (LC1) to district level (LC5).[16] State power, however, is also exercised top-down through the RDC, an appointee of the President, to whom the various district officers (Health, Education, Agriculture, Forestry, Internal Security, etc) report (via the Chief Administrative Officer, or CAO). As I have already indicated, these titles, positions and functions are all clearly rooted in the colonial era. There are also local politicians of greater or lesser influence at the centre and locally, as well as the various military formations in the district, which (inevitably in a rebel-affected area) also exercised state power in a variety of formal and informal ways. 'State's men' is a convenient way of grouping together these not always harmonious forces. I analyse the political

---

[16] The best accounts of Museveni's Uganda are in the collections edited by Hansen and Twaddle (1988, 1991, 1995b, 1998).

role of the state, and local people's attitudes to its institutions and practices, below.

The 'world of the market' involves the formal and informal traders, wholesalers, smugglers and dealers of both the physical market-place and the invisible, international, formal and informal markets for all kinds of tradable commodities (from second-hand clothes to gold and diamonds, cooking oil to marijuana and khat, smuggled petrol to transistor radios) that run through and beneath the visible stalls and shops of the town. The businessmen and women involved in both sectors are in town primarily because they can make a profit there, but it would be simplistic to see the informal sector (referred to throughout Uganda by the Swahili term *magendo*) as some kind of ideal free market. In many cases (e.g. gold, diamonds, drugs) a personal relationship involving considerable trust is essential to the exchange process. The market brings in many from outside the district: some are passing through, others are there to stay. I met second-hand shoe sellers from Guinea and Senegal, Israeli gold dealers, a Yemeni garage proprietor, Sudanese grain traders, Indonesian loggers, Somali truck drivers and many others.

The 'world of the assistance regime' is that of the international (and a few national) intergovernmental and non-governmental organisations. As I have written elsewhere (Leopold 2001), the impact of the agencies, of which they seemed largely unaware, affected every aspect of the local economy and society, from basic infrastructure (UNHCR funded the construction of the first tarmac road through the town) to the formal and informal economy of the town market. The availability of very cheap United States Agency for International Development (USAID)-supplied cooking oil, resold by the refugees, had wiped out the local seed-oil business. At the same time, a group of market youths involved in smuggling and other informal trade, and calling themselves 'the Mobile Team', specialised in providing hard-to-get items for NGOs, such as motor spares and fuel. They would even provide the receipts necessary to keep agency bookkeepers happy. The international agencies were also the biggest employers in the district, especially of relatively educated, English-speaking people, and also wielded political power and patronage, visible in the UNHCR-funded offices of the local government refugee officer, which were newer and smarter than those of the RDC himself.[17] Again, a distinct set of beliefs, norms and ways of operating govern the activities of the assistance economy and determine the ways it related to the other socio-economic sectors.

In the above discussion I have used the conventional distinction between the 'formal' and 'informal' sectors, but my examples show that the reality is more complex. As MacGaffey says (preferring the term 'second' to 'informal' economy):

> The second economy exists for political as much as for economic reasons; its activities are supposedly under the control of the state but either evade this control or involve illegal use of state position. It is important to see them not simply as solutions to

---

[17] The NGOs also appeared to be immune from many regulations applying to other foreign nationals: for example, I never met an NGO researcher who applied for research clearance for their projects from the Uganda National Council for Science and Technology, although this is a legal requirement for them, as newspaper adverts by the Council stated.

household survival or individual subsistence problems, but rather as political options, co-opted by political discourse.... The margin between the legal and the illegal, the legitimate and the illegitimate is often shadowy.... Through the second economy, the citizenry may not only evade civil obligations but also express resistance to the state and to the class which controls it. (MacGaffey 1991: 9–10)

This *magendo* trade (in a narrow sense, the term applies particularly to cross-border smuggling, but it is applied more widely) probably accounts for most of the 'real' economy of Arua, as it did in MacGaffey's study of Mobuto's Zaïre. Green (1981) and Prunier (1983) both date the Uganda-wide *magendo* trade to the collapse of the economy after Amin's expulsion of the Asians. They depict, from very different perspectives,[18] an informal sector out of control, dominating every other sector of economic life in the country, from subsistence farming to the activities of senior civil servants, and generating its own class structures. This process continued through the 1980s, as Hansen and Twaddle put it in 1991:

> [L]ow salaries have ... pushed wage earners ever more deeply into engagement with the magendo economy and the subsistence sector. This process sharply accelerated after Idi Amin came to power in January 1971 and continued into the 1980s.... An unprecedented fall in real wages during the last two decades has forced the economy into an essentially subsistence mode and prompted substantial growth in the informal sector. (Hansen and Twaddle 1991: 11)

In Arua town itself, Meagher (1990) analysed a triangular cross-border trade system linking Zaïre, north-west Uganda and Kenya, and involving gold, coffee and US dollars, as well as lesser trades in food commodities, mercury and clothing.[19] MacGaffey (1991: 18, 43–71) lists the following commodities as being traded illegally across this part of the Zaïre/Uganda border: gold, coffee, ivory, skins, live animals, vehicles, fuel, tea, and papain. Most of these are still traded, though at lower levels, but I did not hear of the coffee trade; perhaps (as with gold, see below) the fall in commodity prices in the 1990s had an effect.

In my time in Arua, the most prevalent, or at least overt, form of *magendo* seemed to be the smuggled fuel and cigarettes business. The main way this worked was that a fuel tanker (say) would enter Uganda from Kenya with papers stating that the load was for transshipment to Zaïre. Therefore no Uganda duties would be levied. The truck is driven through Uganda to (perhaps) the Aru border post, where, for a consideration, the driver obtains stamps on his weigh-bill from the Uganda border post showing that the fuel has left Uganda, and from the Zaïrean customs post to show it has entered Zaïre. The truck may even actually cross the border. Either way, its untaxed contents are siphoned out and taken back to Arua for distribution throughout Uganda.[20] Meagher describes a similar

---

[18] Green is overtly, polemically hostile to the *magendo* business on developmental grounds, while Prunier is considerably more relativist and enthusiastic, demonstrating the two poles between which European attitudes to *magendo* (and similar African illegalities) tend to swing.

[19] According to Meagher, 'Even brand names have a scarcity value. There is a high demand among Ugandans for Lois jeans, imported by Zaire but not by Uganda, while the Zairois prefer Lees, imported by Uganda, but unavailable on the official circuit in Zaire' (Meagher 1990: 77).

[20] This highlights the central role of truckers in the informal economy (they are also central to the operations of the assistance economy). They form a highly cosmopolitan society in themselves, whoever they are working for, with their own hierarchy of convoy bosses, drivers and turn-boys. I met truckers from a dozen countries, including one from a small village in Norfolk where I grew up.

process, and such methods were also used in the smuggling of cigarettes, with the result that in Arua a (smuggled) packet of the Kenyan Sportsman brand was a couple of hundred shillings cheaper than a packet of Ugandan Sportsman, the twist being that both contained tobacco grown, by BAT, in West Nile. Much larger discounts were available on larger quantities.

In 1996–8, the gold trade remained important despite the fact that low international prices, and the poor security situation in Congo-Zaïre had reduced both profit margins and the numbers of people involved since the days of Meagher and MacGaffey. I was told in March 1998 that the difference between gold prices in producing areas of the Congo and that in Arua town was only 5 per cent; potential smugglers therefore had to be very confident in their ability to get the gold across the border, to make the margin worthwhile. Another factor was the (albeit relatively small-scale) mining of gold in SPLA-controlled 'New Sudan'. Here again, margins were low: at least one company involved in mining there eventually found it more profitable to provide transport services for the assistance agencies. By 1998, however (when I was offered one), diamonds were also finding their way to Arua.

Many forms of illegal trade in Arua go unmentioned by MacGaffey and Meagher. One is the drugs trade, which in Arua involves locally grown illicit substances such as cannabis (in Uganda, this is often, confusingly, referred to as 'opium') and khat (known as *mairungi*). There is also a thriving trade in biomedical drugs illicitly obtained from government or NGO stores. Another illegal trade in the region which goes unmentioned in the 'informal economy' literature is that in tropical hardwood species that are protected by the international Convention on International Trade in Endangered Species (CITES) treaties. In 1998, a Malaysian-based company was logging teak plantations near Yei in New Sudan (planted by the British in the 1950s), having come to an agreement with the SPLA/M. Other woods came from the Congo, including the extremely valuable (and protected) 'African blackwood', known incorrectly as ebony, which is used to make woodwind musical instruments. A final category of illegal trade, which is not usually mentioned in the literature on *magendo*, is the arms business. Certainly arms of all kinds were getting out through the district to the SPLA and being brought into the district by the rebels.

By May 1998, forces friendly to the Ugandan government were in power for some distance over both the Congo and Sudan borders. This severely limited the long-standing cross-border economic activities of local traders in the 'informal' or *magendo* markets, such as those for gold, diamonds, fuel, tobacco, drugs and motor spares. Most of my local informants who had been involved in the informal economy believed that the business had not vanished so much as been monopolised by the UPDF and other government agents; but from their point of view, the effect was much the same.

At this time, one 'market boy' in his late teens, an intelligent young man whose Congo connections were proclaimed by his oil-stained Versace T-shirt, complained to me about the lack of business and his straitened financial condition. It occurred to me that we might help each other if I could employ him to gather information about Arua's flourishing market. I improvised a rather rough-and-ready survey, which did not seek to collect information on informal trade, but my assistant interpreted a question on whether the stallholders had any other business to include *magendo* business. The results of the survey are, of course, by no means scientific. Many people refused to answer his questions; I suspect, too, that there may well have been others he simply did not approach, knowing them to have a personal animosity towards him, or perhaps they were simply not in one of his networks. He excluded the vegetable market (with its all-female stallholders) and other specialist areas, such as the side street where hides and skins are sold and the one for fish sellers. The survey seems to have concentrated on the areas with better-established stalls and shops: the results certainly underestimate the proportion of women involved, the extent of *magendo* trade and the participation of people from outside the district. The non-random sample of fifty-five stall/shop holders (spread unevenly over nine streets), out of a population of perhaps 800 sellers in the market area as a whole, provides a picture of the market which is partial in both senses of the word.

Nevertheless, in a qualitative rather than quantitative sense, the study is revealing in several ways. Twenty per cent of the stallholders in the sample admitted to being involved in illegal trades, particularly gold, petroleum and cigarette smuggling. Many shops and stalls sell a variety of goods, which cut across legal and illegal categories; for example, 'the stallholder sells goods like soap, sugar, mattresses, *magendo* trade in petroleum products and Kenya export cigarettes'. More than 7 per cent of stallholders also worked in government, administrative or NGO posts, and some of their trading was related to their salaried employment; for example, a stationery shop owned by an NGO administrator is likely to have an enthusiastic purchaser, and on occasion perhaps supplier, in their owner's employer. Similarly, a veterinary equipment, drugs and services enterprise might be owned by a government vet.

While the survey, as already suggested, almost certainly understates the importance of illegal, *magendo* trade, it is also true that this trade is considerably less than it was in the 1970s and 1980s (Green 1981; Prunier 1983; Meagher 1990). There are several reasons for this. First, the growing power of the Ugandan state, especially the increasing militarisation of the district in the late 1990s, has either closed down or taken over much of the trade (local people involved in *magendo* insist that much of the trade has simply been monopolised by the army, the police or the Anti-Smuggling Unit, but I have no hard evidence of this and the authorities naturally deny it). Secondly, the internal situation in Zaïre and southern Sudan made trade in those countries much more difficult in the late 1990s than ten years earlier. Thirdly, the steep fall in world gold prices in the 1990s had reduced margins for small-scale smugglers to almost uneconomic levels.

Running through and cutting across the socio-economic 'worlds' I have described, are not just the lives of individual people (though most, of course, do inhabit more than one of these worlds) but also social networks. As Sara Berry noted, 'since pre-colonial times, Africans have gained access to land, labour and capital for agricultural production both through exchange and through membership and status in various social units' (Berry 1989: 41). Within the world of the state, for example, there are kinship networks that operate, to a degree, in accordance with the kind of 'traditional' norms I have described as characterising the world of 'the land'. This was one area in which ethnicity had considerable salience; people noted, for example, that particular Madi families were prominent in the district-level state structures. But kinship ties are also linked with both political and religious affiliations, which form interlocking networks. Church networks are extremely important (and the churches engage with the worlds of the market, the agencies and the state in significant ways).

At the same time, *magendo* networks not only run through the overt arena of the market, but extend deep into the assistance economy, as well as state structures. Looser, more informal networks may have great influence; I know a network of friends whose relationships were forged in the refugee camps of southern Sudan and who stay in close touch, helping each other when possible, on an international scale. The refugee experience, for some, especially those 'resettled' in Europe or North America, has opened new opportunities for exercising traditional West Nile skills (for example, the international trading company formed by my Canadian peace-keeping friend, mentioned in the previous chapter). Both more and less formal networks continue to influence access to resources in the complex social environment of Arua town.

Another factor, which cuts across the different social worlds I have described, is poverty. The bustle and activity of the market-place and the scale of the informal economy, disguise the overwhelming fact about Arua, which is that most people are very poor (by, for example, southern Ugandan standards). Even relatively wealthy wage-earners almost invariably have to supplement their incomes by agricultural production for subsistence or sale and, as likely as not, by some degree of involvement in *magendo*. The vast majority of people working in all the fields outlined above were poor and their livelihoods insecure. Neither the assistance economy nor the market offers secure long-term jobs, while the land, though fertile, does not provide a rich living even for relatively large landholders. The state sector pays most of its employees little, and usually late (though, as I was told, at least in the army you are always fed). Most people in and around Arua town get by, in most years, with a complex mixture of livelihood strategies, manipulating membership in various networks and inhabiting more than one social world.

Politics & powers

Political alignments in Arua, as in other frontier zones (see Wilson and Donnan, 1998), are structured around two, potentially contradictory, axes of power. One extends between the town as administrative (and military) periphery and the centre of the Ugandan state in Kampala/Entebbe.[21] The other links the town as regional centre with its wider hinterland, which extends far across the inter-national borders. Over my fieldwork period, power ebbed and flowed around

[21] This axis of power obviously relates to Southall's (1995) 'hour-glass' migration pattern, mentioned above.

these axes in shifting patterns, as electoral results, the fortunes of war and changing economic conditions both caused and reflected shifting local allegiances and expectations.

Chapter Seven examines the relationship between the district and the nation in the context of local attempts at social reconstruction, an important aspect of which has been a series of attempts to negotiate a new relationship between West Nile and Kampala. Chapter One covered my own experiences during the rapidly changing events that characterised my fieldwork period. Here I want to focus on how these events affected power and politics, in terms of relationships between and within the four social fields outlined in the previous section. The central and symptomatic factor at the time was the conflict between the Ugandan government and the rebels grouped in the West Nile Bank Front (WNBF), and later in a splinter group called the Uganda National Rescue Front Part Two (UNRF II). This conflict reflected both axes of power: between the state and its troublesome periphery (and inevitably between the Ugandan state and neighbouring states), but also between Arua town as subordinate centre and its wider region.

The West Nile Bank Front was formed, almost certainly on the initiative of Sudanese intelligence, in 1994. Its leader, Juma Oris, a Madi Muslim from Nimule, had at one stage been Foreign Minister under Idi Amin, and had a long-standing relationship with the Sudanese security services (Harrell-Bond 1986: 38, 141). In 1979, when the Tanzanians invaded, he was Minister for Animal Resources and, according to Peter Woodward, crossed the border into Sudan with 3,000 head of cattle (Woodward 1988: 234). In the refugee camps, Oris's Khartoum connections facilitated the formation of the anti-Obote Uganda National Rescue Front in 1979 (the UNRF came to an agreement with the National Resistance Army/Movement (NRA/M) in 1986 and its former leader, Moses Ali, was by 1995 Third Deputy Prime Minister in the Ugandan government), and Oris is also said to have been responsible for recruiting West Nilers to fight on behalf of the Sudan government in Iraq (*Africa Confidential*, 2 November 1983; Harrell-Bond 1986:38; see also Amaza 1998 :120).

In 1994, following the Sudanese government's capture of the border town of Kajo Keji, and at the same time as it started to support the Lords Resistance Army in Uganda's Gulu and Kitgum districts, the Juba-based Oris began to organise the WNBF. Former soldiers and West Nile youth were offered $300 (300,000 Uganda shillings) to join (according to most of my sources, this was seldom paid) and were promised a bright future for themselves and the district when the NRM fell. Muslims, especially, seem to have been targeted for recruitment (Gersony 1997: 78). Apart from the young men, old soldiers, some of colonial vintage, were driven to join the rebels. One rather sad case was reported in the government-owned *New Vision* newspaper in 1996:

> An 80-year-old man alleged to have been on his way to join the West Nile Bank Front rebels in southern Sudan, has been arrested by the army.... Dario Nyakwa, formerly a soldier with the Kings African Rifles in 1942 and retired from the army in 1979 was arrested at Oleba [Ayivu County].... Nyakwa told the army the group [of rebels] had convinced him to join the rebels in return for 300,000 shillings. Captain Katongole said the old man would be released since the army has established poverty to be the driving force for his wanting to join the rebels. (*New Vision* 29 August 1996)

Initially, the WNBF operated mainly inside Sudan, engaging the SPLA on a number of occasions in early 1995. In Uganda, in the run-up to the presidential and parliamentary elections of 1996, President Museveni promoted two influential West Nilers to the Cabinet.[22] In Arua itself, the government was trying to move an estimated 100,000 Sudanese refugees from transit camps near Koboko to new refugee settlements, particularly Ikafe and Imvepi in Aringa County. Sporadic attacks were carried out against government targets around the district, including a couple of assassination attempts in Arua town itself (newcomers would be shown the splintered concrete of the bar floors, where grenades had been hurled). In April 1996, WNBF forces crossed the border and began to attack the refugee settlements. Fighting intensified over the next ten months, both in the refugee areas and more widely, especially in the northern parts of the district and near the borders. As described in Chapter One, the assistance regime withdrew all but essential services, the state considerably increased its military presence in the district, the peasants and most of the market people suffered from the decline in mobility produced by closed roads, curfews and general insecurity; thousands of people from the countryside flooded into town, which was often cut off from both parts of the West Nile hinterland, and from the rest of the country, by rebel attacks and land-mines. Resentments and tensions increased between the peoples of the state, the land, the market and the assistance regime.[23]

Elders had played a crucial role in earlier reconciliation exercises between the people of the district and central government (explored in Chapter Seven). As Chapter One has outlined, an ad hoc committee of local elders drew up a report for the President in 1995, explaining the situation in the district and attempting to represent the views of West Nilers on the security situation. The Report of the Committee for Peace and Stability in Arua District provides a lengthy analysis of the causes of the antagonism between local people and the national state: from its historical roots in colonial policies and the southern Ugandan identification of West Nilers with Idi Amin, to current concerns about poverty, low educational standards and poor communications (the tarmac surfacing of the main road from Karuma to Pakwach, West Nile's sole link with the south, was and remains the main development aim of local politicians and traders). External factors, such as Uganda's relationship with the Khartoum regime, were also listed, and the document expressed local people's sense of being caught between the larger political forces raging around the frontier zone. As the Report suggests,

> There is a strong belief among many West Nilers that the government has never fully trusted the people of West Nile region, and that is why the ex-soldiers have not been attended to.[24] Government projects in the region are minimal and government has no interest to solve the problems on all routes to West Nile region.... Government has the capacity and the means to have ended the insurgency in West Nile, let alone allow it to develop from a simple disgruntlement to a fully-fledged rebel war as it is today. As we

---

[22] *Economist Intelligence Unit Quarterly Review*, Third quarter, 1995:8-10.
[23] These antagonisms are also examined in Leopold (2001).
[24] Much local resentment centred around demobilisation payments and pensions paid (or allegedly not paid) to former government soldiers of various regimes and members of certain past rebel groups.

talk, the deployment of UPDF in the region is not enough for the size of the problem and logistical support is inadequate.[25]

While the WNBF had very limited support in the district it had, in a confused way, articulated widely held grievances. After the Ugandan military successes of early 1997, described in Chapter One, the new ascendancy of the state set up new expectations. If 'development' had previously been constrained by insecurity, now the government was expected to deliver something. By the time of my second extended field visit in 1997–8, Arua town was certainly, in most respects, booming economically. In place of the curfews, discontent and siege conditions of 1996–7, people were trading more widely, new enterprises had sprung up and the assistance regime had changed its focus from Sudanese refugees in the district (who had mostly repatriated following the SPLA advance) to cross-border assistance into the SPLA/M-held areas of 'New Sudan'. As already noted, in the 1998 local government elections (which were mostly fair, though with a few notable cases of bribery and intimidation), pro-NRM candidates won all the important positions. For the first time, perhaps, the government had a real, if tenuous, base of democratic support in the district. The reconciliation was sealed symbolically with the visit of Presidents Museveni and Moi (the latter endearing himself to locals by delivering his speech – on East African unity – in Kiswahili). Its perpetuation, however, will depend crucially on the economic development of the area, and local expectations of the powers of central government to deliver this may well be exaggerated.

Cultures & societies

Real life in Arua, the town's social and cultural existence, of course transcends the static categories of the land, the state, the assistance regime and the market that I have used here. A walk over the golf-course, for example would reveal its use by a multiplicity of social groups, rather than its symbolic role of exclusion and separation. Behind the garage on the main road one might find a group of youths smoking cannabis. Further up, under the trees, a courting couple may be giggling together. One patch of grass has been appropriated by twenty or so small boys playing a scratch game of football. The small stream that runs through the bottom of the greens is in constant use by young women washing clothes, babies and themselves. On the playing part of the course, a colonel from the south-west of the country might be practising putting with a local businessman while, in the clubhouse garden, now open to all as the 'West Nile Club', a couple of retired civil servants may be sharing a beer with an Oxfam manager from the same part of the district. At the top of the course, a corner has been cut out for building: there are the offices of several assistance agencies (including Oxfam). Round the perimeter run a small group of athletes (Arua is famous in Ugandan sports circles for its long-distance runners, and a group of young men practises twice daily, even in the hot dry season, hoping for a result in national competition that might

[25] Report of the Committee on Peace and Stability in Arua District.

Plate 2.3 Arua golf course

conceivably earn one of them their mutual dream – a sporting scholarship to a US university).

Like the political context, social lives changed over the course of my fieldwork. During the earlier period, with the town under siege, social life was constrained by uncertainty and by material conditions. Fuel and parts for generators and other electrical equipment were hard to come by, while the town centre's public electricity supply was only ever available for three hours in the evenings, and often not at all; the material means of cultural globalisation were therefore rather constricted. For the 1997 European Cup football competition, the sole public satellite TV screen in town (in the Asian-owned Babito's Nightclub) was the most popular evening venue for young males, especially when Manchester United was playing. By the time of the 1998 World Cup, however, more than half a dozen places had satellite dishes, and the canteen in the Catholic Diocesan Centre was forced to acquire one too, faced with losing most of its trade to other bars. Another cultural index of the changes between my two main fieldwork periods was radio. On my first trip, no Ugandan stations were audible in Arua; people listened to the BBC World Service (or occasionally Sudanese stations such as the SPLA's). By the time of my second fieldwork visit, two local FM stations had been established, one playing *Lingala* music, and the other a play list of US Christian pop combined with local news.

Dance, as Middleton (1985) noted, was important in traditional Lugbara society. Such local circle dances are still popular, in and out of traditional contexts. They greet public occasions such as the opening of a new clinic or the arrival of a dignitary. More importantly, dancing (along with drumming and singing) also still dominates the funerals which, during much of my fieldwork, seemed to go on most nights. Dance expresses kinship at multiple levels: variations exist between different Lugbara groups (usually expressed in geographical rather than kinship terms – as specialities of sub-counties), while local historian Lulua Odu claims that the only distinction he has been able to find between the Lugbara and the Madi, in thirty years of research, is that the former simply move up and down during their dances, while the latter tend to sway from side to side as well (see also Middleton 1985: 175).[26] More modern dance forms, especially the *Lingala* music played at parties and discos, were also very popular, particularly, as discussed in Chapter One, during the time of greatest tension in the town.

If the discos in the town centre represent, in a sense, the dance of the market and the circle dances are of the land, then the state and the assistance regime also have their own 'rhythmic bodily disciplines' (McNeill 1995). Parades are popular for both church and state occasions and became especially common during the 1998 local elections, each candidate organising military-looking marches of supporters along the main street, waving branches, posters and flags. Members of religious groups, schools and local NGOs parade together on many occasions and develop their own slogans and styles. Even the international agencies organise dances and parades for occasions such as the retirement or re-posting of staff. These invariably involve strongly hierarchical seating arrange-ments and interminable speeches, before the music (usually *Lingala*) begins. The NGOs also put on plays with moral themes. One I saw was reminiscent of British Punch and Judy puppet shows. It featured a lazy man who did not work and hit his wife. Eventually the wife's father (possibly representing, in the eyes of the NGO, the wisdom of the elders) persuaded her to complain to the local LC officers, who arrived in the family compound accompanied by policemen. After an extended slapstick chase, they caught and beat up the husband, who thereafter learned the error of his ways and performed his domestic tasks without beating his wife. The play was performed and received with vigorous enthusiasm.

The point is, though, that although these different forms of rhythmic move-ment and bodily discipline may be associated, as I have suggested here, with the different 'social worlds' isolated at the beginning of the chapter, they are enjoyed by everybody (except perhaps the funerals, which are more family than public activities). To paraphrase Powdermaker's remarks on the copper-belt towns, local men who participated in a traditional dance to celebrate the opening of an NGO-funded clinic on Saturday afternoon (an occasion well attended by the senior state's men) will get changed into denim and T-shirts to go to a late night *Lingala* disco in a market-area nightclub that evening (alongside the same politicians and soldiers). Generalisations about cosmopolitanism and globalisation elide a more complex social truth. Arua town in the late 1990s was one, varied, world, in which people, like people everywhere, were trying to direct their own lives in circumstances, as ever, not of their own choosing.

---

[26] Lulua is speaking of men's dances, but women's dances, too, have the same general features.

3
Amin, West Nile & the Postcolony
1995–62

Introduction

The roots of any historical phenomenon include both short and lengthier strands. The proximate causes of the situation described in the previous chapter lie in the post-independence period and particularly in the consequences and causes of the refugee experience undergone by the vast majority of the people of the West Nile in the 1980s, together with how these were perceived by others. The flight of the West Nilers and the causes of the rebel conflict, the political and economic marginalisation of the district and the importance of the *magendo* trade and of the assistance regime could be, and sometimes are, crudely traced to one man: Idi Amin. The situation is obviously more complex than this, not least because the causes and consequences of Amin himself can only be understood in light of the earlier history of the district. Nevertheless, for both local people and outsiders, Amin's image dominates understandings of the situation of West Nile at the end of the twentieth century. As the Committee for Peace and Security in Arua District put it, writing of Amin's coup which overthrew President Milton Obote in January 1971, 'Since that day the history and image of West Nile has been read and seen upside down by everyone, Ugandan and non-Ugandan alike.'

In this chapter, I go backwards in time to consider, first, the political relationships between the West Nilers and the Ugandan state when they returned from exile in the 1980s, and then the effects of the flight and return itself. A surprising amount has been written about the latter events, which were in fact an important focus of the first attempts to establish 'refugee studies' as an academic field in Britain, and they also dominate many local explanations of social conditions in Arua today. I go on to focus on the Amin period and how it has been understood, both in West Nile itself and by outsiders (both popular writers and academics), before concluding with a brief look at the district during Uganda's first decade after independence (the period widely known as 'Obote I').

Return & peacemaking in the 1980s

When, after 1985, the West Nilers returned, gradually and often reluctantly, from their exile in Sudan and Zaïre, they found a district whose already minimal infrastructure had been destroyed by the fighting of 1979–80, which had forced them into exile, and by the hostility and neglect of the subsequent regimes of Obote II and its epigones. The appalling situation faced by rural returnees has been well described in a number of papers by Allen, who focuses on the Madi, though much of what he says applies equally to many rural Lugbara people.[1] The situation in Arua town was rather better than that in the countryside, at least for those whose livelihood strategies in the refugee camps had endowed them with trading opportunities. Indeed, the local importance of both the assistance regime and of cross-border *magendo* trade (together with other market activities) may be dated to the return from the camps (although *magendo* has, of course, earlier antecedents). The rebel groups, too, as we have seen, came out of precursor movements established during the period of flight and return.

The literature on the West Nilers' refugee and returnee experience, discussed below, defines various waves of population movements between 1979 and 1996, but such an approach tends to hide the degree to which individual households moved back and forth across the borders, or maintained certain family members in Sudan while others returned to see how things were at home and made initial contacts with local representatives of the new regime. In some parts of the district, many people returned fairly early, in 1982 or 1983. Other counties remained in a fluctuating, lawless state, with the presence of 'Aminist' rebel groups. Little is known about the operation of state power in the district in the earlier part of this period (the later part is considered below).[2]

A few West Nilers never left the country but tried to work with Obote. Ondoga ori Amaza, a Madi doctor later to become a leading NRM cadre, wrote:

> It thus became clear to people from the West Nile region that if they wanted to fit in the post-Amin era of Ugandan politics, they had to behave correctly... West Nilers could only hope to be considered favourably if they supported Obote and the UPC [Uganda People's Congress]....
>
> Consequently, for most of September 1980, I was in Moyo District, walking from parish to parish calling on the villagers to vote for Apiligia and the UPC. 'The UPC regards everyone from West Nile as Amin's supporters. So we must pretend to support them so that when they come to power they will not mistreat us. And whether we like it or not, they are going to come to power anyway.' (Amaza 1998: xv–xvi)

Some local elders took a similar position, collaborating with the UPC in an attempt to moderate the actions of the government. Many of them were Protestants, who belonged to the nationalist generation of the 1950s and 1960s; at one time they had seen Obote's UPC party as their natural home, notwithstanding Obote's later hostility to the people of West Nile. One man told me:

> Well, 1980 was not easy. But I had foresight. Because ... I knew that this was a completely defeated army. There was no question of deceiving ourselves that we could fight back, do counter-whatever ... They started to organise themselves to fight back, but I knew that it was useless. So I went back, I took an active part in the politics and I identified myself with the authorities through the UPC. Of course, there I had a cover, and a very good cover also. I was here as a youth leader, trying to fight the insurgency,

---

[1] Allen (1989a, 1991b, 1992, 1993, 1996b). See also Crisp (1986).
[2] On the political background in this period, see especially the contributions to Hansen and Twaddle (1988) and Rupesinghe (1989).

well, the insecurity. But the insecurity I was fighting was both external and internal, because the official government soldiers were also responsible for the insecurity. There was this problem in the politics of Uganda, of revenge and so on. But because I was now here on the government side I had a ground to stand on. It was not easy, but I managed to restore order, particularly in this area here. I also managed to make it possible for our people to come back, to come back and start to settle down.... By 1983, 84, around here many of the people had already returned.... Because I was a strong fellow, I was here, so the majority came back.[3]

Other leaders, too, were more anxious to make peace than fight. After the Okellos overthrew Obote in 1985, some elements of the military groups which had emerged in exile from the ruins of Amin's Uganda Army made peace with the new government.[4] Colonel Gad Wilson Toko, who had returned in 1984, was promoted to Brigadier and made Minister of Defence, in an attempt by the new regime to placate the West Nilers.[5] Most locals, however, remained suspicious of what they saw as an 'Acholi' regime, and indeed of any Ugandan government. As we shall see, many people who returned after Museveni's 1986 victory did so, not because of any confidence in the new NRA/M government, but because of SPLA attacks on their refugee camps.

The NRA/M, however, made early attempts to reassure the West Nilers that it was not about to persecute people from the northern tribes. In his swearing-in address, Museveni said:

Recently, Buloba was captured by our army, and the commander in charge of the group was an officer called Okecho. He comes from Pakwach in West Nile [the Alur area]. Therefore the so-called division between the north and south is only in people's heads. Those who are still hoping to use it are going to be disappointed. They ought to dig a grave for such aspirations and bury them. Masindi was captured by our soldiers led by Peter Kerim: he too is from West Nile. Dr Ronald Batta here, who is from Madi, has been our Director of Medical Services for all these years in the bush. (Museveni 2000: 7)[6]

At this time, January 1986, the NRA had yet to take West Nile, but they were obviously on the way. At this crucial moment, an initiative by local elders, both in Sudan and in the district itself, prevented the West Nile forces that had fought previous regimes (grouped in FUNA and UNRF) from opposing them. As the later Report of the Committee on Peace and Stability in Arua District put it:

These initiatives were taken because the people of West Nile were sick and tired of running up and down, and they did not want to wage any more wars because of the war fatigue as well as not wanting to suffer again in exile. This effort produced positive results in that for the next ten years our people enjoyed some relative calm and never left their homes to go into exile. The soldiers of FUNA and UNRF struck an understanding with the National Resistance Army.[7]

[3] Interview, Mr Nahor Oya, 6 February 1997. Transcribed from tape.
[4] These were the Former Ugandan National Army (FUNA), under Major General Isaac Lumago, and the (original) Uganda National Rescue Front (UNRF), led by Brigadier Moses Ali. Ali, a Madi from the East Bank (present-day Adjumani district) was a key figure in negotiating the relationship between the West Nilers and the state after he was co-opted into government by Museveni following a period of imprisonment.
[5] See Amaza (1998: 108).
[6] Of all the West Nile groups, Madi people were most prominent in the NRA/M and, as noted in Chapter Two, in local government posts in the late 1990s.
[7] Report of the Committee on Peace and Stability in Arua District.

One prominent figure in the initiative was a former senior civil servant, who told me:

> Before the NRM took over state power, the people of West Nile region made sure that all the fighting forces against the National Resistance Army laid down their arms in the interests of peace and security in the region. Both members of the fighting forces and the civilian population, represented by a few people under me as their Chairman for peace initiatives, agreed to lay down their arms and did not resist when the NRA entered West Nile. The government had already been made aware that the people of Arua, Nebbi, Moyo and Adjumani (West Nile) would not fight government forces on their arrival in the region.[8]

By March 1986, having taken Gulu and Kitgum by force, the NRA were ready to advance into West Nile. As the Madi NRM cadre Amaza recounted the events:

> The NRA's advance into West Nile proceeded along two prongs. One prong moved to Moyo along the Gulu–Moyo road, while the other advanced into the districts of Nebbi and Arua along the Karuma–Pakwach road. As forces of the NRA advanced along both axes, the people of West Nile were busy imploring their FUNA and UNRF sons not to bring war to the region. Having gone through the Obote II days trapped in the crossfire between the UNLA and former UA forces,[9] the elders in West Nile prevailed upon their FUNA and UNRF sons to lay down their arms even before the NRA reached there. Those who resisted were told to go back into exile in the Sudan or Zaïre. In Moyo district, elders and opinion leaders marched to River Ayugi on the border with Gulu and pitched camp there, waiting to welcome the advancing NRA troops into their district. The same scenario awaited the NRA forces advancing along the Nebbi-Arua axis. Elders gathered at the Pakwach bridge, waiting to welcome the NRA. Instead of a gunfire welcome, the entry of the NRA into the West Nile region was greeted by welcoming ululations, drumming and feasting. (Amaza 1998: 115)

While the West Nile elders were negotiating with both rebel groups and the NRA to establish such a peaceful welcome for the new state power, at local level the broader consequences of the refugee experience were having deep and persisting effects on West Nile society. It is to these I now turn.

Perils of return & flight

The present-day salience of the returnee and refugee period may be illustrated by the ways in which many local elders explain features of Arua society of which they disapprove in terms of the effects of the refugee/returnee experience. As one man, the brother of a former prominent rebel commander, put it:

> [As refugees] they cultivated groundnuts, *simsim* [sesame seeds], sweet potatoes, sorghums, and other minor crops, so when they come back even one family ... might come with a full lorry of relief food from his *shamba*. So when he reaches [Arua] he found the price of commodities is booming, so he gets a lot of money. Right from that relief aid business. You find that now some of these people are now rich in the town here, building good houses and so on. You see, they start small business out of their food aid from the United Nations camp...[10]

---

[8] Written statement in my possession. In June 1986, the author, who requested anonymity, was appointed to a senior administrative post by the NRM.

[9] The Uganda National Liberation Army (UNLA) was the official Ugandan army of the Obote era. The former Ugandan Army (UA) groups, as already mentioned, were the FUNA and UNRF.

[10] Interview, Mr Kitami Ali Garawan, 25 January 1997.

Another elder explained the rebel activity of the WNBF in terms of the refugee experience as a contrast to the Amin days:

> You will recall that, around 1972, when Amin was in power, many of these people who are now suffering outside here, they had very high positions,. They amassed a lot of wealth. But, during the time when they went into exile, of course, they lost all those things. Maybe some of them would like to go back, to restore their past glory. It's not possible now. Another problem is, during the time these people were in exile, there's another generation now. Now, there's some youths who were born either there [in Sudan], others went when they were around seven and, when they came back later, they were already seventeen years and they couldn't go to school. So there is a period when you have a generation which has not been to school and has been living freestyle life under the United Nations, just being fed all those years. And then you have the stories their fathers are telling them, how they used to enjoy and so on. No, that period has brought us a problem now. The youth we cannot control. That one is part of it, coupled with the low level of education... now they [the rebels] have backing and training [from Sudan] they can do recruitment, they can be armed....[11]

Contemporary reports described the situation facing the returnees in more harrowing terms. The most thorough account is Allen's on the returnees in East Moyo (now Adjumani district):

> There was not much that was 'voluntary' about this repatriation. Most Ugandans remained refugees as long as they could and only returned to Uganda when the war in Sudan made their continued residence impossible. Back in Uganda, life was difficult. Economic activity was restricted ... and the security situation has remained unpredictable into the 1990s. The relief effort mounted by the UNHCR and other international agencies was of limited help, and Ugandan state services were inadequate.... [I]t took several years for agricultural production to reach a point whereby most families had enough to eat and many people had to rely on gathered famine' foods for prolonged periods. That they survived as individuals and as groups reflected a remarkable capacity to make ends meet. (Allen 1993: 222)

Allen is at pains to stress (eg 1993: 257–8) that the East-Bank Madi were worse off than the Lugbara and other groups in West Nile, but other contemporary accounts suggest that there was little difference between isolated rural groups either side of the river. Many Lugbara and Kakwa speakers, too, lived on famine foods, had poor access to markets for cash crops, and faced an unsafe political and legal environment for a long time after their return.[12]

In these circumstances, more and more people moved into the social world of the market. As Allen says of local traders and stallholders in Moyo town, 'They barely seemed to break even, but trading offered an alternative to farming and some young men seemed to enjoy the excitement of travelling around.... Virtually all the stallholders were young men. Some stated openly to me that they worked in the market in order to enjoy the town life and avoid being stuck in a rural

---

[11] Interview, Mr Nahor Oyaa, 6 February 1997. Transcribed from tape.
[12] See, for example, B.E. Harrell-Bond and G. Kanyeihamba, 'Returnees and Refugees: EEC Mission to Uganda, October 1986' (RSC LU-46), A. Gowers and D. Redhouse, 'A Fact Finding Mission in West Nile, August 1987' (RSC LU-46 GOW). Even Allen, although he claims that people in Arua district were leading 'more comfortable lives' than his own subjects, concedes that 'In 1989, when FAO [the Food and Agriculture Organization] was considering food relief in northwest Uganda, nutritional surveys indicated that some populations in Arua district were in a worse position than people in Moyo district' (Allen 1993: 258).

refugee camp' (ibid.: 241–2). Arua's market was larger, and the cross-border *magendo* trades offered more lucrative opportunities to ambitious young men and women than the sweets and cigarettes stalls of Moyo. The urban economy recovered faster than its rural counterpart. The insecure and poor conditions of agricultural production in the district also sent others to Kampala and the south of Uganda (where so many had worked in the colonial era), creating a strong basis for the informal networks of West Nile migrants, which facilitate both legal and illegal trading (and, indeed, job-hunting for formal employment).

Another route out of peasant production was offered by the assistance agencies. As Allen remarks, 'a considerable portion' of the relief agencies' activities were 'tangential to the everyday concerns of the supposed beneficiaries' (1993: 222), to the point where: 'the relief effort failed, but because there was no publicity about what was going on, and because most senior staff in the aid agencies lived a life so divorced from the surrounding population, many seem to have genuinely believed that it had succeeded' (ibid: 260). Nevertheless, the agencies provided jobs as well as inadequate food aid, and many people – especially but not exclusively the relatively educated English-speakers – were sustained by such employment (not least because, unlike government and private sector employers, most international agencies actually paid salaries in full and on time). One disadvantage of such work (as of *magendo*) was the lack of job security. On 31 December 1993, the 'lead agency' in Arua district, the Lutheran World Federation (LWF) declared the district no longer an emergency situation. In accordance with the eschatological theology of the assistance regime, 'relief' was to give way to 'development'. In practice, however, most of the agencies simply pulled out (leaving a residue of bitterness among many I spoke to). It took the mass influx of Sudanese refugees in 1993–4 to bring back the agencies and restore the assistance regime as Arua's major source of employment.

Most comment on the role of the international agencies, however, concerns not the employment opportunities they provide, but the effects of the 'assistance' they give to their chosen beneficiaries. Both in Arua itself and outside, much of this discussion revolves around the notion of a 'dependency syndrome', as if people *could* have survived by depending on the unreliable and ineffective aid provided by the assistance regime. None the less, the access to food and other items provided by international recognition as a 'returnee', or before that as a 'refugee', did provide a crucial element in many people's livelihood strategies. For people used to gaining access to resources by switching 'ethnic', kinship, or economic personae, as many West Nilers were, the labels of the assistance regime offered a new set of roles with their own opportunities (see Virmani 1996, *passim*, for an elaboration of these points).

The excuse and the occasion for the violent cleansing of the district in the 1980s was its association with the regime of Idi Amin. The accepted view in the literature seems to be that the Tanzanian forces behaved well, and that persecution of the West Nilers began with their replacement by – mainly Acholi and Langi – Ugandan forces in April 1980, after which, as one of Woodward's informants told him, 'If you had a Moslem name, you died, if you were from the Lugbara, Madi, Alur and Kakwa tribes, you died. If you were from the Sudan, you died' (Woodward 1988: 234). However, some local informants claim the violence started earlier; one (Lugbara) man told me 'They started shooting as soon as they crossed the border from Nebbi: it was Luo versus Lugbara, Nilotes versus Sudanics' (a view which gains some support from an expatriate eye-witness quoted in Grahame 1980: 243). Whenever the violence started, when it did West Nile's position on two international borders for once served it well,[13] and some 250,000–350,000 people were able to escape to comparative safety in Sudan and Zaïre. The West Nilers' period of exile itself is one of the most analysed refugee movements in recent African history (e.g. Crisp 1986; Harrell-Bond 1986; Pirouet 1988; Allen 1993; Virmani 1996). Harrell-Bond's rambling anthropological master-work, *Imposing Aid* (Harrell-Bond 1986), was claimed to be the first ever independent academic appraisal of an emergency assistance pro-gramme. It launched a multidisciplinary academic sub-field, refugee or forced migration studies, which now exists in university departments around the world.[14] The book also set a research agenda beyond which few more recent studies have gone, however much more sophisticated their theoretical armoury than that deployed in *Imposing Aid*. The research questions to be answered focused on the relationship between the refugees, their hosts (both local hosts and the host state) and the international assistance regime. These remain the key issues in 'refugee studies', and are reconsidered, in relation to the West Nile refugees, in Virmani's more recent – 1996 – doctoral thesis. I shall not, however, pursue these questions here; rather, I wish simply to note how the 'refugee studies' writers, from Harrell-Bond to Virmani, portrayed the West Nilers: in part as victims, 'deployed as chessmen' in Harrell-Bond's phrase, and in part as agents capable not only of manipulating the aid system to their own advantage, but of introducing new agricultural and marketing practices to their Sudanese hosts.[15]

The southern Sudanese poet, Taban Lo-Liyong, described the West Nilers' exile from the viewpoint of a 'host' political leader (he was MP for Kajo Kaji at the time) as well as that of a former refugee in Uganda himself:

When Amin fell and Oyite-Ojok started chasing his fellow citizens out to every corner of the world.... The Madi ran, the Lugbara ran, the Kakwa ran, the Muslims ran, pursued by the Langi, the Acholi, and the Tanzanian soldiers who, while doing their master's bidding, were filling their purses. Those Ugandans who were in Arua ran to Kaya, a smuggler's meeting point on the Uganda, Zaire and the Sudan border. Some of these were brought straight to Yei and then dispersed in refugee camps. Some headed first for Gulu, and then to Nimule. These were also settled in camps, strung out on the road between Nimule and Juba. Between Nimule in the east and Kaya in the West, there is a long, undemarkated, sparsely populated and unpatrolled border. This is

---

[13] A missionary writing in the *Uganda Church Association Newsletter* noted 'we thank God that Zaire and Sudan were so near otherwise the slaughter might have been much greater than it was' (Pirouet 1998: 248). The Baganda, trapped in the centre of the country, were indeed slaughtered in great numbers at this time. See, for example, Kabera and Muyanja 1994.

[14] The book was, in fact, a relatively late flowering of the original research, between 1982 and 1984, which included a conference in Oxford at which refugees and hosts spoke for themselves about their lives, and field visits to Sudan by Oxford students, several of whom went on to become professional Africanists. The inspiration for much of this, as Harrell-Bond is the first to acknowledge, was Ahmed Karadawi, former Assistant Commissioner of Refugees in Juba and co-founder of the Oxford Refugee Studies Programme.

[15] See McGregor in Wilson et al. 1985: 15–25; Harrell-Bond 1986: 330–46.

where most of the remnants of the resistance took their last stand on the Ugandan side. On the Sudan side, the old, the infirm, the young, the Madi, Lugbara and Kakwa just walked across, chose a location similar to the one left behind, built huts and began cultivating. When the land became congested, latecomers moved inland and bartered with zinc sheets or whatever else they ran with for land. These are my guests. The guests of the hospitable Kuku of Kajo Kaji sub-district. And they are not just a handful, they are many.[16]

One key issue for the refugees, as it is for today's West Nilers, was the anxiety not to be seen as 'Amin's people'. 'We are the forgotten refugees of Africa,' a refugee in Kit 1 settlement told Virmani, 'they have labelled us "Amin's people" and then forgotten about us' (Virmani 1996: 229). Another 'Kakwa refugee in Affa... thought that the expatriate organisations "think that the whole Kakwa tribe supported Amin. Maybe now they want to punish us... They have decided to ignore our problems"' (ibid.: 230). Being seen by others as 'Amin's people' had led to their exile, and it was this perception, they felt, that would label them for ever in the eyes of other Ugandans.[17] One man explained it to me in 1997:

> It was in 1979 up to 1984 ... [we fled] in fear of Acholi soldiers. They were bad; they tortured people, killing, so people had to run away. They still follow people because of the name Lugbara, Lugbara, Lugbara like that. Because they say you Lugbara people in Amin's time you killed us, so now we have a chance to gain back so the army must kill also, tit for tat. They were using tit for tat.[18]

As the report of the Committee for Peace and Security in Arua District summarised the situation:

> Amin phobia has driven most if not all West Nilers into remaining apologetic all their lives. Ugandans know this fact and use it very effectively to silence anyone from West Nile who dares challenge authority on issues. They are smart enough even to use our own brothers and sisters to do the tricks for them. Statements like 'so and so is a former Amin this and that' coming from amidst our own people are nothing but tactics used by those who know us to divide and rule. When you think about it, who was not 'Amin this and Amin that'? Even those who claimed to have nothing to do with him were quietly 'enjoying'.

Ondoga ori Amaza, a Madi medical student in Makerere at the time, wrote later of the events of 1979:

> The idea of getting out of Kampala, even as the war approached the capital, never occurred to me. In my naïve civilian thinking, the war had nothing to do with me since I was not a soldier. This thinking, however, turned out to be a reflection of my underestimation of the extent to which Amin's misdeeds and excesses had been 'West Nilised'. For no sooner was Amin overthrown than everybody from West Nile became not only Amin's agent, but even a foreigner. We were variously labelled Sudanese, Nubians or Anyanya. People from West Nile, the Kakwa, Lugbara and Madi in

---

[16] Taban lo Liyong, 'How to maintain refugees in your midst for the love of humanity whilst the United Nations High Commissioner for Refugees looks out over Khyber Pass and doles out goodies to Afghan and Vietnamese expatriates: a spirited diatribe', paper presented at the symposium 'Assistance to Refugees, Alternative Viewpoints', March 1984, Queen Elizabeth House, Oxford (RSC Conf. box Alt 1984). Taban himself provides an illustration of what Virmani terms the 'situational nationality' characteristic of many in the Uganda/Sudan/Zaïre borderlands. A refugee in Uganda in the 1960s, his poetry was published by Heinemann as that of a Ugandan writer (Virmani 1996: 343).

[17] I consider this ideological dynamic further, from the perspective of Ugandan press reports in the 1990s, in Leopold (1999) especially pp. 231–7.

[18] Interview, Mr Kitami Ali Garawan, 25 January 1997. Transcribed from tape.

particular, found themselves being singled out as those responsible for Amin's misdeeds. (Amaza 1998: xiv)

By the time I arrived in Arua, the 'Amin' reference was ubiquitous in the West Nilers' 'image' in the nation as a whole (see Leopold 1999). It is unsurprising, then, that many of the West Nilers I spoke to were unwilling to speak much of the Amin era (some who did are quoted at the end of this chapter). In a sense, their experience over this period encompassed, in so far as one can generalise, given massive variations in the experiences of different individuals, all three of the classic triad in the anthropology of violence (Riches 1986), simultaneously becoming victims, performers (or perpetrators) and witnesses. This, of course, had its consequences for the kind of oral material I was able to gather, not only on the Amin era, but throughout this book (an issue discussed in Chapter Eight). Silences themselves may speak profoundly, but there is no reason to think that the silence of the traumatised victim, of the scared witness and of the guilty perpetrator may not coexist in any given individual. However, the political settlement on their return was not one which sought to establish individual or even collective guilt or responsibility. By then, too many other, more powerful groups in Uganda had their own reasons for guilt and their own traumatic memories. The West Nilers, though, did make attempts to heal the wounds of the past, which are discussed in Chapter Seven.

Idi Amin: man, myth & magic

If the results of Idi Amin's rule (particularly the flight and return of the West Nilers) are a central theme in the contemporary history of West Nile district, then the literature on Amin himself is dominated by his origins in the district.[19] It is no exaggeration to suggest that almost every writer on Amin's rule uses his West Nile origin in some way to explain his behaviour. In this literature, the area becomes virtually synonymous with violence and marginality, especially in the more popular books on Amin, but also in more academic analyses. In these eyes, Amin did not cause West Nile's violent marginality; *he* was caused by *it*.

So prevalent is this diagnosis that it is easiest to begin with a short list of writers who do not utilise Amin's origins in the West Nile district as an explanatory tool. They fall into two broad camps; in the first place, there are those Marxists who, as was fashionable in the 1970s, sought to explain Amin solely in terms of the structural demands of world imperialism and its consequences for different sections of the Ugandan petty bourgeoisie.[20] The other school which does not blame Amin's actions on his origins treats him as simply insane, clinically psychotic (e.g. Kiwanuka 1979).

---

[19] The literature on Amin is vast and I have by no means read it all. Jamison's bibliography cites 406 'scholarly, research level works [on Amin and Uganda during his rule] in English and housed in libraries in North America' (Jamison 1992: xiii). Before his overthrow, one commentator called him 'Africa's most publicised leader' and remarked on the number of academic discussions of his rule (Woodward 1978: 153).

[20] E.g. Brett (1975), Mamdani (1976, 1983). For a sympathetic early critique of this school see Saul (1976).

These cases aside, the debate is not whether, but how Amin's background conditioned his actions. Some of the material is, of course, purely factual: given the prevalence of the ethnic stereotypes and antagonisms of Ugandan politics, Amin's origins in West Nile district affected (to an extent) whom he was able to call on as allies, while his contacts in the border area also played an interesting role in his rise to power (through, for example, two incidents in which Amin's involvement was alleged, one of which involved ivory and gold smuggling across the border from the Congo as part of a scheme to assist Lumumbaist rebels, while the second concerned an Israeli-sponsored scheme providing assistance to Sudanese rebels). Much of the literature, however, goes further than falsifiable statements of fact to attribute a causal relationship between Amin's deeds and his ethnic background. This works in two ways: in the more popular texts, a racist anthropology relates Amin's atrocities to the traditional ways of his tribe; in the more academic work, his origins link his actions through deep, perhaps submerged historical roots to aspects of the Nile Valley or wider African past.

In the first place, suitably for a fairy-tale figure, there is some dispute over Amin's precise origins. Most accounts suggest that he was born in Koboko, very close to both the two borders, of a Muslim Kakwa father and a Christian Lugbara mother. However, he seems sometimes to have claimed to have been born near Kampala (according to Kiwanuka 1979, Mutibwa 1992), while hostile commentators frequently suggest he may not have been born in Uganda: Smith, for example, remarks that:

> the Kakwa tribe... congregates in the north west corner of Uganda where the southern Sudan and Zaire blur their borders together... They are peoples of a tribe, or tribes, and of a region, rather than of one clearly defined country. In that area borders are clearly defined only on a map ... there is no way of proving whether he was born in a hut in Zaire, in Uganda or in the southern Sudan. (Smith 1980: 25).

while Harrell-Bond refers to Amin as 'a Kakwa speaker (said to have been born in Zaire)' (Harrell-Bond 1986: 33). These stories made it possible to deny that Amin was truly Ugandan:

> To the Lugbara mother and the Kakwa father a son was born, Idi Amin. The precise date of birth is not known. It was some time between 1925 and 1928 in the Koboko district, so close to both the Sudanese border and that of Zaire as to make it very doubtful whether one could call him a Ugandan. What does matter is that his father was a Kakwa. They spoke a Sudanic language and were Nilotic tribes [sic] and whereas about six thousand of them lived in Uganda, a much larger number lived in the Sudan and Zaire. Amin came from a corner of three countries and from two tribes – his mother's Lugbara also Sudanic, also spreading across the borders of three countries. (Smith 1980: 42)

Kiwanuka, too, doubts his birthplace: 'Koboko in Kakwa land may stick as his birth place not because he himself was sure that he had been born there but because the idea had been drummed into his head by the writers' (Kiwanuka 1979: 13).

In the cruder work, the Kakwa are depicted as particularly ferocious. Grahame calls them a 'warrior tribe' (Grahame 1980: 9) and tells us that they and other West Nile tribes engaged in 'sacrifices of animals and humans' (ibid.: 12). Kyemba goes further still:

Amin's bizarre behaviour ... derives partly from his tribal background. Like many other warrior societies, the Kakwa, Amin's tribe, are known to have practised blood rituals on slain enemies. These involve cutting a piece of flesh from the body to subdue the dead man's spirit or tasting the victim's blood to render the spirit harmless.... Such rituals still exist among the Kakwa. If they kill a man, it is their practice to insert a knife in the body and touch the bloody blade to their lips....

I have reason to believe that Amin's practices do not stop at tasting blood: on several occasions he has boasted to me and others that he has eaten human flesh ... he went on to say that eating human flesh is not uncommon in his home area. (Kyemba 1977: 109–10)

As Smith (1980) points out (although it is a close thing), the most bloodthirsty accounts of Amin's violence and cannibalism come from southern Ugandans, rather than racist whites.[21] However, Smith's own position is ambiguous. At first he says that 'there is strong evidence that Amin and his henchmen did engage in this sort of thing, but as an instrument of terror, not as a tribal custom' (ibid.: 34), but he goes on to tell his readers that: 'People in thin, arid places such as the Kakwa area of Uganda[22] would engage more in the shedding of the blood of animals or even human beings. The witchcraft in which blood is shed is stronger than the witchcraft of berries and roots' (ibid.: 40). Several of the commentators mention '[A] Kakwa ... cult called the water of Yakan ... which Amin may have learned to make when he attended meetings in his early youth [which] is mixed with a drug ... called kamiojo ... a powerful drug which causes excitement and elation; taken in large quantities, it leads to elation' (Listowel 1973: 14–15). Smith believes that Yakan or lion water was 'the LSD of Central Africa in the latter part of the last century' (Smith 1980: 41) and an aphrodisiac as well as a war potion: 'Amin's mother was a Lugbara. She was known to be steeped in witchcraft, consulted by soldiers from the barracks for that, and for other services. She would have known how to prepare the "lion's water" of the Lugbara which made men strong for war or love' (ibid.: 42). The Yakan water becomes metonymic for West Nile and for savagery; Amin was: 'A boy wrung from the withers of the tribes around the western Nile, drawn in from the twilight of the witchcraft and the superstition surrounding them [*sic*], a boy of "the waters of Yakan"' (ibid.: 37). This had unexplained consequences for Amin's taste in torture techniques: 'The water symbol touched his life at many points. Its tribal mystical influences on his younger days were later followed by more terrible associations and manifestations, such as the "water treatment" meted out under his rule when the victim's head was held under water until he drowned' (ibid.: 43).

Another approach is to explain the supposed violence of the West Nilers in terms of the relatively stateless, acephalous nature of their traditional societies. The Anglo-Irish aristocrat Lady Listowel, perhaps unsurprisingly, traces the problem to Amin's lack of social advantages:

The Kakwa have a great respect for personalities, but not for rank or position. They

---

[21] *Contra*, for example, a furious article in *Africa* magazine by Godwin Matatu (1974).

[22] Smith repeatedly asserts that West Nile is dry and arid. In fact, average annual rainfall in Arua district (which includes Koboko) ranges from 1,400 mm on the watershed down to 1,000 mm by the Nile floor. This, although drier than much of southern Uganda, is a lot wetter than, for example, most of England.

never had chiefs or recognised clan leaders.... Amin was brought up to believe that all Kakwa tribesmen are equal.... A chiefless African society can have disadvantages. Among the Baganda... a chief's headquarters was in every sense the centre of tribal life.... Parents sent their children to the chief's enclosure to be his men- and maid-servants as only in that way could they obtain advancement.... Amin could have had no such training because the Kakwa had no chiefs. Some of his recent measures illustrate all too well that he had to leap from a peasant background into the complicated politics of the modern world without any intermediate feudal preparation. (Listowel 1973: 12)

If the 'Kakwa'-based explanations, in Mamdani's damning phrase, were 'parading Amin as some sort of anthropological oddity' (Mamdani 1983: 32), another set of explanations based on his West Nile background portrayed him as a *historical* oddity, a resurgence of primeval African tradition. This approach reaches its most intellectually interesting form in a debate between Aidan Southall and Ali Mazrui, which will be discussed in more detail later. First, though, it is necessary to discuss an aspect of Amin's ethnicity which indeed has historical reverberations, the Nubi factor.

In the literature on Amin, the Nubi or Nubians tend to be portrayed as an exclusively martial group. As I have already noted, they were supposedly descended from Emin Pasha's soldiers who had been driven up the Nile in the 1880s by the insurrectionary Sudanese forces of the Mahdi's rebellion. They were taken into Uganda by Captain Lugard, where, as the core of the Uganda Rifles, they assisted Baganda troops in subduing Buganda's neighbouring rival kingdoms, to form the core of modern Uganda. They were later integrated into the Fourth Battalion of the King's African Rifles (4 KAR) and fought for the British in East Africa and elsewhere. The Nubi were Muslims and, in fact if not in theory, the identity became one which many West Nile Ugandans and others adopted when they moved to towns or joined the army, and converted to Islam. Although the Nubi are always presented as 'detribalised', many maintained closer links with their West Nile origins than has often been realised. More will be said about their history later: here I shall simply note that Idi Amin was (probably like his somewhat mysterious father) a Nubi, and that many commentators have seen this as determining, in part, his violent behaviour, just as others explained it in terms of his Kakwa nature.[23]

Martin, for example, says that: 'among their fellow countrymen they enjoyed an unenviable reputation of having one of the world's highest homicide rates. The Nubians were renowned for their sadistic brutality, lack of formal education, for poisoning enemies and for their refusal to integrate, even in the urban centres' (Martin 1974: 14). Grahame, who, as Amin's commanding officer in 4 KAR, would have commanded many Nubian troops, gives a gloss on Nubi history: 'For close on twenty years [after Lugard's formation of the Uganda Rifles] the Nubians became the most feared and influential ethnic group in Uganda, mercilessly suppressing uprisings and tribal disputes at the behest of their British masters. It was the success of these early operations that gave them a contempt

---

[23] On Idi Amin and the Nubi, see especially Mazrui (1975a, b, 1977c), Pain (1975), Southall (1975), Soghayroun (1981), Johnson (1988, 1989), Rowe (1988), Woodward (1988), Hansen (1991), Kokole (1995).

for all pagan and Christian tribes in the country' (Grahame 1980: 9). To be a Nubi was to lay claim to a martial tradition:

> [Amin's mother] was a Christian from the Lugbara tribe, while his father was a Moslem and a Kakwa. Like many West Nilotes, Idi Amin therefore had complex ethnic and religious affiliations for, as a Kinubi-speaking Moslem whose ancestors had come from the Sudan, he was also allowed to consider himself a Nubian. To these people Lord Lugard had given the epithet of 'the best soldiery in Africa'. (Ibid.: 23)

Thus one can explain Amin's violence by either the Kakwa's traditional lack of a state, or the Nubi's historical involvement in the state. Some writers are unsure whether murder and cannibalism are Kakwa or Nubi phenomena. Smith tells us that: 'The southern Ugandans are particularly contemptuous of the southern Sudanese and Nubis (not of other northern tribes) as wild and uncivilised. It is from them that we have reports of Amin and his Nubis tasting the blood of their victims and eating their livers and the explanation that such a custom is either a Nubi or a Kakwa one' (Smith 1980: 34).

Another set of associations deployed in both popular and academic work on Amin concerns gender and sexuality. Amin is portrayed as the epitome of masculinity, defined in terms of both violence (the warrior ethos) and a charismatic sexuality. Lady Listowel describes meeting him for the first time: 'I looked into the smiling face of a tall, muscular officer with shrewd eyes, who invited me to a cup of coffee. He was a hulking figure of a man and I was fascinated by his hands – beautiful, slim hands with long, tapering fingers' (Listowel 1973: 7). As a famous sportsman in his army days (he was heavy-weight boxing champion of Uganda in 1951–2), Amin's 'physique was like that of a Grecian sculpture, and no matter to what form of athleticism he turned his hand, he excelled and he conquered' (Grahame 1980: 34). During a particularly exhausting route march:

> One man was an example and inspiration to us all. As we finally passed the finishing post, Idi Amin was marching beside me at the head of the column, head held high and still singing... for all he was worth. Across one shoulder were two bren guns and over the other was a crippled askari. It reminded me of a translation of another KAR marching song:

> 'It's the Sudi,[24] my boy, it's the Sudi
> With his grim-set, ugly face:
> But he looks like a man and he fights like a man
> for he comes of a fighting race'. (Ibid.: 39).

Masculinity, violence, sexuality – all linked to an atavistic racial primitivism, together with a frontier historical tradition, both exemplified in Amin's West Nile origins – perhaps surprisingly, these themes are pursued most obsessively, not in the popular books on Amin, but in the contemporary work of Ali Mazrui and its critique by Aidan Southall.[25] Mazrui's writings about Amin as they developed over the 1970s and 1980s are complex and sometimes contradictory – matching,

---

[24] Sudi = Sudanese = Nubi. Wendy James (personal communication) points out that this verse builds on the original Arabic connotation of 'Sudanese' as synonymous with 'black' or even 'slave'. It is one of the ironies of Ugandan history that it has there come to have connotations of 'Arab' and 'Muslim': of course, on both counts it implies 'Other'.

[25] See particularly Mazrui (1975a, b, 1977a, 1988). The edited collection (Mazrui 1977a) includes

in this respect, their subject. It is difficult to summarise the work without omitting some of the web of qualifications, rhetorical questions, ifs and buts he weaves around his analysis. Here I aim to avoid caricaturing the overall thrust of his argument, while at the same time emphasising those aspects most relevant to my own. In contrast, Southall's analysis, while quite as subtle, is rather less convoluted and hence more easily summarised.

These two accounts of Amin's historical meaning are developed in adjacent articles in the *Journal of Modern African Studies* (*JMAS* 13.1, 1975) (Mazrui 1975a; Southall 1975), and again in Mazrui (1977a) as well as later articles. Mazrui, invoking Ranger's early arguments about the relationship between 'primary' and 'secondary' resistance movements, suggests that: 'It is General Idi Amin rather than Dr Milton Obote who is the true successor to those early warriors in Bunyoro, Acholi, as well as West Nile, who reached for their spears to strike a blow, however weak, against European imperialism' (Mazrui 1975a: 67). Mazrui develops a pan-African theory of 'the warrior', whether from a stateless society or from the Zulu kingdom. Throughout Africa, the warrior exemplifies self-reliant adulthood: 'the theme of self-reliance involved in this warrior tradition is antithetical to the dependency complex which many Africans later acquired under the impact of colonial rule ... the struggle against dependency as exemplified by Field Marshall Amin at his best is, in an important sense, a reactivation of the ancestral assertiveness of warrior culture' (Mazrui 1977b: 77). Moreover, he exemplifies heterosexual masculinity:

> What should not be overlooked is the sexual dimension of the warrior culture.... In societies otherwise vastly different from each other, one factor remains constant, it was a man who fought for the society on the battlefield. Virtues like courage, endurance, even ruthlessness, were regarded as hard, masculine virtues. The statement 'he is a real man' could mean either he is sexually virile, or he is tough and valiant....
>
> In some African societies, special sexual rites [*sic*] were accorded to warriors.... Given the link between manliness and warfare there could also be an easy link between violence and sexuality. (Mazrui 1975a: 71, 73)

Historically, this link was exemplified by Shaka, but:

> Whereas Shaka had defined manliness in terms of sexual abstinence, Amin has seen it in terms of virile promiscuity.... Even Amin's hostility to the Asians started in part as a reaction against their sexual and social exclusivity in Uganda.... The barrier which the Asians of Uganda had erected against intermarriage with Africans was an important aspect of their tragic fate under General Idi Amin. A new Shaka has indeed cast his shadow across the African continent – but committed to virile masculinity, rather than to celibate manliness. (Ibid.: 81–3)

The sexual, the military and the political are merged in this masculine paradigm:

> When we relate charisma to the warrior tradition in Africa, there is one quality which demands particular attention. We call this quality political masculinity.
>
> As a personal quality political masculinity is a powerful image of manliness in a

25 (cont.) material from eight other papers on Amin and Uganda. Much of this work, as Mazrui explains in the introduction, was first written while he was at close quarters with Amin, teaching at Makerere at a time when Amin was an active Chancellor of the University. It was published, however, after Mazrui had left Uganda. Aidan Southall's main writings on Amin are Southall (1975, 1977, 1980, 1988). He also taught at Makerere in the 1960s. By 1975 Mazrui was at the University of Michigan and Southall at Northwestern.

political leader, which tends to affect his style of leadership and his impact on his followers. In February 1972 I visited Elmina Castle in Ghana.... I was shown round the castle by a tall and broad policeman, who ... said to me: 'You say you come from Uganda? I really like your General Amin. He is a real man.' What struck me was that across the continent in Ghana the manly image of the General ... had been perceived.

The political masculinity of the General does not lie merely in his size, though he is impressively tall and broad. Nor does it lie merely in his insistence that he fears no-one but God. Yet these factors are part of the story, combined with the additional factor that an affirmation of fearlessness and an athletic build have indeed been part of the total picture of martial values within African political cultures. (Mazrui 1975b: 149)

While Mazrui's papers on this theme usually include a token reminder that the warrior tradition is also a cruel one, the overall tendency of his work was to celebrate both that tradition and its current exemplar, Idi Amin.

If, as Nubi, Amin exemplifies the warrior (see especially Mazrui 1977b), as Kakwa he exemplifies the peasant:

Amin's response to his position in power had a deep agrarian factor from the start.... Amin moved from one group of elders to another, from one district to another, vigorously pursuing a primordial system of oral consultation.... Amin has brought other cultural inputs into the political process in Uganda derived from his peasant origins. His entire style of diplomacy is striking for its lack of middle class 'refinements'.... Some of these tendencies are personal to Amin rather than to his social origins. But the very fact that he lets his personal tendencies have such free play while occupying the top office of his nation might have been influenced by the relative spontaneity of rural upbringing among the Kakwa ... humanitarian arguments quite often are arguments steeped in middle-class assumptions and are therefore more likely to impress an African intellectual than an African peasant with memories of having been insulted over the years by Asian shopkeepers or Asian employers. The style of Amin's expulsion of the Asians was in this sense an aspect of his peasant origins (Mazrui 1975b: 46–7).[26]

More than this, it was a reflection of his West Nile origins:

Part of Amin's tribe, the Kakwa, was in the Sudan. The Sudanese Civil War broke out partly because of a de facto heritage of racial stratification in the Sudan. Amin's first rebellion against racial stratification took the form of his sympathy with the southern Sudanese movement.... He disliked the Sudanese heritage of racial stratification and resented the economic dominance of the Asians in Uganda.... Could he oppose racial stratification in the Sudan and southern Africa without confronting it in his own country? It was not long before the fate of the Ugandan Asians was sealed. (Ibid.: 283)

Whether *qua* warrior or *qua* peasant, Amin represented African tradition:

General Amin is in some respects deeply primordial in his attitudes and presuppositions. His demands on the Asians echoed some of the anthropological findings about traditional political societies in Africa. Amin has been primordial in his demand for cultural identification and biological intermingling; he has also been primordial in his tendency to regard complete aliens as basically potential enemies; and ·thirdly he has been primordial in his distrust of private choice in matters of public concern. (Ibid.: 76)

In contrast to Mazrui, Southall, while accepting Amin as the incarnation of a warrior tradition, wholly deprecates it. He relates Amin to local rather than continental history and to a developmental process rather than an episodic

---

[26] Elsewhere he refers to Amin's attitudes to the Asians as (in a phrase borrowed from Senghor) 'anti-racist racism' (Mazrui 1975b: 285) and, more flippantly, as 'Idi-ology' (ibid.: 225).

recrudescence from the precolonial past. Evoking the martial history of the Nubi and the geopolitical marginality of the Kakwa, alongside the problem of Baganda dominance in Ugandan politics, Southall presents Amin as 'an exceptional person ... [who] is the product of a series of events and a concatenation of forces which seems ineluctable' (Southall 1975:101). 'Central to my interpretation', he says, 'is the fact that General Amin is a Nubi, and that the history of the Nubi is important for the understanding of contemporary events. The present regime is more and more predominantly a Nubi regime, and its core strength is a Nubi strength' (ibid.: 85).

West Nile marginality is again emphasised and linked with Amin's violence. The Lugbara, for example, were:

> really only known by south Ugandans until recently as unskilled migrant labourers, especially on the sugar estates. Their language and behaviour was utterly foreign to the rest of Uganda. Remote from the centre and from the benefits of education and income opportunities, they seem fertile ground for fairly bitter resentment and potential hostility to other Ugandans, which may have found its outlet through the army. (Ibid.: 90)

The Nubi are once again presented as wholly deracinated and the Kakwa as barely Ugandan:

> Among the more closely informed, Amin is indisputably regarded as a Kakwa. He treats the Kakwa country in the far northwest as his home, though some argue that he is Sudanese, and others that he is Congolese, for the Kakwa have the melancholy distinction of being chopped into three by colonial boundaries.
>
> I suggest that Kakwa is a strategic identity for Amin since it carries at least the possibility of being a native Ugandan, whereas the Nubi are still looked upon as of alien Sudanese extraction. (Ibid.: 101–2)

However, Southall parts company explicitly and forcefully with Mazrui's valorisation of the warrior tradition, which, in a prescient analysis, he traces to an imperial stereotype:

> I will be bold and state my conviction that the warrior tradition is neither relevant nor useful for contemporary Africa. It inevitably summons up the colonial image of the noble savage, poised on one leg in nilotische stellung, fierce, courageous, independent every inch a man and visibly male, honest and clean, lion-spearing, the virtuous though primitive contrast to the lying, thieving, spoilt 'mission boy'....
>
> The adulation of the warrior image never hampered the efficient suppression of resistance to imperial rule by local patriots fighting to preserve their freedom. Such local valour was soon quashed, and quite forgotten... until recent Africanists dug them up again out of the archives and popularized them as 'primary resistance movements'.
>
> In so far as the warrior tradition continues to find expression in the verbal bellicosity and excessive military spending of some African leaders, it is a suicidal mockery, effectively destroying any hope of sound economic development....
>
> Moreover, the African people whose poverty and economic backwardness are exploited to perpetuate the sentimental warrior image ... are not for the most part even those who posed the greatest military threat to the Pax Colonia ... they are those who have been left high and dry in inaccessible and inhospitable areas ... so that, faute de mieux, their primal existence has continued colourful and unchanged.
>
> There are deep and insidious dangers, as well as intellectual fallacies, in fostering the warrior image as a positive symbol in contemporary Africa and, as an example of it, flattering Field Marshal Hajii Idi Amin Dada as a mystical heir of Shaka the Zulu. (Southall 1977: 166–7)

Some effects of postcolonial rule among the Lugbara

While Amin was rising to prominence in the army under Milton Obote's first government and the latter was manoeuvring against Baganda dominance in the non-military institutions of the post-independence Ugandan state, the people of the West Nile area were little known to other Ugandans. Their marginality was not that of the famously primitive Karamojong, who had been preserved as curiosities in a kind of human game park during much of the Protectorate era and were (are) still regarded in much the same light by most Ugandans. Instead, the West Nilers, in so far as they had a presence in the rest of Uganda, occupied inconspicuous positions at the bottom of the labour market, as unskilled plantation workers, soldiers, very petty traders and small farmers. In the eyes of most Baganda they probably blurred into a northern Nilotic mass.[27] Within the ethnically stratified economy created by the Ugandan version of British Indirect Rule, the West Nile district occupied a proletarian position – it had nothing to sell but its labour, and that was unskilled and poorly paid.

This position changed little under the Obote I regime, though most West Nilers acknowledge the building of the Pakwach bridge as a major step in the development of the region. Nor did Amin himself do much to improve conditions in his home region. He did build the airfield (somewhat grandiosely called Arua International Airport, and opened by President Mobuto in 1976) and nearly completed a satellite earth station which would have given the district advanced telecommunications facilities, had it been finished. Aside from that, Amin did little for the West Nile as a district. What he did do was provide many opportunities for the West Nilers, who increasingly piled into his army, to take over the ruined businesses of the expelled Asians, and to use their status as members of what Mazrui termed the 'lumpen militariat' to enrich themselves in diverse, usually illegal, ways. This undoubtedly affected a lot of people, especially young men. One West Nile exile who attended a local secondary school in the late 1970s told me of army lorries turning up at the school empty, late at night, and returning to their bases full of recruits for the forces, sometimes almost entire classes of boys.

However, the enrichment of the West Nilers was a temporary phenomenon and left few traces in the district. When asked what the effects of Amin's rule were for the West Nile, one local elder explained the situation to me as follows:

> Oh, nothing, nothing. During Amin's time here it was nothing. Because when he came here, what he did based here was recruit all the youths: even teachers were taken to join the army. OK, from the army they got ranks and so on. That is what they benefited from. But there was no tangible development here, not here, but people were enjoying themselves all over, all over the big shops in the city, everywhere and so on. [They became] directors of factories, ministers without qualifications, and what, what, what.

Like many others who had joined the army earlier, and had acquired a professional military ethic, he distrusted the new recruits, and left the army before the end:

---

[27] The generic Luganda term for West Nilers, 'Balulu', derives from 'Alur', see Chapter Four.

I was in the army, but personally I knew by 1977–78 there was no army. The situation we were in really showed militarily. There was no army. I am afraid a similar situation could even be in Zaïre right now. Because at that time, all soldiers were now acquiring big shops, otherwise they had factories, in every town they were just celebrating. The military life, that way of life got lost completely, completely. The war just took them by surprise. They were now living lifestyles, extravaganza lifestyles, and civil ones, not military at all. So when war came, seriously speaking, there was no fighting.... Even if one took the death toll of soldiers, you would not find many soldiers there have died. Everyone protected their riches, how could they die? Everybody said, 'I'm going home to take my car, to take my this, take my family that.' They were coming home everywhere, so nothing, nothing.[28]

This professional soldier's view of the realities of Amin's 'lumpen militariat' seems to me to expose the shallowness of Mazrui's fantastic 'warrior tradition' as acutely as Southall's well-justified argument did.

Put crudely, then, the effects of the postcolonial era among the people of West Nile were to reinforce the economic marginality of the district, established under colonial rule, and then, under Amin, to divert the human resources of the region (especially young males) into the army and thus into a freebooting, pillaging lifestyle. The strange fantasies about Amin cultivated by both international and Ugandan commentators were based on pre-existing ideas about his home district, and grew to determine how the inhabitants of the area were seen by other Ugandans (and thereby perhaps also by elements of the assistance regime). The West Nilers became, ineluctably, 'Amin's people'. The marginality of the district was embodied in Amin's huge frame. But he himself was symptomatic (as the fantastic elements of both the popular and academic accounts eloquently testify). In the context of regional history, his position as the quintessential Nubi turned the ordinary army NCO into a symbol of the return of the colonial repressed – a role he himself made explicit and celebrated in his many famous insults to the British empire.

The ideological legacy of the colonial period was developed in the postcolony into what I have elsewhere termed the 'Ugandan master-trope' (Leopold 1999). Broadly speaking, since the beginning of British rule the north of the country (characterised as Nilotic, and traditionally lacking in strong state structures) has been marginalised in relation to the south (Bantu-speaking, with powerful kingship traditions and regarded by the British as much more civilised, especially the largest group, the Baganda). The articulation of this tribal/spatial theme with a religious one, involving divisions between Catholic, Protestant (i.e. Anglican) and Muslim believers, gave (pre-NRM) postcolonial Ugandan politics its particular flavour. As Michael Twaddle put it: 'In Uganda, political alliances at the centre of the country sometimes follow an ethnic line, sometimes politico-religious allegiances, sometimes a racial difference. More frequently, they cluster along some combination of these allegiances' (Twaddle 1972: 107).

To consider these divisions as thematic tropes is to emphasise their discursive nature. As Christopher Wrigley emphasised (Wrigley 1988: 28–9),[29] they are not

---

[28] Interview, Mr Nahor Oyaa, 6 February 1997. Transcribed from tape.

[29] These issues are considered in relation to post-1980 Ugandan history by many of the other contributors to Hansen and Twaddle (1988, 1991), especially Gingyera-Pinycwa (1991), Low (1988), Mazrui (1988), Obbo (1988), O'Connor (1988), Southall (1988), Woodward (1988, 1991). See also Gingyera-Pinycwa (1978, 1989, 1992), Twaddle (1989) and other contributors to Rupesinghe (1989).

the inevitable result of anything objective in the linguistic or ethnic composition of Uganda. They have been created out of stories men and women have told and retold each other about their circumstances. One of the most powerful themes in this Ugandan master-trope, the British belief in Baganda superiority, is explicitly introduced as a fairy story by one of its more influential proponents; Churchill wrote in 1908:

> The Kingdom of [B]Uganda is a fairy tale. You climb up a railway line instead of a beanstalk, and at the end there is a wonderful new world. The scenery is different, the vegetation is different, the climate is different and most of all the people are different from anything elsewhere to be seen in the whole range of Africa.
> In the place of naked, painted savages, clashing their spears and gibbering in chorus to their tribal chiefs, a complete and elaborate polity is presented. Under a dynastic King... an amiable, clothed, polite and intelligent race dwell together in an organised monarchy. (W.S. Churchill, *My African Journey*, quoted in Grahame 1980: 52)

It was an influential fairy story, which has structured much of post-independence Ugandan history, as it did the differential treatment of Ugandans under British rule.

One of the subsidiary effects of the 'fairy tale' has been to mask the degree to which West Nilers are, or regard themselves as, culturally marginalised within the north, for example as predominantly speakers of Sudanic, rather than Nilotic, languages (Leopold 1999). The structure of the discourse of marginality in Ugandan society can be seen as a set of binary oppositions, within which Buganda dominates the south and typifies or encompasses the other southern kingdoms; the south dominates and encompasses the north, within which the central northern peoples, the Acholi and Langi, come to stand for the region as a whole, encompassing the more marginal West Nilers and (on the eastern side) the Karamojong and similar peoples. The system is similar to that of Dumont's theory of hierarchy as 'an encompassing of the contrary' (Dumont 1970: 239). It is only possible to deconstruct its oppositions if one bears in mind that the structure is an intellectual one, discursively formed through time, rather than the natural or inevitable result of any anthropological or historical 'given'. The deeper roots of both the discourse and the realities of West Nile marginality are discussed in the next three chapters.

4
Drawing a Margin
West Nile under colonial rule
1961–1925

Introduction

It is convenient to treat the colonial period in West Nile in two parts. This chapter is concerned with the period during which British imperial rule and the place of West Nile in the Uganda Protectorate were firmly established. Chapter Five will focus on the earlier period, which saw the gradual and contested imposition of this regime. The year 1925 is a suitable caesura, for both material and discursive reasons: the year the migrant labour system became established and the first professional labour recruiters arrived in Arua, it was also the year of publication of the first full-length ethnographic essay on a West Nile 'tribe', the Lugbara (McConnell 1925).

The present chapter concerns a period in which the colonial regime had stabilised affairs in West Nile: some years the harvest was poorer than others, some years the administration was concerned about incursions from the Congo, some years there were serious epidemics. Aside from such events (and the effects of the Second World War) little changed for the people of the district. Accordingly, this chapter is not structured chronologically (or reverse-chronologically), but in two main parts: the first focuses on West Nile perceptions of colonial rule and its effects (from the viewpoints of both the 1990s and the 1970s); the second reverses the question, examining colonial-era discourses of the West Nile, especially the important anthropological work of Middleton on the Lugbara and Southall on the Alur.

'The Engereza is like a rat': local perceptions of colonial rule

The early years of Amin's rule were characterised, as the NRM period has been, by a certain resurgence of traditionalism in Uganda. Unlike the resolutely modernist Obote, Amin made a practice of consulting traditional leaders; he even allowed the Kabaka's body (though not his heir) back to Buganda for burial. One element in this revival of tradition was a new concern with Ugandan history. At Makerere University, the History of Uganda Project sent dozens of undergraduate historians back to their home areas to collect and disseminate 'traditional histories'. The results naturally varied in quality, and the methodology involved somewhat uncritical use of oral sources (for example, using genealogies linking the present day with mythic hero-ancestors to establish precise chronologies). Nevertheless, much interesting material was produced, including several dissertations from West Nile.[1] Two of these provide contrasting evaluations of the brief period of British colonial rule. Samson Geria, author of 'A traditional history of the Northwestern Lugbara of Uganda' (1973), wrote:

> When the present writer asked his informants to compare their colonial rulers, the British ranked first. The British are reputed for having established peace by abolishing inter-clan wars.... [and] introducing modern Court system through which more humane punishments were decided as opposed to the brutal and outrageous punishments the Belgians gave. Cattle raids which had been prevalent in the earlier regimes were no more. The only complaint against the British being the increasing pressure of taxation and forced labour, particularly in public works, that the local people experienced.[2]

A more ambiguous response to British rule is given by James Boliba Baba, whose dissertation was entitled 'Adiyo: the coming of the Kakwa and the development of their institutions' (1971). One of Baba's informants, a Kakwa elder from Nyangilia, Mr S.K. Dada, told him:

> If the Engereza [English] had not come, I think that few of us would be around today. I do not mean that the Engereza were good, but they were tactful with us. You see, the Engereza is like a rat, he bites you hard and then blows a cool air over the bitten part. But all the same, we were able to breath freely when they came. They never raided us, never even killed, but they ate us slowly until we got our independence.[3]

Such ambiguity seems always to have accompanied West Nile perceptions of colonialism, from the time of Middleton's research to that of my own. The student historians of the early 1970s were the same generation (and in some cases the same individuals) as the elders I interviewed in the late 1990s. They were the nationalist generation of educated West Nilers and most had been supporters of the UPC during the first post-independence years. Nevertheless, intellectual honesty forced them to concede that their interviewees saw much that was positive in the colonial years, especially measured against the chaos of the post-contact, pre-effective administration period. As Middleton noted:

> The Lugbara were in general uneasy at the thought of independence, which for them meant not so much the end of colonial rule, which they had felt relatively lightly, as the probable intensification of Nyoro and Ganda economic and political hegemony over northern Uganda (and even the spread of Arab rule from the Sudan). The southern Ugandan people had for years exploited the Lugbara and other northern Ugandans as cheap labour and sharecroppers; they despised them as 'millet eaters', as people whose men were poor and whose women wore little clothing. The Lugbaras' fear was justified after the independence of Uganda in 1962. (Middleton 1992: 100)

The disastrous events of the postcolonial era, however, had clear roots in the policies of British Protectorate administration, and not just the prejudices of the southern Ugandans (real though these were and are). There is little disagreement

---

[1] I have been able to consult three of these in the library of Makerere University: Baba (1971), Geria (1973) and Loro (1971).
[2] Geria 1973: 93.
[3] Ibid.: 37.

on the key factors involved; to simplify, the economic underdevelopment of the district and its political marginality were instigated and reinforced by its 'closed area' status for most of the colonial era. Successive colonial regimes in Entebbe clung to this status against complaints by commercial pressure groups. As early as January 1925, the Chief Secretary for the Protectorate wrote to the Uganda Planters' Association

> The question of the retention of the West Nile as a 'closed district' has been engaging the attention of this Government for a number of years. Apart from the fact that the tribes resident in the area have been truculent and troublesome up to comparatively recent times, the proximity of the Sudan facilitates the ingress of very undesirable influences, while the long international frontier, which forms the Western boundary of the district, renders it particularly important that every precaution should be taken to avoid trouble among the various tribes. (UNA:A46/1275 (SMP4102) 'West Nile District, Opening Up of')

When Middleton went to begin his research twenty-four years later, he found that 'Lugbaraland was a closed area, so that no one without government permission could enter it' (1970c: 227).

'Closed status' meant that cash-crop production was discouraged, and West Nile was treated as a labour reserve, particularly for the sugar and sisal plantations of southern Uganda, where the West Nilers were regarded as particularly strong and reliable labourers. When, in 1930, a sleeping-sickness outbreak forced the government to consider halting West Nile recruitment for the sugar plantations, the Indian entrepreneur R.K. Metha, owner of one of the largest, wrote to the Chief Secretary that:

> for practically all the plantations in Uganda the number of porters required is available from the West Nile area and if recruiting in that area be prohibited for any time, I am afraid it would mean great difficulty to all owners of plantations in Uganda and to me particularly it would mean considerable loss, for the work of plantations would be very largely hampered thereby. (Quoted in Ahluwalia 1995: 106; cf. Okot 1989: 74, quoted below)

At the same time, the British, influenced by Lugard's myth of the Nubians as 'the best material for soldiery in Africa' (see Chapter Six, below), recruited disproportionate numbers of West Nilers for the lower ranks of the army and police. West Nilers also figured largely in the other coercive trades of the colonial state: I interviewed several who had worked as policemen, spies and informers or as prison officers based elsewhere in Uganda during the period. According to one interviewee, the Kabaka of Buganda, who maintained his own prison in Mengo outside the Uganda Prison Service of the colonial Protectorate, staffed it largely with West Nilers because 'they were frightened of us, the Bantus, so they used us also to frighten their prisoners'.[4]

Other important factors in shaping the later history of the region included the introduction of trading and markets (see Middleton 1962) and the implementation of a system of 'chiefs' which bore little or no relation to indigenous social hierarchies. The next chapter will examine the early imposition of colonial rule and the events which led up to the Lugbara being placed under the control of

---

[4] Interview with anonymous respondent, 16 March 1997.

Nubi 'agents'. By the time of the period I am discussing here, as Middleton sum-marises it:

> the situation had attained some degree of stability. There were a dozen 'counties', each under a chief, the sultan. Each of these was divided into three or four 'subcounties', each under a subchief, the *wakil*. Within the subcounty were 'parishes', under a chief called *mukungu*, and under him were several 'headmen' or *nyapara*. The subchiefs were the highest authorities set over indigenous units. (Middleton 1971b: 32)

As the Officer-in-Charge of the Madi sub-district put it in 1955, 'Most chiefs here seem to have been former teachers, etc., and few, if any, possess hereditary powers and authority.'[5] The Lugbara historian Lulua Odu wrote,

> The Lugbara saw these chiefs as agents or puppets of the White men. They were given the title of *Ogara'ba* or *Mundu'ba* (people of the Europeans). They were collaborators and spies of the new order. There was little the people could do to reverse the trend of events. Eventually they had to submit and accept the changes of the new order. (Lulua 1996: 42)

The Committee for Peace and Stability in Arua District gives an eloquently negative account of the overall results of colonial rule in the area:

> The colonialists ... allocated many West Nilers quasi-slavery careers. As Africans were shipped across the Atlantic to tend sugar and cotton plantations in the Americas, so were the people of West Nile transported by trucks and river boats as 'Kasamvu' to tend coffee, tea and sugar plantations along the fertile shores of Lake Victoria. The Southerners were regarded as incompetent and inefficient in these areas.
> At the same time, a segment of the West Nile human resources was diverted to military service in the defence of the colonial interests of the British where, during the days of the Kings African Rifles ... many West Nilers distinguished themselves in expeditions against Italians in the deserts of Libya and the dense forests of the mid-Orient, India and Burma, to protect allied interests against Japanese invasion. Totally lacking in ambitions of their own, many returned home with possessions that were lifted in single trunks, plus only the uniforms and medals they wore, which became their only valued souvenirs, plus the endless tales of their journeys in faraway lands. These were their achievements and ultimate possessions until death. Back in their homes, they continued to live the same lives as their predecessors, simple and monetarily unproductive.[6]

During the period of my fieldwork, the issue of the colonial legacy in West Nile became briefly a matter of national political controversy. In August 1996, a major parliamentary inquiry was launched into the causes of, and possible solutions to, the instability and war in Uganda's north and north-west. This represented the first attempt by the newly established Ugandan Parliament to hold the executive branch of government, Museveni and his Cabinet, to account for its actions in such a sensitive area of national security and foreign policy. After a 'long, heated debate on the northern insurgency',[7] the matter was referred to the Sessional Committee on Defence and National Security, which established the inquiry. Most of its hearings were held in public and many received near verbatim coverage in the newspapers. Sessions were held in the

---

[5] UNA U/C:ADM/21/Mpt. II, Madi District Council, Minutes of meeting held on 15–16 June 1955.
[6] Report of the Committee for Peace and Security in Arua District.
[7] *New Times* newspaper, 28 August–2 September 1996.

north itself and witnesses included local leaders and other public figures from the north, as well as government and opposition politicians and senior military officers. A wide range of views was expressed and reported over the six months the committee was sitting.

In September 1997, West Nile's most powerful and controversial political leader, Hon. Brigadier Moses Ali, Second Deputy Premier and Minister of Tourism (MP for East Moyo), gave evidence to the Committee. He told them:

> It would be unfair of me to talk about the causes of this war without going back to history. The root causes are historical. Since the British came here, the way they handled different ethnic groups determines our history now. We in the north have been graded as warriors; we are fit for army because we are tall people; we are hunters because of our cultural activities. For many years we were locked up in the security forces. Northerners did not participate in other sectors. We were tailored to poverty straight from the time of British rule. We in the north are poorer than people who grow permanent cash crops. There is also a false belief that we are the only ones suitable for the army.... But the belief that a particular tribe excels in the army has been overrun by those [i.e. the southerners] who were thought weak and are now warriors. They are now the ones holding the gun. It was not true that only northerners were expert in the army.[8]

The government-owned newspaper, *New Vision*, has an English editor named William Pike, a supporter of Museveni since the time the NRA itself was a rebel group. Pike put Ali's testimony as a front-page lead under the headline 'Northern poverty blamed on Britain'[9] and attacked the Deputy Prime Minister the next day in an editorial entitled 'Wrong, Mr Ali'. The editorial stated:

> Ali is wrong on two fronts. He is insinuating that there was a deliberate policy to gag development in the north, while the other regions prospered – that the colonial authority discriminated against the north – and he is wrong on the economics of the cash crops.... But most of all it is obscurant of Ali to still blame the British in 1996. True though it may be that many distortions in our social, economic and political structures were caused by uninspired policies, it is unrealistic of us to still blame the colonial administration, long after it has departed.[10]

Ali responded a few weeks later, citing colonial records to support his claim of deliberate underdevelopment. He quoted (from Powesland 1957) the response of central government in 1925 to an attempt by the Director of Agriculture in West Nile to introduce cotton production in the district: 'The policy of this government is at present to refrain from actively stimulating the production of cotton or other economic crops in outlying districts on which it is dependent for the supply of labour for the carrying out of essential services in the central or producing districts.' Ali concluded:

> I am not saying that the British colonial policies are the only variables in understanding the present crisis in the north. There are other components to the problem. But it is necessary to comprehend the impact of British colonial policies on Uganda's development in order to understand the present crisis in the north.... Present Ugandan society as structure is, to a large extent, a creature of British colonial policies.[11]

[8] *Crusader* newspaper, 1 October 1997.
[9] *New Vision* newspaper, 21 September 1997.
[10] *New Vision* newspaper, 23 September 1997.
[11] *New Vision* newspaper, 20 November 1997.

A more nuanced assessment of the colonial legacy is given by the Lugbara historian Lulua Odu, writing of the nation rather than the district:

> As a matter of fact, Colonialism may be said to have brought some advantages as well as disadvantages.
>
> *Advantages*: 1. The building of schools, hospitals and dispensaries and the subsequent expansion of educational and health services. 2. The construction of towns, roads, bridges, railways and factories. 3. The introduction of modern transport system by air, rail, road and steamer. 4. Prevention of inter-clan and inter-tribal wars followed by the maintenance of an atmosphere of relative safety. 5. Introduction of cash crops and other income generating activities. 6. Laying down the foundations for a nation-state with a system of Administration, Education and Law.
>
> *Disadvantages*: 1. The colonial policy of 'Divide and Rule', which led to divisive national policies based on tribal, religious, racial and party differences. 2. The killing of indigenous technology such as hoe-making, fire-making and local medicine. 3. Economic exploitation of the colony in favour of the colonial power through unfair exchange and looting of treasures. 4. Cultural alienation which was done by promoting ignorance through education and religion by instilling a sense of inferiority complex in the minds of the subject peoples. (Lulua 1996: 50–51)

Cultural alienation notwithstanding, one aspect of colonial discourse much appreciated in contemporary West Nile is the work of the British social anthropologists who studied its people, notably John Middleton on the Lugbara and Aidan Southall on the Alur. I was frequently surprised during fieldwork by how much people knew of their work and how many remembered their presence in the district. As often as not, an elder questioned on local tradition would refer to their work rather than (or as well as) to oral sources. When I took a copy of Middleton's 1992 edition of his synthesis *The Lugbara* to the officers of the Lugbara Literature Association, one elder was able to point to a photograph of his grandmother, almost naked but for ear and lip rings. I was embarrassed, but he seemed delighted. The next section concentrates on the work of the colonial anthropologists, using it in particular to examine the effects of the migrant labour system on the district.

'Suitably remote & unknown': West Nile in colonial discourse

The generation of West Nilers that grew up in the later Protectorate period, such as most of the elders I spoke to in the late 1990s, saw the district and its people emerge simultaneously on to the Ugandan public stage as migrant workers and into academic discourse as the objects of social anthropology. This combination was no coincidence: the Protectorate wanted to know about the massive alien labour force it had drawn into the plantations of southern Uganda, and deployed a bevy of (later eminent) social anthropologists to tell it.[12] Meanwhile, the very

---

[12] Protectorate officers, even those stationed in West Nile, were frequently confused as to the nature of its inhabitants. In 1936 the Acting Provincial Commissioner for Uganda's Northern Province wrote, 'The West Nile, with its gradations of country and climate ... its mixture of tribes and its potentialities for production is a most interesting and complex District. Nor is the task of administration so simple in dealing with tribes the individuals of which range from the most primitive types to that very unsatisfactory person, the sophisticated gentleman who has spent

marginality and air of violence that clung around the West Nilers, which worried the authorities, attracted the anthropologists.

The result was an explosion of knowledge about West Nile and its people, especially the Alur (in the work of Aidan Southall) and the Lugbara (in that of John Middleton). To take the latter case; before 1950, outside the somewhat specialised pages of *La Nigrizia* (the internal journal of Catholic missionaries, the Comboni (Verona) Fathers), only five articles had been published on the Lugbara: two in Belgian journals, two in the *Journal of the Royal Anthropological Institute* (*JRAI*) and one in *Anthropos*.[13] In the 1950s, the volume of this material would have more than doubled even without Middleton's prolific pen, while he brought out ten articles (in addition to his doctoral thesis, conference papers and a report for the Colonial Office) over the decade, culminating in the publication of his classic book, *Lugbara Religion* (1960a).[14] Other West Nile groups remained somewhat obscure (there is still, for example, no sustained ethnographic work on the Kakwa) but the Lugbara and Alur at least were made known to a European and American audience for the first time, though they remained without honour in their own country.

In this section, I am concerned with this material in two ways: one is to examine the versions of West Nile marginality rehearsed in its pages, the other is to look at its articulation with the political and economic system which reproduced this marginality. John Middleton, looking back on his fieldwork twenty years later, wrote with some honesty about what attracted him to the Lugbara:

> I was romantic enough to want to find a relatively 'untouched' society.... The Lugbara live in a remote part of northern Uganda.... In addition, I knew that the Lugbara actually existed because I had met Lugbara troops during the war.... But other than their being a tall, very dark-skinned and apparently both cheerful and somewhat easily quarrelsome people, I knew little about them.... They seemed suitably remote and unknown, and my teacher, Professor E.E. Evans-Pritchard, agreed that they would make an admirable first study where I could learn my job. (Middleton 1970a: 2–3)

Naturally, Middleton found the marginality he sought. On his first arrival in Kampala, he says: 'I never found anyone in the capital who had actually set foot in Lugbaraland, but I was told it was savage, remote, cold at night, and was regaled with various secondhand anecdotes about past administrative officers who had gone mad, drunk or permanently sullen while serving there' (Middleton 1970c). Getting to 'Lugbaraland', he found that it: 'was remote from centres of government and ... literally closed to unauthorized visitors. During my stay there were seven British officials responsible for the district of some half a million

---

12 (cont.) several years working down country and associating with the detribalised elements around Kampala and Jinja' (UNA OS. Uganda Protectorate Annual Report 1936: Annual Report of the Provincial Commissioner, Northern Province by E.D. Tongue, OBE: 32).

13 See Dalfovo's (1988) *Bibliography of Lugbara Studies and Literature*. In addition to the five articles, Dalfovo lists only three books which contain references to the Lugbara, one of which is purely a passing mention. This early material will be considered and cited in the next section.

14 The non-Middleton work of importance over this period includes Crazzolara (1950–54, 1960), Posnett (1951), Baxter and Butt (1953), Lanning (1954) and Collins (1960). Middleton's papers of the 1950s include Middleton (1954, 1955a, b, c, 1958, 1960b), as well as Middleton and Greenland (1954).

Africans, half a dozen Protestant and a dozen Catholic missionaries, a dozen Indian shops, one Indian labour recruiter, and three British tobacco growers and buyers' (Middleton 1992: 6). The local people had *'virtually no contact with European officials'* (ibid.: 7).

Although almost all Lugbara men were forced out of the district to work as migrant labourers in order to pay taxes and their land was ruled by a wholly alien system of government appointed chiefs, Middleton still thought that: 'Lugbara social relations may ... be described as they are today with the knowledge that they are not greatly different from what they would seem to have been traditionally' (Middleton 1953: iii). The West Nilers, in his account, seem curiously impermeable to their colonial experience:

> Although European economic, political and other activities impinge upon and affect Lugbara society at all points, Lugbara still carry on most of their traditional activities much as they have ever done, and still consider the world of the Europeans as something quite distinct from their own. For most of the adult population the Government is still a novelty, something extraneous and strange, although it is now taken for granted as existing for some purpose of its own. Most heads of families have taken part in feuding and have killed men in the traditional way.... Lugbara, with the other peoples of their District, are still regarded generally and with justification as being the most 'backward' peoples in Uganda. It is well known throughout the Protectorate that it is only these savage people from the north-west who still give their women neither cloth nor venereal disease, two rough and ready criteria of progress in this part of the world. (Ibid.: 19–20)

Aidan Southall was a good deal less attracted by the notion of timeless tradition and static ethnicity. As early as 1954 he was attacking (in a little-known but important article in the *Uganda Journal*) prevailing notions of synchronicity in anthropology, and attempting to recover from a variety of sources a history of the people who called themselves Alur which was dynamic and complex:

> Alur society developed embryonic political institutions of a specialized type. This, combined with the continuous mobility and fluidity of Alur groups in space and time, rendered necessary and habitual the recollection of past events as a charter of present political relations. The high degree of ethnic variability and of temporal and spatial fluidity and mobility provides some of the fascination of Alur studies, but involves formidable difficulties of presentation.
>
> This paper is intended to provide some concrete evidence of the influence of differing types of social structure, and of the temporal processes inherent in them and the particular oecological environment, on the quality of recollection of past events. From this, the reader may assess the advisability of relating the traditions of particular tribal societies to the possible sequence of historical development. (Southall 1954a: 165)

Southall's Alur may have been living in the same district of Uganda as Middleton's Lugbara, but they seem to inhabit a different intellectual universe. Although '[t]he Alur today count as one of the backward tribes of Uganda... [for which] their remote geographical position is mainly responsible' (ibid.: 267), they did not remain unaffected by British rule:

> Apart from the obvious cessation of tribal warfare, with the profound structural modifications which this entails in a flexibly balanced social system, the Alur very often appear to be leading the old life unchanged in many essential respects. But even apart

from the rigid framework of external political control Alur society has ceased to be a closed system. For the rural peasant who is observed one day cultivating with his peers according to an immemorial system, sacrificing to ancestral spirits, seeking guidance from diviners in any critical decision, and carrying out a host of complex and highly ritualised traditional obligations, is the very same individual who also ties a few essential belongings into a cloth bundle and goes off to seek his fortune in the extra-tribal world, travelling by bus and Nile steamer to Buganda and Kampala, working for wages or more likely growing cotton to sell for cash, fending for himself in the increasingly impersonal and commercialised world which the Europeans have brought. (Southall 1953: 279)

Although 'the Uganda Alur give the superficial impression of being a primitive people' (ibid.: 268), tradition itself is continually being reinterpreted; 'traditional Alur political values have been prohibited, curtailed, modified and transformed into compatibility with the contemporary system of administration' (ibid.: 340), and the attempt to ignore this is portrayed by Southall as a delusion:

The Alur are still greatly tempted to feel that the working of the District administration is a concern of the intangible government and not of theirs at all.... What is felt to be the sphere of Alur responsibility includes only their own homes and fields, the few shops so far started by them, and the remaining traditional authorities of localised lineage and clan section, chieflet area and chiefdom. Few perceive the artificiality and complete lack of autonomy of this dream world. (Ibid.: 344)

To be fair, the Alur did have both a different history and a different response to the demands of the Ugandan economic system from those of the Lugbara, but a good deal of the contrast between Middleton's and Southall's accounts has to be traced, not to such material differences in the subject group, but to the writers' own contrasting predilections.

At this time, so-called 'British' social anthropology in Africa invariably required working with the imperial authorities,[15] and both Southall and Middleton produced officially sponsored accounts of the role of West Nile people in the migrant labour process. These studies were prepared as part of a wider study of migration in Uganda coordinated by Audrey Richards as Director of the East African Institute of Social Research, and published as Richards (1954). For some reason, Middleton's contribution was produced separately by the Colonial Office, rather than being included in the collective volume.[16] Taken together, these reports provide both an account of the process that was changing the lives of the people of West Nile in the period between the 1930s and independence, and an insight into how they were perceived: by other Ugandans, by the colonial

---

[15] Middleton was open about this link, 'It is important to stress that I was a protégé of the then government. This was deliberate. I have little sympathy with those anthropologists who set themselves up in some kind of personal opposition to government, usually to show that they are anti-colonialist in spirit (who isn't?) free and independent, on the side of the oppressed Africans and the like.... Lugbaraland was a closed area, so that no one without government approval could enter it; the Lugbara trusted the then European government a good deal more than they would a future independent government, which they feared would be controlled by their hereditary foes from southern Uganda' (Middleton 1970c: 227).

[16] Middleton's report is listed in bibliographies such as those in his own books and Dalfovo's (1988) as published by the Colonial Social Science Research Council for the Colonial Office in 1952. I have been unable to trace a published copy, and instead have used a typescript of the report in Rhodes House (RH mss.Afr.s.1220). Another separate publication linked with Richards's study is Powesland (1957).

authorities and by the academics who were pursuing their own interests and inclinations. In the course of these events and this intellectual and political concern, the discourses of West Nile marginality were both maintained and expanded.

Individual motivations for migration were always complicated. As Southall noted:

> All [the Alur migrants] have, in fact, left Alurland partly in order to escape from.... kinship obligations.... To a large extent Buganda offers freedom from the traditional restrictions imposed at home by elders in the kinship system and by chiefs in the political system.... The women who go to Buganda also prefer it.... The full motivational picture is therefore complex. (Southall 1954b: 150–51)

Despite the clear effect of the combination of taxation and a lack of opportunity for earning cash in forcing people into migration, it is a curiosity of this kind of research that people seldom say they were forced to migrate to earn money for taxes: they say they quarrelled with their brother, or their father, or neighbours; that they wanted to see the big city, or their family did not have enough cattle to get a wife. However, the structural process by which the West Nilers were forced into migrant labour is fairly clear. To finance itself, the Protectorate government needed money; all households were therefore taxed. However, there were virtually no sources of cash income in West Nile; it was far from the southern economic hub of Uganda, and cotton and other Ugandan cash crops were believed to grow poorly there. To pay their taxes and escape arrest, therefore, West Nilers had to travel to work in the richer districts of the south, particularly the former Kingdoms of Buganda and Bunyoro. They were joined for the purpose by other Lugbara, Alur, Kakwa, and neighbouring peoples from over the border in the Congo and Sudan, who also had taxes to pay and no convenient source of employment within their own colonial borders. As the southern Sudanese poet and politician Taban Lo-Liyong (who on occasion described himself as Ugandan; see Chapter Three, above) wrote, in 1984:

> Which cotton ginnery in Uganda never employed a young stalwart from Kajo Kaji earning his bicycle or dowry? Which sisal estate never had a Kuku on the payroll? My father cut sisal for an Indian tycoon. Who produced the sugar of Kakira and Lugazi? How many Kore songs lament the hardships faced in the sugar estates of Mulubai and Mehta? As indentured labourers, recruited by entrepreneur Indians, smuggled in either as Madi or Kakwa, we Sudanese refugees laid the foundations for agricultural and manufacturing industries in Uganda. (Taban 1984)

From the mid-1920s onwards,[17] the system grew until, by the time Middleton and Southall's fieldwork began in the late 1940s, most West Nile men, and some women, spent some time working in the south, where they formed the second largest migrant group, after the 'Banyaruanda' from present-day Burundi and Rwanda. The Alur tended to rent land from southerners and to farm it themselves until they had earned enough to return. They stayed away longer at

---

[17] The early 1920s for the Alur and Madi, later for the Lugbara (see Powesland 1957: Ch.II; Powesland in Richards n.d. [c.1953]; Ch. II; Middleton, RH mss. Afr.s.1220: 3–5). The early primacy of the Alur was reflected, in the collective Baganda term for West Nile migrants, *Balulu* (RH mss Afr.s.1220: 5 fn 1, see also Southall 1953: 143 fn. 2).

a time and earned considerably more than the Lugbara, who tended to be plantation workers and lived in small, mono-ethnic settlements near the plantations. In
1948, the three biggest employers (all 'Indian'-owned) formed the West Nile
Recruiting Organisation, sending local hirers out all over the district (and into the
Congo) to pick up Lugbara workers (Middleton 1971b: 22). Middleton concluded
that:

> the general pattern of development elsewhere in the Protectorate has been accom
> panied by the growing of cash crops but this development in Lugbara has involved the
> use of its manpower outside the district, a process which in general may be said to have
> benefitted other parts of Uganda rather than the Lugbara themselves.... In the south of
> Uganda Lugbara have played the role of cheap, unskilled immigrants who, together
> with the far greater number of Banyaruanda immigrants into Buganda, form the
> lowest stratum in the economic structure of the country....
>
> In the West Nile labour migration may be seen as a regrettable accompaniment to
> the changes that have been taking place since European administration of the country.
> Such changes however have been taking place in the peripheral areas of other
> developing economic units. They have occurred in the northern parts of Nigeria and
> the Gold Coast and in the areas on the periphery of the Rhodesian industrial areas and
> the Witwatersrand.[18]

The effects of this process on the economy and society of the West Nile were
indeed regrettable. The area suffered considerably from the absence of its young
adult men (and some women). In 1943–4, as in earlier years,[19] famine struck the
district. In the previous year, its Agricultural Officer had reported that:

> Labour recruiting in the West Nile has always been a major obstacle to agricultural
> progress. During the past years the insatiable appetite of the armed forces and the
> continued exploitation of the manpower for cheap plantation labour have prevented
> agricultural expansion and limited food planting.... Unabated recruiting with
> progressive increase in the number of women and children left as a charge on those
> men who remain behind will shortly endanger the internal food supply of the whole
> District which is at best precarious – It is extremely dangerous to regard the West Nile
> as an inexhaustible source of manpower and so to deplete the district of men that no
> surplus exists to balance the most common misfortunes of drought and locust
> invasion.[20]

The social, as opposed to strictly economic, consequences of the system were
and are obvious enough: As John Middleton pointed out (e.g. Middleton 1971b)
it weakened family structures and traditional authorities and norms. Those
district officials who tended to romanticise the traditional worried about this from
the late 1920s, but romanticism aside, the system generated real enough strains
on social norms, as many of my own interviewees testified from experience. One
prevalent aspect of these social strains was (and is) the ritual cursing of those
leaving the district, to ensure they will return. Such curses are frequently taken
very seriously. The stigma of migration was perhaps particularly strong for

[18] Middleton, RH mss Afr.s.1220: 25.

[19] E.g. 1936, when 'A small famine occurred in the Aringa County... which necessitated the
distribution of some 20 tons of relief food' (UNA OS. 'Uganda Protectorate Annual Report 1936:
Annual Report of the Provincial Commissioner, Northern Province: 27).

[20] District Agricultural Officer, West Nile, Annual Report, 1943, quoted in Middleton, RH mss.
Afr.s.1220: 23. It should be noted, however, that most subsistence agricultural work in West Nile
was done by women.

women (usually ignored in the literature on West Nile migration). The end of one Alur cursing song I was taught goes:

Obola, peri nik	Whore, even if you
Icidi Kampala ibidwogo se	Go to Kampala, you will come back on your own
Obola, peri nik	Whore, even if you
Icidi Rwangara ibidwogo se	Go to Rwangara you will come back on your own
Obola, peri nik	Whore, even if you
Icidi Entebbe, ibidwogo se	Go to Entebbe you will come back on your own
Obola, Kathari na ni obola	Whore, Katherine, you are a whore
Ibidwogo se	You will come back on your own

In the south itself, the (male) West Nile migrants had a reputation as violent and aggressive. Audrey Richards found that among the Baganda:

there was general agreement... that the Alur and also the Lugbara were the most difficult to handle although they were the hardest workers. We did not hear any comment in their favour, except as to their physical strength. They were accused of making the most [legal] cases and of refusing, in the first instance, to pay their taxes and even of assaulting the chiefs who came to ask for these. They were regarded almost as raiders who came into Buganda to make as much money as they could and then returned home.... Typical comments were 'The Lulu (Alur) are the worst. They stay the shortest time. They go without burning the cotton plants or paying the dues. And then they drink most.' 'They are rough. They pull out spears quickly when they are angry.' 'They are bad! They commit murders. They have no laws.'

Richards concludes that: 'The West Nile people are in fact a group that differs in culture and does not want to be assimilated either economically or politically and does not understand the system of central government and delegated chieftainship of the Bantu' (Richards 1952: 165).

However, the West Nilers' image of violence, masculinity and primitiveness persisted, not only among the hierarchical Bantu, but among their fellow migrant workers from elsewhere in the north. In his novel *White Teeth* (originally published in the Acholi language in 1953) the writer Okot p'Bitek depicts an Acholi migrant looking for work in Kampala:

At that time, rumours were going round in Kampala that many young men were required to go and work on the sugarcane plantations at Kakira, Jinja. This kind of work was not really for people from Acholiland. Most of the workers there were recruited from the western side of the Pakwach river [i.e. from West Nile], for they were tough people. It was manly work, requiring young men who were healthy and tough. Young men who had not yet been weakened by drinks and women. (Okot 1989: 74)

As late as 1966, Parkin spoke of 'the extreme socio-economic separation' of the Lugbara migrants from their fellow urban workers (Parkin 1966: 92).

Interestingly, the Nubi are portrayed in Middleton's work, not as violent, deracinated soldiers, but largely as a group of petty urban traders with strong links to local 'traditional' ethnicities:

there are also full-time peripatetic traders.... They are mostly 'Nubis' from Arua town. The town consists largely of Nubis, who are said to be the descendants of Emin Pasha's Sudanese troops who were settled in various parts of the region after the Mahdi revolt and the Uganda mutiny. Today, however, there are very few pure-blooded Arab or Sudanese Nubis in Arua, most of them being Lugbara, Kakwa or members of other tribes who have become Muslims and married into Nubi families. They control the hide and skin trade, and deal in other goods in which the profits are too small for larger traders. In addition they control the illicit gin trade in Arua, perhaps the most profitable trade in the district. (Middleton 1962: 571)

Nevertheless, military recruitment continued to be an important source of employment for West Nile men. As the Committee for Peace and Security in Arua District noted, the West Nilers (whether or not they considered themselves 'Nubi') in the Fourth Battalion of the King's African Rifles (4 KAR) as well as the other, temporary, formations created during the war, fought for the British empire against both Italians in the Horn of Africa and the Japanese in Burma (Moyse-Bartlett 1956: 504–686; see also his Appendix F: 702). The word 'violence' and stories of cannibalistic practices are notable by their absence from descriptions of this period in Nubi military history.

Conclusion: the material effects of an ideology

The archaeological 'layer' of West Nile history between independence and 1925 is characterised by a relatively peaceful incorporation into the imperial system of the Protectorate, albeit into a highly marginal position. Both Middleton and Southall depict the Lugbara and Alur as relatively passive victims of this process. Such a perspective is not simply to do with functionalist assumptions about stability and tradition: colonial rule really did serve to fossilise (as well as invent) some aspects of social relations. Moreover, the earlier period, from 1925 to West Nile's first incorporation into Uganda, is portrayed as peaceful by no one.

Middleton's account of the effects of colonial rule is, however, somewhat contradictory. In successive paragraphs of Middleton (1971b), he writes:

> The way of life of the older men of today – or at least of the period of my stay among the Lugbara – is very similar to that of their fathers, according to the men themselves, with two important reservations: the colonial system introduced taxation and they altered the traditional jural system by the prohibition of warfare and feud.

and then:

> Lugbara awareness of the effects of colonial rule is considerable. Older people maintain that the country, its people and their culture, have been largely destroyed; whereas younger men are more aware of some of the advantages of colonial rule. (Middleton 1971b: 7)

As the first section of this chapter showed, however, the West Nilers' own assessments of the colonial legacy are as ambiguous and contradictory as Middleton's. Both versions, to my mind, suffer from underestimating the effects of the earlier period before the establishment of effective colonial administration, which will be discussed in later chapters. Most of the elements of the image of West Nile, as a marginal place, inhabited by intrinsically violent or warlike people, were in place before British rule was established. This discourse played a decisive part in the decision to maintain the district as a closed area and a labour reserve, and thus in the ensuing events of the postcolonial period.

The racial fears which lie beneath the violent and marginal image of West Nile are well demonstrated in a vignette from the hinge date between this and the next chapter: 1925. This was the year the Swiss psychologist Carl Gustav Jung visited East Africa, and passed through West Nile on his way from Mombasa to Khartoum.

In a village on the way from Lake Albert to Rejaf in the Sudan we had a very exciting experience. The local chief, a tall still quite young man appeared with his retinue. These were the blackest Negroes I had ever seen. There was something about the group which was not exactly reassuring. The mamur of Nimule had given us three Askaris as an escort, but I saw that they as well as our own boys did not feel at all easy....

When the chief proposed that he give a n'goma (dance) in the evening, I assented gladly. I hoped that the frolic would bring their better natures to the fore. Night had fallen and we were all longing for sleep when we heard drums and horn blasts. Soon some sixty men appeared, martially equipped with flashing lances, clubs and swords. They were followed at some distance by the women and children; even the infants were present, carried on their mothers' backs.... [A] big fire was kindled and women and children formed a circle round it. The men formed an outer ring around them, as I had once observed a nervous herd of elephant do.... The men's chorus began to sing, vigorous, bellicose melodies, not unharmonious, and at the same time began to swing their legs. The women and children tripped round the fire; the men danced towards it, waving their weapons, then drew back again, and then advanced anew, amid savage singing, drumming and trumpeting.

It was a wild and stirring scene, bathed in the glow of the fire and magical moonlight. My English friend and I sprang to our feet and mingled with the dancers. I swung my rhinoceros whip, the only weapon I had, and danced with them. By their beaming faces I could see that they approved of our taking part. Their zeal redoubled; the whole company stamped, sang, shouted, sweating profusely. Gradually the rhythm of the dance and the drumming accelerated.

In dances such as these, accompanied by such music, the natives easily fall into a virtual state of possession. That was the case now. As eleven o'clock approached, their excitement began to get out of bounds, and suddenly the whole affair took on a highly curious aspect. The dancers were being transformed into a wild horde, and I became worried about how it would end. I signed to the chief that it was time to stop, and that he and his people ought to go to sleep. But he kept wanting 'just another one'.

I remembered that a countryman of mine, one of the Sarasin cousins, on an exploratory expedition in the Celebes, had been struck by a stray spear in the course of such a n'goma. And so, disregarding the chief's pleas, I called the people together, distributed cigarettes, and then made the gesture of sleeping. Then I swung my rhinoceros whip threateningly, but at the same time laughing, and for lack of any better language I swore at them loudly in Swiss German that this was enough and they must go home to bed and sleep now ... capering, they scattered in all directions and vanished into the night. For a long time we heard their jovial howls and drumming in the distance. (Jung 1983[1963]: 301)

Jung was by no means the first European to exhibit superstitious fears about the violent potential of the people of West Nile, nor the first to respond with his own violence (see, for example, van Gennep (1967 [1911]) quoted in Chapter One). The ideological foundations which underlay West Nile marginality had in fact been laid earlier. In the next chapter, I look at the role of such fantasies in the establishment of British rule over the decade between 1924 and 1914.

5

'Rather a Difficult Tribe to Tame'
The invention of an uprising
& the creation of a colonial district 1924–1914

From Rebellion to Incorporation

In this chapter, I deal with a shorter period of time, at greater length, than elsewhere in the book. The period in question is the decade which saw the establishment of effective British administration in West Nile District, following the area's incorporation into the Uganda Protectorate in 1914. Before this, as later chapters will show, the people of the district were indeed affected by outside forces and events, but only after 1914 were the West Nilers to feel the systematic control over their everyday lives produced by the imposition of effective colonial rule.

None of my informants' memories stretched to this early period in the district's history, and oral traditions are influenced by the written material produced by outsiders – academics and others – who have seen this period as crucial in the shaping of subsequent West Nile history. The key event, on which this chapter will concentrate, was the so-called Yakan or Allah Water uprising of 1919, which became a central metaphor for the supposed violent and warlike nature of the West Nile people. This 'water' and this 'uprising' have already been mentioned in Chapter Three, in connection with the literature on Amin. There, the 'water' of Yakan is presented as having a somewhat contradictory set of properties; at the same time a hallucinogen, an aphrodisiac and a drug which roused previously timid men to warfare. In the literature on the 1919 uprising, it is the latter property which predominates. The drug was said to be used in the rites of a subversive cult implicated in an outbreak, in 1919, of violent opposition to the imposition of British imperial rule. The 'Yakan' or 'Allah Water' rebellion has thus passed into history as the last desperate act of a prophetic 'primary resistance movement'. It also had the unusual distinction of being written up by the man who put it down, Assistant District Commissioner turned social anthropologist J.H. 'Jack' Driberg, whose account in the *Journal of the Royal Anthropological Institute* in 1931 rested heavily on depositions gathered during his police investigations of twelve years previously. These also formed the core of subsequent, more elaborate accounts of the 'uprising' produced by Middleton (especially 1963, 1971a, b) and by Anne King (1970), who supplemented them with other archival material and interviews undertaken decades after the events. In this chapter, I argue, based on previously unused primary archival sources, that the local British officials relied on an inaccurate account of the Yakan movement's origins and intentions, that their evidence for a widespread, Yakan-inspired, uprising in West Nile in 1919 is very thin, and that later commentators have been mistaken in adopting uncritically their account of Yakan.

The earliest published account of Yakan occurs in the first ethnographic essay on a West Nile people, 'Notes on the Lugwari[1] Tribe of Central Africa', published by Driberg's colleague, Assistant District Commissioner R.E. McConnell in the *JRAI* in 1925. This dismally characteristic example of the 'Notes and Queries' school of anthropology featured tables of cephalic indices, nose measurements and the rest of the intellectual apparatus of scientific racism, decked out with anecdotal accounts of picturesque local customs. It portrays in a fairly straight-forward manner the 'primitive' and 'violent' people we find throughout the century's writing on the region:

> Though not aggressive, the Lugwari are a fearless and warlike people in defence or in revenge for a grievance ... in recent years [they] fought largely among themselves, rather than as an organized people against adjacent tribes....
>
> On account of their intractability the Belgians made little effort to administer them. One of the elephant poachers of twelve years ago told me that when he had to traverse their country he did so as quickly as possible. Since our administration small punitive affairs have been not infrequent, and on the whole they have been rather a difficult tribe to tame.
>
> Killings among themselves are common, particularly in the dancing and drinking months of January and February....
>
> The missionaries find them very 'wild' to begin with, but report that with persistent instruction they give good promise. The Italian Fathers state that with respect to their neighbours they do not share the Alur's laziness and have more capacity than the Madi.... In the King's African Rifles, during the war, they furnished some excellent soldiers. The officers have told me that they despaired of them in the beginning, but that when their minds did at last awake to the meaning of their instructions they were among the best of the native soldiers. (McConnell 1925: 442–3)

McConnell concludes, in similarly elegiac tones to those of Middleton thirty years later: 'In this short survey of the tribe it is evident that the Lugwari, in respect of attainments and customs, are among the least advanced of the African tribes, and should receive further study before their civilization is submerged by that which slowly but surely will flow in upon them' (ibid.: 467).

As the previous chapter related, 1925 saw, as well as the publication of McConnell's essay in London, the arrival of the first professional labour recruiters in West Nile. The growth of the West Nile migrant labour system from 1925 onwards depended crucially on a number of events between 1922 and 1925, which acted as 'pull' and 'push' factors, generating a powerful impetus to go south. In the south of the country, extensive railway construction and the opening of the Lugazi sugar works occurred at the same time as a considerable growth in the Bunyoro timber plantations. In West Nile itself, as we shall see, while poll taxes had theoretically been in place since 1918, the authorities were at first lenient, recognising the inability of most West Nile households to acquire cash. Increasing pressure to pay, however, coincided with a series of disasters: in

---

[1] The spelling 'Lugbara' was only established after Middleton's work. From now on in this book, various spellings will be encountered.

1922, severe drought and crop failure accompanied an influenza epidemic, while in 1924–5 an outbreak of rinderpest killed nearly half the cattle in some areas of the district, wiping out many West Nilers' only saleable assets.[2] At the same time, the Acting Provincial Administrator was able to report that 'Demand for West Nile labour is steadily rising'.[3]

In 1922, the District Commissioner, West Nile, had written that, although Alur and Madi men often went south to earn their tax money, 'very few Lugwari go outside their own country for employment'.[4] By 1925, his successor was able to report that, 'The Lugwari, in particular, have responded well to calls for labour.' The migrant labour system was, however, seen by the authorities not just as a way of satisfying economic demand, but as a tool for social engineering, a means of civilising the West Nilers and thus preventing revolutionary upsurges such as (they believed) had occurred in 1919. In support of his preference for keeping West Nile as a closed area, the Provincial Commissioner, Northern Province, wrote to the Protectorate's Chief Secretary in 1925:

> I anticipate that in a year's time that [sic] a very considerable proportion of the Madi, Lugwari and Kakwa natives will have been out to work, and have become more sophisticated and less likely to be imposed upon either by traders or Somali cattle buyers, or by recruiting agents or, on the other hand, to flare up under the influence of Allah Water, which constituted a distinct factor in the Administration a few years ago.[5]

The 'Yakan uprising' in context

The most significant figure in the establishment of imperial rule in West Nile was the first District Commissioner, Alfred Evelyn Weatherhead, who was in charge of the district from 1914 to 1922, and became a legendary figure to local people.[6] As Southall wrote: 'the methods by which Weatherhead established British domination over the population of West Nile district are of unusual interest. It is rare in this part of Africa that peoples who had barely come in contact with Europeans, let alone had any experience of European rule, should have been brought under control so largely by a single individual' (Southall 1953: 287).[7] If Weatherhead was the key individual in the process of establishing imperial rule,

---

[2] RH mss Afr.s.1220: 3. See also Southall (1954b: 142), Middleton (1971b: 22).
[3] Northern Province Quarterly Report, Quarter ended 30 June 1924 (UNA A46/797). As it happens, A.E. Weatherhead, the first DC West Nile (see below), was Acting Provincial Commissioner at the time. After his departure in 1922, West Nile came for some years under a series of short-term DCs. It is interesting to speculate how the underdevelopment of West Nile would have transpired if a dedicated and respected (by his superiors) DC such as Weatherhead had been in charge of the district when the labour demand arose.
[4] Quoted in RH mss Afr.s.1220: 4.
[5] UNA A46/1275 (SMP 4102), 'West Nile District, Opening Up of'. Provincial Commissioner, Northern Province (PCNP) to Chief Secretary, 13 October 1925. The Chief Secretary replied agreeing on 22 October.
[6] For Weatherhead's reputation in the district, see especially Middleton (1953: 15, 1971b: 16), Southall (1953: 287), Allen (1991c), CAP (1993: 15).
[7] It is therefore surprising that no historians seem to have consulted Weatherhead's diary, available in Rhodes House library, RH Mss Afr.s.1638 (32 annual volumes), which I use widely in this chapter.

Plate 5.1 West Nile District Chiefs, with DC A.E. Weatherhead &
ADC B.A. Warner, 1918

(Photo by unknown photographer, copyright Bodleian Library, University of Oxford, Mss. Afr. s. 1638 (36), II)

the key year in the process was perhaps 1918. In that year, for the first time,
significant numbers were forcibly recruited into the army.[8] Even more signifi-
cantly, the Lugbara were finally introduced to taxation.[9] As King remarks: 'the
collection of tax very quickly became the most vivid symbol of government. It
was the first aspect of government chiefship mentioned by interviewees in 1969
when questioned about the work of the early chiefs' (King 1970: 22ff, 63). The
chiefs were in a difficult position; they were:

> Expected to carry out regular duties such as raising recruits for the K.A.R. for labour
> duties and so on, and after 1917 they were responsible for the regular collection of tax.
> If the chiefs wanted to maintain their positions, which had considerable pecuniary
> advantages, they had to make sure that they could carry out these duties and in this
> way the interests of the administration gradually became their own. As the gap closed

[8] Only 14 had been recruited in 1916, 300 by 1918, see Middleton 1971b: 17.

[9] Middleton says that taxation began among the Lugbara in 1918 (1971b: 16), King (1970: 22)
says it was 1917. UNA A46/248 ('Poll Tax in West Nile District') makes it clear that it was more
of a process than a date. The Governor wanted tax collection to begin on 1 April 1917, but local
officials disagreed. The compromise was that the tax would not be 'unduly forced on those portions
of the district least able to bear it' (ibid., Actg DCWN to PCNP, 4 December 1916). Collection was
'left to the discretion of the DC' (ibid., Chief Secretary to PCNP, 12 January 1917). The first
mention of tax in Weatherhead's diary is on 13 March 1918, the entry for that day reading 'To
Agondua, awaiting tax registers. Harelhurst and son over, out with them to view Mission site.' The
same source records the first attempts to chase tax defaulters as being in January 1919, see below.

between the chief and the administration, that between the chief and his people was in danger of widening. (King 1970:22)[10]

For the people of West Nile, chiefs or not, this attempt to introduce state (or quasi-state) structures, combining executive, legislative and judicial functions in the same individuals, came at a bad time. Human and animal diseases were hitting epidemic levels. According to Middleton, 'severe outbreaks of cerebro-spinal meningitis and rinderpest occurred ... about 1912. In addition, there was at least one outbreak of smallpox in the years immediately following, and also further cattle epidemics. Finally, in 1918 there was an outbreak of Spanish influenza' (Middleton 1971b: 17). Weatherhead's diary records several cases (mostly Europeans) of smallpox, meningitis and blackwater fever in late 1917 and 1918.[11] In March 1918 he responded to a serious smallpox epidemic by attempting to establish an 'isolation camp' for smallpox victims in Arua.[12] By May, a famine was under way. Hundreds of bags of food were supplied from southern Uganda by boat and distributed around the district.[13]

It appears that this period saw the revival of a healing religious movement among the people of the area, which may have been important during a previous series of epidemics in the 1890s. Known to local people as Yakan or Yakani, and to the Europeans as the 'Allah Water Cult', this was believed by Weatherhead, and by the writers of subsequent accounts of this period in West Nile history, to be a dangerous anti-British conspiracy. As one influential account put it, 'On every occasion [the movement arises] the medical aspect is shortly superseded by the revolutionary idea' (Driberg 1931: 420). Middleton suggested that the Lugbara associated disease with the arrival of Europeans,[14] and certainly the Yakan movement employed syncretic ritual elements derived from European motifs.[15] In my view, however, the evidence for seeing the movement as being behind the opposition Weatherhead faced in 1919 is weak. In the next section, I shall examine the historiography of the Yakan movement in West Nile. Here, I want to attempt a reconstruction of what actually happened in 1919 from primary archival material, particularly Weatherhead's daily diary, and a full set of depositions from the ensuing government inquiry, which are held in the UK Public Records Office.[16]

By the end of 1918, the chiefs were supposed to have collected the poll tax.

[10] Forced labour was the alternative to poll tax, for those unable to pay. Resentment against this was noted among Geria's interviewees (Geria 1973: 77), and was also mentioned to me in 1996–8.
[11] Provincial Reports for 1917 record hundreds of 'native' deaths from 'CSM [Cerebrospinal memingitis]' in West Nile in 1917: UNA A46/794, 810.
[12] Weatherhead, Diary (RH Mss Afr. s. 1638), 4 March 1918, 22 March 1918.
[13] Weatherhead, Diary (ibid.), 13–30 May 1918. The Northern Province Annual Report for 1918–19 records that 'the distribution of relief food in West Nile was continued from May until December 1918' (UNA A46/811).
[14] He is somewhat inconsistent in this. The Lugbara remembered well the epidemics of the early 1890s when, according to Middleton, they had experienced only 'very slight' contact with Europeans or Arabs (Middleton 1971b: 13). He also described their pre-contact life in Hobbesian language, as 'an everlasting succession of epidemics, droughts, famines, and population movements going back for centuries' (Middleton 1992: 2).
[15] Driberg (1931: 419), Middleton (1963:101), King (1970: 15).
[16] The trial papers are in the Public Records Office (PRO): WO 106/253: 39–125. One of the state-ments in this file forms the basis of most previous accounts of the 'uprising', see below.

During the year, Weatherhead's staff had been augmented by the arrival of a KAR detachment large enough to be headed by three British officers.[17] Two new British administrators had also been appointed; R.E. McConnell arrived in August and Weatherhead's new Assistant District Commissioner (ADC), J.H. (Jack) Driberg, in mid-December.[18] Both, unlike Weatherhead himself, were keen amateur anthropologists.

Weatherhead's diary entry for New Year's Day 1919 reads: 'Alarm 3.30am. Turned out to be Fad.[Fadl el Mula] Murjan firing at hyena. Out on station to Baraza [public meeting] noon to 4pm. Tennis and Bridge.' On 8 January, the diary for the first time records an operation to round up tax defaulters. The campaign was to continue for much of the month as Weatherhead and Driberg moved round the northern part of the district: typical entries read: '9 January 1919. Checking tax-defaulters at Terego, 12 January 1919. Left for Wadri hunting tax defaulters.' '16 January 1919. At Omugo on tax defaulters.' By the end of the month, Weatherhead was in Aringa County, where the county chief was the 'Nubi' Fadl el Mula Ali. The last day of January was spent at a major meeting in the northern county of Offudde: '31 January 1919. Aupi to Offudde. All chiefs in for diwan. About 5,000 people present. Sermon on heinousness of drinking "Allah water".' The *diwan* (meeting) continued for three days, following which Weatherhead sat down to write a long report on the 'Allah Water' movement for his superiors. There had been, he wrote, 'a certain amount of unrest' among the Lugbara, the cause of which was the drinking of 'a magic water sold by two agents in the Yei River District of the Sudan'. The result of this to date had been 'a little unrest among the Lugwari, resulting in individual cases of refusal to take share of communal labour. I have no immediate fear of any severe trouble but unless the two men are removed and dealt with the movement may grow.'[19]

Weatherhead's optimism proved unfounded. In the following weeks there were two further incidents of opposition to county chiefs, which caused him to revise his assessment of the situation. These form the substantial events of the 'Yakan uprising', although, as we shall see in the next section, the published accounts vary widely. Unfortunately the original sources I have seen give only a sketchy account, but it is more than enough to cast doubt on the accuracy of previous versions. The first outbreak occurred only days after the *diwan*, in Maracha County, where the chief was a man named Aliga. On 5 February, Weatherhead's diary records: 'word rec'd from Aliga, Retiko [a parish in Maracha] Heads out. Six police sent out; large nos of Lugwari said joined in.' The next three days' entries read:

> 6 February 1919. Started in direction Yei [southern Sudan] then turned back along border to intercept Paranga [another Maracha parish] Camped at Paranga
> 7 February 1919. Out along border south, Driberg do. north. Returned camp 2pm.
> 8 February 1919. At Paranga. Rain 11 to noon. Mail arrived 10pm. Strolled out to border to get in touch with Paranga.

---

[17] Weatherhead, Diary, 7.3.18 and subsequently.
[18] Weatherhead, Diary, 21 August 1918, 14 December 1918.
[19] This is the report King refers to as Weatherhead's 'Secret Memorandum', it is in PRO:WO 106/253: 108–11.

The second and more serious conflict occurred in Udupi Parish, Aringa County. According to Sultan Fadl el Mula Ali's statement at the ensuing trial: 'The Udupi trouble came ... when I and my party were attacked by the Udupi people when I went to arrest a man. I heard one man shouting "bullets cannot hurt us, we have drunk Allah Water, we can catch the people with our hands".'[20] Weatherhead's diary appears to record ten days of trouble, by which time the British forces had the upper hand, proceeding (in a standard punitive action) to impound the cattle of the rebels:

17 February 1919. 4.15am. News of Udupi catastrophe received. Left @ 6.30am arrived Terego 9.30am where found Riddick and McConnell. Left Terego 1pm. Arr'd Omugo 13.30pm.
18 February. Left Omugo 7am, proceeded to Udupi which intact. Thence to Ezappi. Tentative scrap. Returned Omugo 5.45pm. Riddick and McConnell apparently gone Arua. Fired: 19+11 self + 4 misfires.
19 February. Moved on to Udupi. Police on patrol. In contact with people. C.D. Brodie of KAR arrived 6pm.
20 February. Swept through Lubari and back via Ezappi. Juma Said recovered abt 79 [...?]. Brodie with me.
21 February. Brodie returned to Arua.
22 February. At Udupi. Nothing doing.
23 February. Left camp 3am through Lubari; on to low veldt on Anau [river]. Got 200 odd [...?] Returned via Mveppi; reaching Lubari 4.30pm. No camp, no nothing. Dossed under googoo top.
24 February. Safari turned up 11pm. Note from Driberg who at Mveppi. Out to Stoney Hill S. of camp 4pm. Chased off lookouts.
25 February. Good scrap in Devil's Pass above Mveppi. Got an arrow in knee. Driberg came up R. bank of Anau; afterwards on to camp with me. Camp moved from Lubari to Ezappi.
26 February. Moved camp from Ezappi to Mveppi, joining up with Driberg.
27 February. Driberg & I patrol R bank Anau. Arua police & KAR left bank. Self in camp all day. Knee dickey.
28 February. Patrols out. S[elf] & Driberg in camp all day
1 March. Returned to Udupi. Ezappi sent in rifles.

Neither Weatherhead's diary nor the account of the events of February in the papers of the ensuing government inquiry seem to indicate a very violent sequence of events. As the Acting Governor of Uganda described the affair in a report to the Colonial Secretary the following year: 'For some time past there have been periodical phases of unrest among the natives in the West Nile district. For instance, in February last it was necessary to send a machine gun and team under a British officer, and the presence of these troops, with the help of some additional police, averted the trouble.'[21]

Whatever the precise events of February 1919, however, this was all there was to the 'Yakan uprising'. Both Weatherhead and Fadl el Mula Ali himself blamed the Yakan movement for the trouble. Driberg was given the task of gathering evidence about the extent of support for the movement. He became

[20] Statement of Fademulla Ali, alias Akuti, Chief of Aringa County, PRO:WO 106/253: 102.
[21] W.M. Carter, Acting Governor, Uganda Protectorate, to the Rt. Hon the Secretary of State for the Colonies, 21 February 1920, in PRO:WO 106/253: 40–42. In fact, the machine-gun team, as Weatherhead's diary shows, did not arrive until 6 March, after the fighting was over.

Plate 5.2 Fadelmulla Murjan,
One time bugle boy to Emin Pasha

(Photo by A.E. Weatherhead, copyright the Bodleian
Library, University of Oxford, Mss. Afr. s. 1638 (36), II)

convinced that further trouble was brewing, and in August Weatherhead
requested further armed assistance. A substantial detachment of soldiers arrived,
but no further disturbances occurred.[22]

Driberg also returned with a fully-fledged conspiracy theory. As one account
puts it, 'He became convinced that all the county chiefs and most of their people
were involved in the cult' (King 1970: 8). This may be something of an
exaggeration. As we shall see, at least one of the chiefs, Fadl el Mula Ali, was one
of the main sources of Driberg's theory and, together with another Nubi in
Weatherhead's service, Fadl el Mula Murjan,[23] his testimony formed the basis of
the government case against fifteen men considered to be behind the Yakan
conspiracy. They included the County Chief of Terego and sub-county chiefs from
Terego, Aringa and Maracha counties. On the basis of the information gathered
by Driberg, in September Weatherhead arrested them and forwarded depositions

---

[22] Weatherhead, Diary: '21 August. K.A.R. arrived. Place, Stevens, 140 R&F [rank and file soldiers] 1
Maxim + 2 Lewis guns.' The Governor's report to the Colonial Secretary of January 1920 stated,
'In August the District Commissioner considered it sufficiently serious to warrant a request for
military assistance. 125 rank and file, with machine guns, were therefore sent up and, though no
active operations were eventually found to be necessary, their presence in the district had a
steadying effect. They have now returned to headquarters' (PRO:WO 106/253: 40). In the
government files on the issue collected in UNA A46/1870 (SMP 5592) 'West Nile District: Unrest
in Arua District', the telegram announcing the arrival of the troops in Masindi (DC Bunyoro for
PCNP to Chief Sec. 15 August 1919) is annotated (probably by the Chief Secretary himself): 'As Mr
Weatherhead asked that the troops shd not arrive later than the 31st, there does not seem need for
desperate hurry – no rising had occurred, he wanted to have troops there when he made certain
arrests' (i.e. of the supposed Yakan ringleaders).

[23] This is *not* the Fadl el Mula Murjan whose life was recounted by Lanning (1954), who was a
younger man. I am not clear which of them was responsible for the false alarm on New Year's Day
1919; both seem to have been in Weatherhead's service at the time.

to the Protectorate authorities recommending that the fifteen be deported from the district.[24]

At this point, the conspiracy theory met a hitch. The Attorney-General of Uganda, Alan Hogg, was unconvinced by the quality of Weatherhead's and Driberg's evidence that the Yakan cult was behind the February 'uprising'. He requested additional evidence, and Weatherhead supplied further affidavits. However, on 5 January 1920, Hogg concluded:

> I have carefully read these supplemental affidavits and I regret that I cannot advise His Excellency to grant Deportation Orders. I do not think that they show that any of the persons named have caused disaffection or have actually intrigued against the Government. As far as I can gather from the affidavits, 'Allah Water' appears to be particularly intoxicating drink but does not appear to be necessarily anti-governmental.[25]

He was, however, overruled by the Acting Governor General, William Morris Carter, on the grounds that:

> the persons in question were all active members of the cult, and were engaged in dispensing the water and in other practices connected therewith. Although, therefore, there is nothing to show that they have intrigued against the government if the dispensing of 'Allah Water' is to be regarded as of no political significance, yet on the evidence produced as to the meaning and objects of the rite I am satisfied that they have been conducting themselves so as to be dangerous to peace and good order in the West Nile District and that their deportation is justified. It is, moreover, in my opinion clearly advisable.[26]

Neither the Attorney-General nor the Acting Governor-General, therefore, agreed with Driberg and Weatherhead that the events of February were evidence of a coordinated conspiracy against British rule led by the Yakan movement, but the Governor was convinced that the 'meaning and objects' of Yakan were dangerous. The fifteen were deported from West Nile to Masindi District, to be followed the next year by a further eight 'Yakan leaders' (King 1970: 8).[27] Weatherhead at last had the opportunity to place his own people in the vacant chiefly positions. The Lugbara as a whole were placed under the rule of a Nubi 'Agent', a post which was not abolished until the late 1920s (Middleton 1971b: 32). The Nubi, Fadl el Mula (or Fademulla) Murjan, whose testimony had helped to convict the men, was first made Sultan of Terego (Lanning 1954: 180, fn. 5; Middleton 1963: 106, fn. 1) and then became the overall Government Agent.[28] Other deportees were replaced by men loyal to Weatherhead. As Lord Hailey's official report for the Colonial Office on 'Native Administration in the British

---

[24] Weatherhead, Diary, February 1919. Depositions in PRO:WO 106/253: 40–42.

[25] Hogg to Chief Secretary, 5 January 1920, in PRO:WO 106/253: 112.

[26] Carter to Sec. of State for the Colonies 21 February 1920. PRO:WO 106/253: 40–42.

[27] Weatherhead seems to have used the weapon of deportation from West Nile on at least one previous occasion. According to Aidan Southall, a troublesome Alur chief named Amula was deported to Masindi, in Bunyoro district in 1917 after having been 'shown to have twice attempted by witchcraft to kill District officers and to bring guns into the country to drive out the Government' (Southall 1953: 283).

[28] The Northern Province Quarterly Report for July–September 1926 (UNA A46/798) noted his death in office: 'In West Nile, Government has lost a valuable servant by the death of Fademulla Murjan, the Lugwari Government Agent, who unfortunately died of dysentery in July. His influence over the Lugwari was good and they too have lost a good friend.'

African Territories' put it in 1950, 'In the West Nile District ... the British at the outset ... relied on sultans chosen on grounds of [Belgian] service or local position. Trouble which occurred in 1918 [*sic*] led to a more careful selection of chiefs and the adjustment of administrative units in closer conformity with tribal boundaries' (Hailey 1950: 62).

Weatherhead continued to extend British rule, remaining in post until 1922. Driberg stayed as his ADC until 1921, when he transferred to the Sudan administration (see below). The 'Yakan uprising' became a part of Ugandan history.

The historiography of the 'Yakan rebellion'

Any critique of the written history of West Nile district should perhaps begin with the recognition that most of it has been produced, not by professional historians, but by social anthropologists. In the case of Yakan, a further caveat is necessary. The inevitable relationship between knowledge and power is complicated in this case by the dual role of Jack Driberg as both government official and (later) academic analyst. Although McConnell produced the first published account of what he called 'Yakani' (McConnell 1925: 464) it is a brief one, amounting to no more than a paragraph of his paper, with only a sideways reference to the uprising. Driberg's paper in the *Journal of the Royal Anthropological Institute*, entitled simply 'Yakañ', formed the basis of most subsequent accounts. Although, as we have seen, Driberg in his earlier role as colonial administrator had spent several weeks investigating the 'Yakan movement', his account of its history and beliefs is very largely based on the testimony of Fadl el Mula Murjan.

Jack Driberg was an interesting man, and a most unusual colonial administrator, a fact which was recognised by the authorities when he was allowed to 'resign on medical grounds' from the Sudan government service in 1925. According to Collins, Driberg, stationed with the Didinga people of eastern Mongalla district, had sought authority to take over the neighbouring area of the Toposa people:

> His perception of the Toposa as the malevolent marauders who had to be brought under his governance in order to protect his beloved Didinga soon became an obsession.... He was flatly informed that action against the Toposa should not be undertaken.... What followed was a combination of fact and fantasy. Driberg reported that the Toposa were looting Longarim cultivations and inflicting casualties.... Unknown to anyone but Driberg, all of his reports were sheer fabrication of his own making. There was no Toposa raid.... His only thought was 'to force the government to consent to the action he desired to take' ... he reported a devastating Toposa raid ... involving some six hundred Toposa of the Karingek section who were routed by police.... Upon learning of the supposed raid... the government ordered a strike force to punish the Toposa for a raid they never committed. This was too much for Driberg. He confessed ... that his reports were inventions. (Collins 1983: 93–6)

Driberg seems to have given a rather different version to his brother, the somewhat infamous journalist and Labour politician Tom Driberg. According to the latter's memoirs:

Plate 5.3 J. H. Driberg, colonial administrator and anthropologist

(Photo by A.E. Weatherhead, copyright the Bodleian Library, University of Oxford, Mss. Afr. s 1638 (36), II)

One day a signal came from Khartoum ... to say that His Excellency the Governor would be visiting Jack's district on a certain day and instructing him to gather all the tribal chiefs and village headmen at a central spot on that day, to pay homage to H.E. Now, Jack knew that the appointed day happened to be a day of great local importance ... and the headmen could not be away from their villages. Jack put this urgently to the bureaucrats in Khartoum. No, they said, H.E.'s schedule could not be altered. There must be a full attendance for him. As Jack had foreseen, many headmen stayed away – and he was now ordered to conduct a punitive expedition against the absentees and to burn down their villages. He would do no such thing: instead, he drafted and sent to Khartoum a vivid but purely imaginative report on the punitive expedition. When the truth came out, of course he had to resign.... Jack's 'war that never was' became a legend in the service. (T. Driberg 1978: 30–31)

As Marilyn Fetterman felicitously puts it, 'Deemed crazy, Driberg was sent back to England where he decided to become an anthropologist' (Fetterman 1994: 2).[29] E.E. Evans-Pritchard, in a generous and carefully worded obituary in the anthropology journal *Man* when Jack Driberg died in 1947, called him a 'romantic figure'. He was 'gay, versatile, lovable and adventurous, an Elizabethan. He was a rare spirit and his weaknesses were consistent with the heroic in his personality.' Among Driberg's anthropological works listed by Evans-Pritchard is a pseudonymous volume on how to play poker, and 'it was not for nothing that he was an expert poker player. He gambled with life, and did not always win.' Evans-Pritchard remembered him as an 'inspiring tutor, stylist and brilliant talker

[29] Fetterman's paper gives an interesting and enlightening view of Driberg from a Didinga perspective, based on interviews carried out in the 1980s with old people who remembered his time in the district.

– at his best *splendide mendax'.*[30] (Evans-Pritchard 1947: 12–13). Jack Driberg sounds like very good company at dinner but, to say the least, a somewhat unreliable witness.[31]

John Middleton's account of the Yakan movement (e.g. Middleton 1963, 1971a, b) is based on oral material gathered in the early 1950s, as well as on Driberg's work and the testimony of Fadl el Mula Murjan. It has been influential among later writers on West Nile more through its analysis of the social function of the Yakan cult as an attempt to control the impact of alien forces through the ritual inversion of traditional Lugbara norms, than for its account of the origins and history of the movement.[32] In terms of the latter, Middleton relies largely on Murjan's testimony, and where he does not he is frequently inaccurate, at least in the details. For example, his account of the February events is misdated to April:

> At the beginning of 1919 it was realized that there was considerable unrest among the Lugbara and a rising was feared. In early April of that year a party of government police tried to close a Yakan meeting near Udupi, in north-eastern Lugbara. They were attacked and eleven police and a sub-county chief were killed. The attackers used spears, shouting 'Yakani, Yakani'. There were several later affrays but all were beaten back by police. Extra police and a company of troops were sent from Masindi, and except for a serious fight at Parange, in Ole'ba, the centre of Rembe's [an early Yakan leader] activities, there were no further alarms. (Middleton 1963: 90)

Aside from the misdating, Fadl el Mula Ali's own testimony to the inquiry, quoted above, contradicts Middleton's account of the initial trigger for the Udupi events (he went to arrest a man for unspecified reasons, not to close a meeting). It is strange, too, that if police were killed, this was not mentioned in the inquiry testimony.

An even more violent account of the events of February 1919 is provided by Anne King, who gives the most extensive published historical account of Yakan (King 1970). The only historian to have published a full-length paper on Yakan, she also used oral material gathered in 1968 and 1969, as well as the evidence produced at the enquiry, but she tends to cite Weatherhead's 'Secret Memorandum' of 3 February, rather than Fadl El Mula's post-uprising account. Her article confuses the latter's testimony with that of Weatherhead's translator, another Nubi named Murjan Ramadan. She writes:

> Murjan Ramadan Lemerijua ... suggested that the cult was moving towards the launching of a full scale attack on the government and that the Udipi affair had been merely premature. Weatherhead took up this argument, insisting that strong preemptive measures should be taken to nip that possibility in the bud. A consideration of the history of the cult, as it was presented by Murjan Ramadan, also gave the impression that the cult's sole aim was to organise violent resistance to alien intruders. (King 1970: 11)

---

[30] Chambers Dictionary translates the Latin phrase as 'Splendidly false, nobly lying'.

[31] Driberg was not the only member of the Sudan Political Service to fabricate evidence of a religious uprising in the interest of convincing a sceptical central authority to grant unusual powers. See Johnson 1985 for the case of C.A. ('Chunky') Willis and the 'Cult of Deng'. In 1919, as we have seen, Weatherhead and Driberg were in just this position *vis à vis* the central authorities, when the Attorney General refused to sign their deportation orders (see Anne King's comment, quoted below).

[32] Middleton's theory is well summarised and its later impact assessed in Allen 1991a: 380–81.

There is a confusion here. Weatherhead's translator did give evidence to the government inquiry, but it was a brief statement as to the bad reputation of 'Allah water' among the Nubi. It contained neither a history of the movement nor a prediction of all-out revolt; these were in Fadl el Mula Murjan's lengthy statement.[33] Despite the misattribution, it is clearly this latter document that she has read and uses in her account.

King's version of the February events seems to be largely from oral sources, though her referencing is somewhat confusing:[34] 'On 4th February 1919, men from four parishes [a footnote names Retiko, Paranga, Natika and Aroi] in the Lugbara county of Maracha attacked the government-appointed sultan, Aliga. He and his askaris were embattled for two days before the Assistant District Commissioner, J.H. Driberg, arrived with reinforcements and managed to drive the attackers across the border' (King 1970: 6). She sees the Udupi events as following from an attempt by Fadl el Mula Ali to impose on Udupi an unpopular sub-chief named Olea:

> a large hostile force had gathered, cutting off Fadimulla Ali and his party.... and before reinforcements could reach him, four of the police constables had been killed, as well as Olea, two of Fadimulla's own askaris and sixteen other people.... Between 18th and 25th February the Udupi managed to hold down the district force which, despite the loss of eight rifles, had a far superior firing power. On the 25th a detachment of Protectorate police arrived, armed with a maxim gun. The hard core of the rebels was located in caves near the Anau river, and, in a three day battle, were finally overcome. Weatherhead estimated that some two hundred men were killed, about one quarter of the male population of Udupi. (King 1970: 7)

There is no mention, in the papers of the government inquiry, of either the number of rebels killed or the death of any police or soldiers. The evidence is far too weak to be conclusive, but none of the primary sources I have seen offers much support for the more dramatic aspects of King's account. The figure of 200 dead is a very large, and suspiciously round, number. Moreover, the diary indicates at least one basic error in King's account: the machine-gun team did not actually arrive until after the action was over, on 6 March.[35]

King's paper goes on to make an important point, the scepticism of which is unfortunately not pursued in the rest of her account: 'It should be borne in mind, however, that the information collected in 1919 and presented to the Entebbe government was largely done to convince a sceptical Attorney General that it was necessary to deport certain members of the cult, and that this could only be done by bringing a charge of sedition against them' (King 1970: 11).

This 'information', which failed to convince Mr Hogg, seems nevertheless to have convinced the academics who have written articles on Yakan and, through them, the others who have cited the movement as a classic example of religious-based peasant resistance to colonial rule. This later discourse on Yakan is

---

[33] Murjan Ramadan's statement is in PRO:WO 106/253: 79–80. Fadl el Mula Murjan's is in PRO:WO 106/253: 97–100.

[34] The only source cited in a page-long paragraph is an 'oral record', though it may be that a later-cited letter from Weatherhead to the Provincial Commissioner, Northern Province, which I have not yet been able to trace, is also relevant.

[35] Weatherhead, Diary: '6 March. Laing & machine gun arrived. Tennis. Fathers over.'

considered below. First, it is necessary to look more closely at the material assembled by Weatherhead and Driberg to convince Hogg of the existence of a Yakan conspiracy. This consisted of:

1. Fifteen sworn statements from each of them that each of the proposed deportees had 'conducted themsel[ves] so as to be dangerous to peace and good order in West Nile', together with a summary of the evidence against them, Driberg's statements being witnessed by Weatherhead and vice versa.

2. Forty-two witness statements, some of which inculpate more than one of the deportees, mostly by men described as 'Lugwari, heathen' (i.e. not Muslim Nubians), many of whom held sub-chief or other positions under Weather-head. Most of these statements are brief and simply say that one or another of the deportees was associated with drinking or dispensing 'Allah water'. Only three of the Lugbara informants asserted that the Yakan movement had any insurrectionary intent: two sub-county chiefs from Terego and a police constable based in Arua.[36] These assertions are not backed up by much detail. The statements were all taken down and signed by Weatherhead and Driberg, translators must have been used in each case, and no witness was able to read or sign his own statement. Exceptional in its length and detail is the statement of the Nubi, Fadl el Mula Murjan. Fadl el Mula Ali supplied a shorter statement.

3. Weatherhead's original memorandum on the cult, written before the Udupi events.

Aside from the fact that the (five) witnesses who attributed an insurrectionary motive to the Yakan all worked for Weatherhead and Driberg, who (as King noted) had a strong motivation to emphasise the guilt of the accused, a further reason for scepticism is that the key Nubi witnesses had every reason to wish to convince the Englishmen that Yakan was not an Islamic phenomenon, that the Nubi had nothing to do with the insurrection. As King suggests:

> a conspiracy theory was advanced by Driberg to suggest that there were substantive links between the early activities of the Yakan in Equatoria, the Sudanese [ie Nubi] mutiny against the Uganda Protectorate in 1897 and the Maji-Maji revolt [in present-day Tanzania, 1905–7]. Meanwhile Weatherhead was considering another district officer's bogey, the possibility that Yakan was a Muslim-inspired opposition to the government. (King 1970: 10)

Weatherhead's memorandum indeed stated that 'It is impossible to ascertain here whether the movement is a Mohammadan one emanating from far afield. It

---

[36] The most detailed of the three is the statement of Burua, Sub-chief in the County of Terego, which said (in its entirety): 'When Allah Water was introduced lately among the Lugwari I refused to allow anyone to keep it. It was introduced years ago because the Dervishes were here and we wanted to get rid of them. Allah water was in those days sprinkled over the people so that the Dervish rifles should not kill them, it was to make them invulnerable in case of war. Allah Water is a war measure. The common idea this year and what was given out was that when we had all drunk the water we could make war on strangers all together. My father died from being sprinkled with the water during the time the Dervishes were here, that was one reason why I would not have it, and I also knew that it meant war and many people killed and I preferred to listen to the word of the white man. Allah water is a very bad thing' (Witness statement No.11, PRO:WO 106/253: 84).

maybe that it is merely a cunning device... to obtain large profits at little cost.'[37] The memorandum is also the source of a bizarre list of Yakan beliefs, which has frequently been cited:

the following promises are made to partakers of the water:-

(a) The water will preserve them from death.... (b) Their ancestors will come to life. (c) Their dead cattle will come to life. (c) They can flout all government orders with impunity, and need not pay their tax. (e) They need not fear fighting against the government as the government rifles will only fire water against those who have drunk Allah water.... (f) That in a few months time rifles will be received from 'German' (sic) then be issued to the people, whereupon they will be able to clear the country of Aliens including the administration... (g) People who refuse to drink the water will become termites when they die.[38]

Many of these beliefs are unattested by any other source on Yakan: point (f), for example, which is, however, reminiscent of the promises of Nongqawuse, the South African prophetess of the Xhosa cattle-killing movement of the 1850s (at that time, it was the Russians, Britain's opponents in the recent Crimean War, who were to assist the Africans to get rid of the British).[39] Weatherhead, it may be noted, had seen service in South Africa before coming to Uganda.

The key document in the case, however, was not the rather confused analysis of Weatherhead, but the statement of Fadl el Mula Murjan. This was one of the supplementary affidavits, produced to convince Hogg after he had asked for more evidence. More than twice as long as any of the other depositions, it formed, not only the most important piece of evidence against the deportees, but the basis of, first, Driberg's account and then the subsequent analyses of Middleton and King. It is worth examining in some detail. One notable feature is the confidence with which it asserts specific details of the history of the Yakan movement, in contrast to the somewhat vague terms in which every other document speaks of it:

This water started with the Dinka, who wiped out the boma of Rumbe [sic],[40] killing some 800 soldiers, after drinking the water, which they believed to give them irresistible strength. About two years later, the Dervishes attacked the Sudan post of Madi.... Shortly after this the Dinka came down and sold the Allah water to the Bari, telling them it would render them invulnerable if they attacked the government. (I was a bugler [in Emin Pasha's service] in those days).... The whole Bari tribe arose and attacked Rejaf, and it was only by calling up troops of Silal, Kiri, Mogi, Lebere, Kuraya, Dufile, Patiko and Wadelai that we were able to defeat the Bari.

After the Dervishes again came and drove us from Dufile to the Alur country, Magoro chief of the Mondo obtained Allah water from the Dinka.... The whole tribe drank this water in the expectation of a Dervish raid, and when the Dervish attacked they drove them back with great loss. The Abukaya then went to Magore and asked him how he had managed to defeat the Dervishes... Magore replied that it was due to Allah water which made them invulnerable both to spears and guns. The Abukaya

---

[37] PRO:WO 106/253: 111.

[38] PRO: WO 106/253, 109-110.

[39] See Pieres (1989:72): 'The Russians, it gradually came to be believed, were not a white nation at all, but a black one, the spirits of Xhosa warriors who had died fighting [against the British]... the Xhosa posted lookouts on the higher hills to watch for the arrival of the Russian ships.... By the summer of 1855, more than five prophets had sprung up within British Kaffraria itself, asserting they were in contact with the black nation over the sea, who were on their way to help the Xhosa.'

[40] Presumably a reference to the Battle of Rumbek in 1883.

bought the water, and were followed by the Moro, the Pajulu, the Nambara. After drinking the water these five tribes combined and waged a victorious war against the Makraka, the most powerful tribe at that time in the vicinity.

At a later date (about 28 years ago) Lagere, a Pajulu, bought some of the water from Magore, and Rembe obtained it from Lagore ... [one of the deportees, Mba, chief of Terego, and six other Lugbara chiefs are then inculpated]

After Emin's retirement with Stanley 4 companies were left at Wadelai under Fademula Bey. A patrol of 80 men was sent towards Terego and was engaged by the Lugwari, who had been drinking Allah water, and were completely wiped out....

At a later date Major Preston[41] found us and took us to Masindi, with innumerable natives of different tribes who were either 'boys' or porters. They eventually enlisted. I was sent with 30 men to establish Mahagi, and on my return to Masindi found that some of the Makraka porters had taken over Allah Water and that the cult was flourishing among the troops.... From Masindi, the cult spread to Kampala and Entebbe.... It was said that if a European even tried the [sic] arrest a member of the cult his hands would wither up. The cult developed most strongly in Busoga ... and when disaffection culminated in the mutiny all the Nubis were members of the cult....

In 1918 I gave one of my Mkungus Geria some bags as instructed by the D.C. and he refused to take them saying that he had drunk the water of Allah and would owe no allegiance to authority. In December 1918 finding that the cult had really taken root I learn from a woman Marotia that all the Lugwari except the west and south of Arua had drunk the water and were members of the cult and she said that in a short time they would drive out the Europeans: that there was only left this small area and all would be ready, but that any who refused to drink would be killed for refusing to listen to Yakany. She added that all the Lugwari including all the chiefs were in the conspiracy....

This drinking of Yakany water has only one object, a concerted rising and expulsion or massacre of Europeans. At the time of Udupi rising the tribe was not ready, the rising being premature, but had instant measures not been taken or had the punitive police received a reverse the whole tribe would have risen and destroyed Arua. As it was, a cordon was ready between Udupi and Arua cutting off the DC. After Udupi the cult still continued secretly, and had no further measures been taken there would undoubtedly have been another rising as soon as Yakany was ready.

xxxxxxxxxx

Affirmed before me 19.11.19
Sd. J.H. Driberg, A.D.M.

Fadl el Mula Murjan's tale is very clearly a Nubi history. Yakan water is shown as accompanying the Nubi on their travels, from their time under Emin Pasha in southern Sudan, to the period when they were pinned down by the Mahdi's 'dervishes' in West Nile, and on to their British army experience in southern Uganda, before returning to West Nile under Weatherhead. It is associated primarily with the 'heathen' tribes against whom the Muslim troops were pitted by their European masters, and features as a factor in many of the conflicts of the period, from the Battle of Rumbek in 1883, in which an Egyptian garrison was destroyed by a combined Nuer/Dinka force (see Johnson 1994: 249), to the Udupi events of 1919. A regional, anti-colonial conspiracy is clearly outlined. No mention is made of any healing function for the Yakan rituals, although all authorities from Driberg on have seen the movement as originally concerned with healing.

[41] In fact, Major A.B. Thruston, see Moyse-Bartlett 1956: 59.

As an account of the origins of Yakan, Murjan's story about the Dinka has been echoed by Middleton, King and later writers. It is, however, ill-founded. No accounts of the attack on Rumbek speak of a magical or religious element, while no signs of any movement oriented around a water ritual have been found in southern Sudan prior to the 1919 events in West Nile,[42] after which administrators sought strenuously and unsuccessfully for evidence of a Sudan connection for Yakan. As Douglas Johnson has written:

> The Yakan or 'Allah water' cult in Equatoria Province and Northern Uganda ... was associated in administrators' minds with the appearance of a 'holy lake' among the Atuot...; the spread of the magic root matthiang goh among the Jur-beli and Dinka of Rumbek district; and the 'rebellion' of the Dinka prophet Arianhdit in 1922. Each had seemed capable of attracting followers across social and even international boundaries, and was all the more subversive for that. Though there was no direct connection between these different movements and events, administrators constantly tried to find one, attributing a Dinka origin to Yakan, and searching for cultic similarities between the Zande societies, matthiang goh and even the Nuer prophets. (Johnson 1994: 27)[43]

The administrators did not, however, invent the conspiracy themselves: they listened to the Nubi. As already noted, they also rewarded them with chiefly posts over the Lugbara. The Nubi also had other good reasons for insisting on the 'heathen' (Lugbara, Kakwa or Dinka) roots of Yakan; Weatherhead's initial memorandum had raised the spectre the authorities most dreaded (in the wake of the Mahdist uprising in Sudan and the Muslim military revolt in Uganda), that Yakan was linked with Islam. On the contrary, the Nubi witnesses insisted, it had been used against Muslims throughout most of its history.

John Middleton points out that 'most of' Driberg's account of Yakan is based upon' Fadl el Mula Murjan's account, which he 'used almost verbatim' (Middleton 1963:80, 91). This is also the main origin of Middleton's own account of Yakan's origins and involvement in the violence of 1919. He believed, for example, that, in the Rumbek attack of 1883, 'both the Dinka and ... others were led by prophets of cults of which the central part was the mass drinking of magic or sacred water' (Middleton 1971a). By the time of his own research, however, Yakan was seen as primarily a healing movement.[44] King, too, adheres to the conspiracy line. While Driberg concluded that 'On every occasion, the medical aspect [of Yakan] is shortly superseded by the revolutionary idea.... The military character of the organisation is evident' (Driberg 1931: 420), King writes that 'the association of the Yakan cult in the attempted risings in 1919 ... suggest that it played a major role in organising violent resistance to colonial rule' (King

[42] Douglas H. Johnson, personal communication.
[43] Another authority has referred to the Yakan movement as an example of how colonial governments handled outbreaks of 'religious fanaticism' in 'a localised manner'. Holger Bernt Hansen argues that, while the Protectorate authorities were simultaneously dealing with the Nyabingi movement in the Great Lakes region and the Yakan, 'Officials would appear to have seen no parallel between Nyabingi and Yakan, and no mention of the former phenomenon exists in the documentation dealing with the Yakan cult' (Hansen 1995: 158). This is inaccurate on both counts. Weatherhead and Driberg both had geographically widespread conspiracy theories about Yakan, while the latter explicitly mentions Nyabingi in the last sentence of his paper (Driberg 1931: 420).
[44] By which time, he says, the movement took 'a different form, and it has continued to the present day as a disease cult' (Middleton 1963: 91).

1970: 9). As we have seen, there is little evidence for such an association, and none for a Dinka water movement in the early 1880s.

This is, however, how the Yakan movement has passed into history. In the 1960s, radical academics at the University of Dar el Salaam had directed attention to various revolts in the early years of colonialism in Africa, linking such 'primary' resistance movements to contemporary nationalist movements.[45] When, in the same year King's article appeared, Idi Amin seized power in Uganda, the Yakan movement was, as we have seen in Chapter Three, widely mentioned as a precursor. There is an irony in the fact that an account of events in West Nile in 1919, which was originally produced as part of an attempt to assert colonial authority, lent itself so easily to the requirements of anti-colonial historians. In Jan Jorgensen's *Uganda, a Modern History*, he associates Yakan with a series of other 'resistance movements' against the imposition of British rule (including the *Nyabingi* cult). His brief summary of events is fairly typical, 'In 1919 ... the Kakwa prophet Rembe and collaborative chiefs turned resisters led the Yakan revolt of the Lugbara in West Nile' (Jorgensen 1981: 61).

A more recent and extensive account, which follows the full Murjan/Driberg line (though occasionally confusing the original account) is in Louise Pirouet's 1995 *Historical Dictionary of Uganda*:

> The cult appears to have started among the Dinka in the Sudan who in 1883 rose against a Mahdist garrison and wiped it out, attributing their victory to the drinking of protective medicine which became known as Yakan or Allah Water.... In the late 1880s it reached the Kakwa, Madi and Lugbara of northern Uganda who all obtained it through the agency of a man called Rembe....
>
> [In 1919]... the British officials were surprised to be faced with possible widespread rebellion. Many chiefs were found to be implicated in Yakan and were believed to be involved in plotting against the government.... At this stage the cult appeared to pose a real danger and measures were taken against it. Several chiefs were exiled to Ankole until 1925 and Rembe himself was caught and hanged.... Through Emin Pasha's troops... the Yakan Water cult is said to have been passed to the King's African Rifles. Those who mutinied in 1897 are all alleged to have drunk the Allah Water. (Pirouet 1995: 367–8).

This is inaccurate on several points: in Fadl el Mula Murjan's account, which is the only source for all this, it was an Egyptian garrison, not a Madhist one, which was attacked in 1883, while Rembe was not involved until the 1890s and 1900s. His fate is unclear. Middleton says he 'was taken to the Sudan and hanged there in 1917' (Middleton 1971b: 18), while King thinks he 'had been discovered in Aringa County in 1918 where he was arrested and later sent back to the Sudan' (King 1970: 6). No contemporary source suggests his direct involvement in, or presence during, the 1919 events, or that he was hanged after them.

By the mid-1990s, there had been a move towards greater scepticism about the interpretation of African healing or religious movements primarily in terms of

---

[45] The 'Dar School' has been the subject of much analysis. See, for example, the references in McCracken (1997), Sunseri (1997).

'resistance' to colonial rule.[46] The classic nationalist histories of movements such as Maji-Maji in Tanzania and Nyabingi in the Great Lakes region were challenged by 'revisionist' accounts stressing factors, such as gender conflict, which had been absent or minimised in the works of the theorists of 'primary resistance'.[47] Questions were also raised about the Yakan movement. Douglas Johnson's doubts about its regional spread, quoted above, are supported by Tim Allen's conclusion, in his discussion of Yakan in the context of a recent Northern Ugandan rebel movement: 'It has been argued that the movement had a history dating back to the previous century, and had already affected neighbouring ethnic groups over a large area. However, it seems likely that its importance has been exaggerated' (Allen 1991a: 379–80).

In this chapter, I have concentrated on only two aspects of the Yakan movement: its origins and history, and its association with violent revolt. I have not discussed Driberg's, Middleton's or King's wider accounts of the healing functions of the movement, or the latter's view of it as a 'cult ... [which] incorporated aspects of the new world which was beginning to be experienced through alien incorporation' (King 1970: 15). While few of the inquiry statements attributed armed insurrection to Yakan, many mentioned rituals which apparently incorporated European symbols of power: a cashbox, square buildings, flag-pole-like 'Yakan poles' and a 'parade-ground' on which a sort of drill was practised with imitation wooden or grass rifles (see King 1970: 15). However, it is apparent from the witness statements that some of this material has been misleadingly interpreted by both the British authorities at the time and later commentators: the 'poles' were usually trees of specific species associated with the Yakan movement, and the 'parade-grounds' are described by the Lugbara witnesses as places for dancing, rather than 'parading'.[48] Even if it is true that the cult had a social function of coping with alien intrusion, there is no good evidence that this included plotting insurrection against colonial rule.

We should, however, beware the too easy assumption that Yakan was 'about' the encounter with British colonialism. As Douglas Johnson warned in the case of European perceptions of the Zande 'secret societies':

> The fact that the European stereotype of secret societies was immediately and automatically transferred to Africa ought to induce some scepticism regarding official reports describing the closed associations. These reports presented an overtly political interpretation, and have linked the rise and spread of the associations to the European

---

[46] A good brief discussion of the general issues is in Johnson and Anderson (1995).

[47] For Maji Maji, see the discussions in Wright (1995) and Sunseri (1997). For Nyabingi, see Berger (1995).

[48] The 'poles' seem to have been either trees themselves, or to have had branches attached to them – see Driberg's testimony against Njikania, an Aringa sub-chief, 'I found what was clearly a Yakany pole in an open space suitable for parades, the timber being the tree called by the Lugbara Kuzu and surmounted by a branch of another shrub called inzu' (PRO WO 106/253: 54). The 'parades' are described by almost all the Lugbara (as opposed to Nubi) witnesses as 'dances': e.g. testimony of Tunjia of Maracha, 'Ojok held a big dance one day. There had been no death [i.e. it was not a funeral dance] and it was not an ordinary beer dance. There was no pole because Ojok knew that Allah Water was forbidden and he said that if he had no pole the bwana would think it was an ordinary dance' (ibid.: 80).

colonial presence. The very forcefulness of the colonial reaction to the societies has made it difficult to analyse the role of the associations independently of the activities of colonial governments. (Johnson 1991: 197)

It seems at least equally, and perhaps more, plausible that, rather than imitating symbols of *European* power, the ritual elements cited above represented an attempt to incorporate *Nubi* symbols, and may have been as much to do with protection as healing.[49] The encounters of local people with the soldiers of the Egyptian army, and the slave armies which came before[50] (which were particularly intense in Aringa and Maracha counties), predated their acquaintance with Europeans, while the spread of British authority even before 1919, was often via Nubi officials (especially in Fadl el Mula Ali's Aringa County). Certainly, both Murjan's story and whatever the real Yakan movement was trying to do with its 'parade-ground' symbols, come out of an environment characterised by the long-standing, complicated and ambivalent interaction between Lugbara and Nubis, many of whom, in fact, had a good claim to similar ethnic origins to those of the Lugbara (see Chapter Six). Yakan surely has its roots in the disturbed, violent period which predated colonial rule and which is the subject of the next chapter.

In terms of the events of 1919, it seems far more likely that the opposition Weatherhead's chiefs in Maracha and Aringa faced in February had to do with localised reaction to the recently increased demands for forced labour/army enlistment, and particularly with the recent imposition of taxation and punitive raids against non-payers, than it had to do with Yakan. The only detailed source for the conspiracy is Fadl el Mula Murjan, whose account, as we have seen, is less than reliable.

On the other hand, I am not proclaiming a rival conspiracy theory. Although it is true that both the British officers and their Nubi assistants had plenty to gain from the conviction and deportation of the Yakan chiefs, and that Driberg appears to have a record of deliberate invention, I do not believe that the conspiracy was entirely fabricated. It seems entirely plausible that Weatherhead really did fear a conspiracy, and that Fadl el Mula actually believed at least some of the elements of his story.

Nor can I claim to have proved conclusively that there was no Yakan conspiracy, no widespread insurrection planned. It is difficult to prove a negative, and there remain many loose ends. Nevertheless, I believe that the full set of papers from the inquiry demonstrates the paucity of the evidence for the Yakan conspiracy theory of what happened in February, while Weatherhead's diary suggests that the scale of these events has been exaggerated. Although Murjan's testimony has often been used, and misused, the evidence as a whole has not been assessed, and nor have the judgements of the Attorney General and Governor been quoted, in previous studies of Yakan. Weatherhead's diary has also not been used before.

---

[49] I owe this idea to Wendy James.

[50] A fascinating account of the way in which the slave armies in another part of southern Sudan appropriated symbols and ranking systems of the Egyptian state is in O'Fahey (1973).

The build-up to Yakan: 1917–1914

The Yakan events and their eventual resolution merely added the finishing touches to Weatherhead's programme of social engineering in West Nile. He was an able, energetic and conscientious administrator who, from the time of his first arrival in the district in February 1914, devoted himself to the task of bringing the West Nile under effective British rule. Weatherhead's diary reveals the vast distances he travelled (on foot or by mule, bicycle and boat) throughout his period as DC.[51] When off-duty, his obsession, unusually intense even for his class and time, was with sports and games. By 1916 he had begun the construction of the golf-course in Arua town, and many evenings were spent playing tennis with friends or football with teams of police, soldiers or workmen. Other evenings were spent playing card-games or working at carpentry or leatherwork. He attacked his job with equal vigour, frequently working a twelve-hour day or more. Counties and sub-counties were demarcated, and chiefs and sub-chiefs recognised. Local conflicts were adjudicated, roads and bridges were built (initially with workers imported from neighbouring Bunyoro District, but increasingly with forced labour supplied by West Nile chiefs)[52] and elephant hunting was halted.[53] A number of local men were recruited, at first forcibly, into the wartime army (Middleton 1971b). Traders arrived, and the first shop was opened in Arua in 1915, operating at first mainly on a barter basis (Middleton 1970a: 16).

Much of this activity was contested by local people, with the forced labour being particularly resented, and all of it was achieved with remarkably little support. From the beginning, the Protectorate government had been unwilling to expend much on this outlying district. Weatherhead's initial staff in 1914 consisted of one other English administrator, two Indian clerks and a theoretical establishment of eighty Ugandan police.[54] After the outbreak of the First World War in August, however, the authorities in Entebbe initially withdrew the newly appointed officials, relenting in Weatherhead's case after he made strong representations that British 'prestige' would be 'seriously injured'[55] if the administration of West Nile were to be abandoned altogether. He was left with only twenty-five policemen and one clerk. Nor were the police entirely trustworthy; the first

---

[51] David Harris, ADC West Nile 1957–9, in an unpublished typescript entitled 'Notes on the early history of West Nile District of Uganda', explains Weatherhead's Lugbara nickname, 'Ejerekedi' (there are various transliterations), as 'given to him by his askari of Nubian origin. I am informed that it is of Arabic designation and means "one who walks swiftly", a reference to the phenomenal rate at which Mr Weatherhead could travel' (RH mss Afr.s.1350).

[52] Local labour seems sometimes to have simply been extorted: Aidan Southall, who corresponded with and interviewed Weatherhead in his retirement, wrote that 'Weatherhead got the Arua–Rhino Camp road [still a main internal artery in West Nile] built by capturing cattle from the Lugbara and Madi and returning them to their owners after the latter had done the required amount of road-cutting' (Southall 1953: 286).

[53] For Weatherhead's early activities, see the Provincial Commissioner (PC)'s Annual Report 1914–15, Middleton (1963: 88, 1971b: 15–17), Southall (1953: 283–347), King (1970: 6). On his work against the elephant poachers, who had operated virtually uncontrolled in the district since about 1908, see Collins (1971: 265).

[54] Figures from Weatherhead's first 'Annual Report on West Nile District, Uganda, 1914–15', in RH mss Afr.s.586.

[55] Guy Eden, PC's Report for 1914–15. RH mss Afr.s.586.

Annual Report for West Nile District remarked that, 'in addition to the conviction of Murder against one Constable, there have been signs of misconduct by detached parties, which makes me distrustful of allowing them from my sight'.[56]

Weatherhead's basic task was the establishment of government authority in West Nile. The Uganda Protectorate as a whole was run, and with such a small staff West Nile would certainly have to be run, on the principles of indirect rule. The problem was that the bulk of the people of the area were wholly unused to any kind of rule at all, or at least to any kind that would be recognisable to a British official. The Lugbara and the Kakwa had no institutions at the level of the tribe; theirs had been a society where political structures rarely went higher than a three-generational lineage group, and never higher than the level of the clan. The Belgians had attempted to discern chiefs, officially appoint them and govern through them, but their relationship with the local people had been very poor and, in any case, they had made no attempt to introduce the kind of administration Weatherhead planned. This began with initial restrictions on hunting and the widespread use of coerced labour on public works, and was designed to lead towards the introduction of taxation and the establishment of a monetary economy. The British project inherently involved far greater incursions into local people's lives than they had experienced before.

Previous acquaintance with foreigners who had hostile intentions, from Arab slave-traders to European and North American ivory hunters, may well, as we shall see in the next chapter, have made many local people suspicious of outsiders.[57] On the other side, previous British experience with 'the local tribes' had certainly made *them* suspicious. Weatherhead was particularly wary of the majority Lugbara (or 'Lugwari', as he called them). He arrived with distinct views on their '*intractable*' nature. In his first Annual Report, he wrote:

> The variety of tribes and languages does not tend... to make Administration easy. The Madi and the riverain Alur have had considerable experience of Administration, the Northern section of the Lugwari a little, the Highland Alur, central Lugwari and Madi Ai-ivu [a section of the Lugbara] none....
>
> [The 'Lugwari'] ... had a reputation as a fierce intractable tribe.... They are somewhat intractable and proved themselves not amenable to Belgian Administration and on that account were considerably *harried*....
>
> The general policy is to strengthen the pepole [*sic*] as much as possible under big-chiefs, to strengthen their hands, and to throw responsibility and onus onto them. As far as possible the natural chiefs are made, but a preference is given to a man who *can be a chief*, and if necessary a man is imported.... Among the Alur every petty chief wants to be independent. Among the Lugwari every *man* wants to be independent....
>
> The task of the Uganda administration has not been rendered easy by previous Administrations. The Belgians closely occupied small parts of the district, whilst leaving other parts entirely to elephant hunters. The Sudan Administration could not afford full protection to the district.... The Uganda Administration has been met among the Lugwari with distrust, the prevalent idea being that we shall only occupy the country

[56] Weatherhead, DC's Report for 1914–15. RH mss Afr.s.586.

[57] Middleton says that 'the Lugbara were never seriously troubled by outsiders except on the northern and eastern borders of their country' (1992 [1965]: 3), but this is contradicted by both oral histories collected in Geria (1973) and my own interviewees in 1996–7. See the next chapter. Further evidence of the effects of ivory poachers is in Collins (1960a), and some of their own testimonies are in Bell (1923, 1960), Boyes (1928), and Moore (1931).

for a time like the last two Administrations, or that we were merely a glorified band of elephant poachers who would pass on very shortly.

He concluded:

> Under these head [sic] may I be allowed to explain my position by a homely simile. I am in the position of having bitten off enough for two mouths with two full sets of teeth to chew, but by the withdrawal by Mr Warner and of the Police, I am left with one mouth and that with half its teeth drawn. I am aware that my orders are to sit tight, but as you know it is impossible to turn back, when once the natives have experienced our hold.[58]

Weatherhead established from the outset his plans for bringing the West Nile people 'under control'.[59] They amounted to an ambitious programme of social engineering, the creation of a hierarchical system of chieftaincy on tribal lines. Three levels of chieftaincy would be established, with fiscal incentives for chiefs to combine into larger units. A meritocratic element would be introduced into the selection of chiefs and, unlike the often widely dispersed clans, which were the largest social units recognised by the Lugbara, the new chiefdoms would be territorially based. The plans were outlined in detail in his first Annual Report:

> Eventually therefore I propose to have three forms of chief fully recognised both for purposes of justice and tax rebate. Many of these posts for a time being unoccupied. My proposal is that every recognised chief should eventually as renumeration draw 5% rebate on his tax collections, but that the Administration should be prepared to pay out 5% three times over for the same tax, making a total of 15% rebate. No chief owing [sic] to say less than 200 men would be recognised as such. (It is impossible to fix an arbitrary figure). Thus Mulla with 10,000 men would draw 5% on their tax and Nyaku with 200 men 5% on 200 taxes. Mulla with that number would be divided into sub-chieftainship [sic], each of which sub Chief would draw 5% on the tax for which he was responsible. Each sub-chieftainship would be again divided, so that each assistant sub-chief would draw 5% on the tax for which he was responsible, making a total of 15%.
>
> Nyaku's district would act vice versa. No one under Nyaku would be recognised for rebate, but if he and three or four other chiefs could combine under one, that one would also draw 5% on the whole, without affecting Nyaku and the others. If that man and four or five such others would combine under one big chief, that big-chief would then draw a further 5% on the whole. All appointments would of course be made by the District Officers, and only where they considered the man sufficiently strong to exercise due authority. The amount of rebate would for some time vary in various localities, until responsible chiefs can be found or imported. This arrangement in its elasticity would I consider be suitable to such a district as this, and would obviate that tendency of petty chiefs to claim independence in order to obtain the tax rebate. It affects his rebate not, whether he is independent or not.
>
> I trust this is clear. No man claiming seventy men only and entire independence would be eligible for rebate, but must combine before any rebate can be paid out. Apart from the question of rebate, which is eventually the renumeration paid to a chief, these are the lines on which the district is being organised. In the first degree is the chief who will always be independent. In the second degree, such as over several of whom it is hoped eventually to place one of the first degree. In the third degree such as over several of whom it is hoped eventually to place one of the second degree. After them

[58] Weatherhead, DC's Report 1914–15 RH mss. Afr.s.586. All emphases in original.
[59] On Weatherhead's methods, and his legendary reputation in the district, see especially Middleton (1953: 15; 1971b: 16), Southall (1953: 287), Allen (1991c, 1996a), CAP (1993: 15).

the Administration cannot recognise a chief, though at first he may not be embodied in a larger community. (RH mss Afr.s.586)[60]

Allen (1996a) has discussed in detail the ethnogenetic aspects of Weatherhead's programme as it related to the Madi. He argues that:

> Weatherhead played a particularly important role in the creation of a Madi tribe, because in West Nile he came across more groups speaking Sudanic languages. He might have chosen to have called all these people Madi, but instead decided to divide the groups living near the Nile... from a larger population which he called 'Lugwari'.... He decided upon an arbitrary dividing line between the two, and in early 1919 could proudly report that 'the tribal boundary between Madi and Lugwari has been more definitely drawn by removal of many Lugwari from close proximity to Luferri [the forest which marked his tribal border]. (Allen 1996a: 6)[61]

One aspect Allen omits here is that Weatherhead had to distinguish between the Madi and the Lugbara, since the former were not supposed to be under his 'West Nile' district, but to be administered, along with the East Bank Madi, from Gulu (as West Madi was from 1915 to 1924). In fact, control over the West Bank Madi oscillated between Arua and Gulu throughout the colonial period.[62] According to the Lugbara historian Lulua Odu, the only basis for the distinction drawn by Weatherhead was the difference between the characteristic dance styles of the two groups; the Lugbara moving more up and down, while the Madi sway from side to side.[63]

In fact, neither Weatherhead's tribal definitions nor his chieftaincy structure was devised by himself. In both, he leaned heavily on the work of an English officer working for the Sudan government named Bimbashi (i.e. Major) Chauncy Hugh Stigand. Stigand was a remarkable man who had spent considerable time hunting and travelling in the Lado Enclave.[64] His had been a leading voice in defining the boundary between Sudan and Uganda on a supposedly tribal basis (Collins 1962a: 141). His posthumously published book on the land and people of the Enclave (Stigand 1923, written in 1913–14) introduced the ethnic definitions used by Weatherhead (for example, the distinction between the riverine Madi and the Lugbara). Stigand's views on the tribes (discussed in the next chapter) were both explicitly quoted and implicitly adopted in Weatherhead's first Annual Report. Weatherhead also followed Stigand's recommendations for siting the District headquarters, at the place which became known as Arua (Stigand 1923:

[60] See Weatherhead, DC's Report for 1914–15, RH mss Afr.s.586: 'With the settlement of the district there will be a considerable amount of movements among the natives, and when they have had time to settle down, the chieftainships will be divided up by natural boundaries, so as to avoid some chiefs having people at a distance settled amidst another chief's men, as is the case when a chief claims allegiance according to family groups.'

[61] Allen cites Weatherhead's report as 'Weatherhead to PCNP 3.2.19. Entebbe Archives Boundaries and Stations in Nile Districts 1991' (Entebbe archives). I was unable to find this file

[62] See a 1957 DC's report headed 'Notes on Madi Sub-District' in UNA UC/ADMI/4/M. PCNP Files, Gulu–Madi Annual Reports 1954–60.

[63] In an unpublished paper, 'A Survey of Lugbara History and Tradition', compiled by Asafu Lulua, October 1993: 3. Copy in my possession.

[64] Collins (1962a: 141). On Stigand's reputation as one of the early 'Bog Barons', the powerful and independent-minded British Governors of southern Sudan, see Collins (1983: 6–10, 176, 413-14). See also Wingate's memoir in Stigand (1923).

90–91). Stigand and Weatherhead met shortly after the latter's arrival in West Nile, and Stigand visited again in 1919.[65]

In 1914, Stigand had published *Administration in Tropical Africa*, which provided a blueprint for introducing colonial rule. Stigand's methodology for establishing 'law and order' in a highly decentralised society seems to have been the basis for Weatherhead's administrative plans, with their emphasis on strengthening the role of chiefs. Stigand wrote:

> Imagine a tribe in which the worst possible existing form of government is found, one split up under numerous small headmen, acknowledging no superior and having themselves but little authority over their people.... The magnitude of the task of evolving an organisation of law and order under such conditions is one that may well appal the official. To accomplish it will require infinite tact and patience. He may start at the top by nominating big chiefs and making certain headmen acknowledge one of the created chiefs, a thing they will do their utmost to evade; or he may start at the bottom by strengthening and establishing the authority of the various headmen. Undoubtedly, the latter will be the best course to pursue. (Stigand 1914: 83)

This was certainly the course pursued by Weatherhead, with his incentive scheme for establishing a three-layer hierarchy. As Robert O. Collins put it, 'A.E. Weatherhead established an administration with policies strikingly similar to those employed in the Sudan' (Collins 1971: 278).

In addition to Stigand's advice, however, Weatherhead had another, even more important, source of support in establishing his rule: the Nubis, both those who were officially attached to his establishment and those he found living in the district, especially in Aringa County, where the Congo authorities had recognised Fadl el Mula (or Fademulla) Ali as Sultan. These men understood what the British meant by 'administration', and spoke Kiswahili (or even a little English) as well as local languages and Kinubi (which is closely related to the trade language commonly known today as 'Juba Arabic'). They were a vital link between Weatherhead and the local people, and much of his information about the latter came from Nubian sources.[66] Fadl el Mula Ali seems to have been one of Weatherhead's biggest suppliers of labour in the first couple of years of his administration although, on at least one occasion, Weatherhead expressed doubts about his control over his Lugbara subordinates.[67]

---

[65] Weatherhead's diary, RH mss Afr.s.1638, establishes that Weatherhead arrived in West Nile on 25 February 1914, and spent 8–9 March 1914 with Stigand in Kajo Kaji (just over the border in southern Sudan). Stigand visited Weatherhead in Arua between 22 and 25 October 1919, shortly before the former's death in December, fighting the Aliab Dinka.

[66] Accounts of this period in the Nubi's existence are in Furley (1959), Moyse-Bartlett (1959 Ch. 3), Collins (1962b) and Soghayroun (1981: Chs.2–4). On the history of the Nubi in general, and in particular the way in which it became an elective ethnicity available to those who moved into towns to trade or joined the army, see also Mazrui (1975a, b, 1977c), Pain (1975), Southall (1975), Johnson (1988, 1989), Rowe (1988), Woodward (1988), Hansen (1991), Kokole (1995). On their role in the creation of Uganda, see for example Twaddle (1993). An interesting biographical account of one of Weatherhead's Nubian protégés is Lanning (1954). My interviews with Nubi men confirmed an oral tradition of the close relationship between the Nubi and Weatherhead, as well as the widespread tendency to settle in West Nile (especially Aringa) after army service. Anne King, who undertook archival and oral research in the district in the late 1960s, quotes one informant as saying 'Aringa was already civilised when the whites came ... and Ajirikedi [Weatherhead] took the bright people of Aringa to help him run the district' (King 1970: 5). A Nubi interviewee said much the same thing to me in 1996.

[67] Weatherhead, Diary, 1914–15. Weatherhead's doubts were expressed on 31 October 1914, after

At the heart of Weatherhead's activities, then, was a combination of pre-conceived ideas about the local people stemming from Stigand and the Nubi, together with the difficult circumstances and limited establishment available to the first DC. Together they led to the violent and contested process by which British rule was established in the district. As Middleton summarises it: 'Weatherhead waged continual war against Lugbara groups for the first few years, as his early reports show.... They required "severe measures" before sub-mitting to the administration, unlike the Alur' (Middleton 1953: 15–16).

Conclusion

I have concentrated at some length in this chapter on a single event and its subsequent discursive elaboration. This is in part because the Yakan events had such an influential afterlife in the discourse of West Nile, but also because they exemplify a process uncovered throughout this book, whereby fact is elaborated into fantasy and subsequently deployed to marginalise the West Nilers both materially and ideologically. In such a context, the analysis of discourse cannot be separated from the process of trying to uncover 'what actually happened'. This also explains why the methodology adopted in this chapter is based largely on archival history rather than a more conventional anthropological approach. Only by a close interrogation of sources can the ideological component of subsequent accounts of West Nile history be disinterred.

Local accounts of the period, in fact, echo the published ones, not least in their vagueness about where the Yakan movement began and what its ceremonies actually involved. Some respondents insist the movement still continues, but invariably elsewhere than in their own area.[68] Even the usually reliable Lugbara historian Lulua Odu is misled in his account of the Yakan movement; after giving an abbreviated version of Murjan's story about 'the Dinkas at Rumbek', he states that: 'Many chiefs also collaborated with the followers of "Yakani". One well-known chief with such sympathy was Kamure of Maracha-Yivu who was deported to Ayivu-Muni. The descendants of his family group have remained there and are called "Ofude" in Muni Parish' (Lulua 1996: 38).

In fact, as the inquiry documents in the Public Records Office show, 'Kamurri, Chief of Offudde County' was a pro-government, anti-Yakan witness, who gave evidence against two of the chiefs, who were subsequently deposed and deported.[69] Difficult though it is to discover today the truth about the Yakan movement, I have argued that its roots must lie in the violent disturbances in West Nile life that preceded the Protectorate take-over of 1914. In the next chapter, I examine this period in the history of the district and its resonances today.

[67] (cont.) travelling to a meeting in Aringa: 'Mulla failed to produce his chiefs, does not appear to have great hold over them.'

[68] For example, an Aringa elder interviewed on my behalf stated that the movement started in Terego County where, 'to date, it is used as magic' (interview, Mr Eliakim Amuri, 14 June 1998).

[69] See PRO: WO 106/253: 90.

6
Imperial Encounters
The Lado Enclave & the Birth of the Nubi
1913–c.1850

Into the pre-colony

This chapter examines the period before the establishment of effective colonial administration in West Nile under the Uganda Protectorate after 1914, but after the first contacts between the people of the area and outsiders with radically different technologies and social systems, which occurred around or shortly after the mid- nineteenth century. Over this period, the future 'West Nilers'[1] were in the situation variously termed the 'contact zone' (Pratt 1992) or the 'tribal zone' (Ferguson and Whitehead 2000), in which their ways of life were being transformed by the effects of expanding polities based far away. Unknown to them, their homeland was the object of imperial competition between the ruling powers of Europe. Before becoming part of Uganda, as the southern part of what was called the Lado Enclave, the area later known as West Nile was part of the Sudan Condominium. Four years earlier it had been ruled as part of the Belgian Congo. These changes in power, as I noted in the introduction, have had their consequences for our categories of knowledge and explain why the area has variously been imagined as part of West Africa, as part of North Africa and as part of East Africa. Even before becoming an object of imperial desire, the southern Lado had been affected by empires to the north, notably during the flight of Emin Pasha's forces from the Mahdist revolt in Sudan, and, earlier still, with the incursions of slave armies from Turko-Egyptian (Ottoman)-ruled northern Sudan.

The long-term effects of this period under an intense European gaze have been pronounced, and are material as well as ideological. The various 'tribes' began to be named and characterised in this period, and the violence and warfare produced on this rim of expanding and competing empires became attached to the people who were its victims. European actions were guided, I argue, at least as much by fantasies (for example, those oriented around the idea of controlling the Nile) as by prospective economic gain. In these fantasies of a violent 'heart of darkness' in the middle of Africa lie the images of the inherent violence and marginality of the area which I have traced back from the present day, and which have functioned

---

[1] The name 'West Nile' was approved in May 1914, after an earlier suggestion by local officials that the new district be called 'Bahr-el-Gebel' was firmly turned down by the Governor. UNA A46/1168 ('Sudan–Uganda Boundary: Transfer of Territory').

as Austinean performatives, or self-fulfilling prophecies. To paraphrase Karl Kraus's famous remark about psychoanalysis: European 'civilisation' in West Nile was itself the disease of which it professed to be the cure.

In this chapter, therefore, I go backwards through the various substrata of this historical layer, from Condominium rule to the earliest incursions by slavers, examining at each stage the elements which have had later resonances in West Nile history, and especially those which aid the understanding of the present-day situation in West Nile. For this period, however, there are few oral traditions or useful archives (most are more relevant to diplomatic rather than social history). I therefore rely, to a greater extent than previously, on secondary sources, and focus on an analysis of the emergent discourse, which developed around the historical events, of the time before the West Nile was part of Uganda.

The Sudan Condominium (1913–1910)

The area handed over by the Sudanese authorities to the Ugandan Protectorate in 1914, the southern part of the Lado enclave (see Map 1.2), already had a bad reputation. As the Chief Justice of Uganda wrote to the Governor in January, 'I understand that part of the country is the resort of a number of bad characters.... The possibility of Europeans of doubtful reputation taking advantage of the technicalities of the law is in my opinion a real danger.'[2] In fact, throughout the period of Condominium rule, the Lado had this reputation and its attendant administrative problems. In 1910, the Sudan authorities had acquired a piece of territory which had, for some years, been under no de facto imperial authority and had become (as we shall see) a playground, and a killing ground, for European ivory hunters. Local people had become adept at manipulating the tripartite (Sudan/Congo/Uganda) borders: for example, living in the Congo but keeping their cattle in Uganda to avoid paying hut tax in the latter and tribute in kind in the former (Collins 1962a: 140). They had also learned to be very wary of Europeans.

Paradoxically, after so many years of imperial scrambling over the place, the Condominium authorities always found the Lado Enclave something of a headache. As the historian Robert Collins commented: 'Ironically, British officials in Egypt and the Sudan did not... welcome the opportunity to extend their control over the Enclave.... Wingate in Khartoum and Gorst in Cairo foresaw nothing but expensive difficulties.... [Wingate] was ... required to occupy an area of nearly 18,000 square miles and all the troops he dared spare was half a battalion of Sudanese regulars' (Collins 1968: 306). The Condominium authorities handed the problem over to a highly regarded young officer, Bimbashi Chauncy Hugh Stigand (subsequently Weatherhead's mentor), who had hunted widely in the

[2] Chief Justice, HM High Court of Uganda to HE the Governor, 5 January 1914. UNA A46/1215 (SMP 3807) 'Lado Enclave: Legal Position Of'. The Chief Justice was pointing to potential problems arising from the fact that the transfer of territories had not been formally ratified by an Order in Council. This was only to happen at the end of April, after the Governor had seemingly invented a spurious story about the possibility of finding gold in the area, in an attempt to get the Foreign Office to take the issue of its legal status seriously.

Enclave (Collins 1962a: 141) and also made something of a speciality of 'native administration'. In his textbook on the subject (Stigand 1914), one of Stigand's emphases was on fitting administrative borders to tribal boundaries and, in general, he distinguished far more sharply between different groups of Africans than did many of his contemporaries. Before his death in 1919, at the hands of the Aliab section of the Dinka, Stigand developed a complex ethnic theory of the Enclave,[3] which, through Weatherhead, was to have great influence on later administrators. His unfinished book on the Lado (published posthumously as Stigand 1923), which provides an unparalleled picture of the Enclave at the time, uses many of the same phrases to describe some of the tribes as Weatherhead did later:

> the Kakwa and Makaraka are intelligent, civilised and progressive, and so are the Moru, Mundu and Avukaya to a rather lesser extent. The Bari are worthless, indolent and retrograde, and the Fajellu are superior Baris or inferior Kakwas. Many of the Madi and all the Lugware are shy, savage and unsophisticated. At the north end of the Enclave, the further one proceeds from the Nile, the more intelligent are the people. If one proceeds still further westwards, over the Congo border, the rule still holds to a certain extent, as one meets the A-zande [sic] and Mombettu, who are particularly intelligent and civilised for Central African natives.
>
> If one follows the Nile upwards one also meets a progression of better types of people. Commencing with the Bari again, to their south are the Madi, a slightly superior people; south again are the Alurr who, taken as a whole, are distinctly more intelligent than the Madi. However, these latter people are ... a composite tribe, under chiefs of foreign extraction. (Stigand 1923:25–6)

For the area that was shortly to become West Nile district, Stigand used the usual contemporary language of racial degeneration:

> the Belgian ... posts ... had been abandoned some years before, and the bulk of the people had relapsed into a state of savagery and disorder....
>
> The greater part of the Lugware country was found in a state of utter disorganisation, practically every village was hostile to its neighbours, whilst it had been the practice of the better-armed and more organised tribes to the north and east to make continual raids on them. (Ibid.: 78)

But he is capable of distinguishing between the (European, and probably in part Nubi-inspired) discourse on the Lugbara, and the reality:

> The Lugware have been credited with ... an evil and truculent disposition.... Their bad reputation had been chiefly fabricated for them by the neighbouring tribes, who have made profit out of their helplessness and capital out of the supposed necessity of inflicting on them incessant punishment.
>
> Although a shy and primitive people, and turbulent and quarrelsome amongst themselves, the Lugware are very well disposed towards the European, directly they are assured that he has not come to rob them, destroy their villages, or capture their stock, women and children.
>
> The Lugware are not a warlike people as far as I can see, whatever has been said to the contrary. Cohesion, and a military organisation, are essential to a warlike people, qualities which the Lugware lack altogether.... Although unwarlike, insensate killing or stabbing appears to be a hobby of theirs, provided little danger is attached to it....
>
> With the Lugware, people seem to be stabbed for the pleasure of stabbing; frequently someone is wounded at night by an arrow or spear, and it is seldom known who did it.

[3] Unfortunately, Stigand makes no mention of the Nubi.

Arrows are stuck into the paths and concealed with grass in the hope of maiming anyone who passes, it matters not who. (Ibid.: 79–80)

Stigand recommended to his superiors that this 'disordered' southern part of the Enclave be transferred to the Uganda Protectorate, and this was agreed in principle as early as 1912. A boundary commission was appointed, whose basic premise was 'to separate the Bari speaking tribes from the Madi and the Lugware' (Collins 1962a: 144). Meanwhile, although certainly more control was exerted than in the latter period of Belgian rule, little could be done to keep ivory poachers at bay. Yet somehow, despite the inability of the Sudanese authorities effectively to police the area, the ivory hunters seem to have disappeared by the time Weatherhead arrived. This is still a mystery to me. It may be that, as Collins suggests, 'thanks to the efforts of the Intelligence Department of the Sudan Government, the more flagrant poachers were well known to the Sudan authorities' (Collins 1960a: 220). Stigand, as I have said, had been a semi-professional hunter in the Enclave; at the time he was theoretically employed as a soldier, but Stigand was famed for his ability to get his superiors to do what he wanted (for example, he was allowed to marry, when this was forbidden to Sudan administrators in the south, see Wingate's memoir in Stigand 1923), and he seems to have spent much of his time hunting. It is possible that his contacts enabled the authorities to stamp out the trade. Certainly there are tales of his diligence in arresting poachers (Collins 1960a: 220–21). It may be that the European poachers found alternative employment once the First World War broke out. It is also possible that elephant had largely been hunted out of the area. In any case, when the exchange of imperial overlords eventually occurred on 1 January 1914 (Collins 1962a: 145) the transfer of power over the southern Lado to the Uganda Protectorate had none of the ceremony which had greeted the Belgian hand-over to the Sudan authorities, three and a half years earlier.[4]

Borders, big game & Belgians: the Lado Enclave (1909–1893)

The violent, wild and disturbed image of the Lado Enclave had some basis in reality. Belgian occupation, always partial and sporadic, declined dramatically after the 1906 Anglo-Congolese Agreement, which provided that the area would not *de jure* be part of the Belgian Congo, but the personal property of King Leopold, to revert to Sudan following the king's death (Collins 1960: 217–18; 1968: 289–305). The Belgians lost interest in every sense, and the Lado rapidly became the arena for what the historian of imperial hunting, John MacKenzie, called 'the swansong of the professional European ivory hunter' (MacKenzie 1988: 164).

Towards the end of the nineteenth century, demand for ivory products had risen dramatically among a growing European and (especially) American middle

---

[4] The 1910 handing over occurred on 16 June. The process is described in Collins (1968: 305–10). Some additional details (such as the final cost of the transfer – £Egyptian 4,631, 570 milliemes) are in PRO FO 407/175, items 101 (Gorst to Grey 27 June 1910) and 110 (extract from *Soudan Gazette*).

class. For their pianos, their billiard balls and the handles of their cutlery, the new bourgeoisie needed ivory if they were to hold up their heads in society (ibid: 147–9). As R.W. Beachey described the trade:

> A vast quantity went to England, where the Victorian love of ornate furnishing and decor was expressed in ivory inlaid work in myriad forms, ranging from ivory-handled umbrellas to ivory snuff boxes and chessmen. There were also large imports for the great cutlery works of the Midlands; William Rodgers of Sheffield used up to 20 tons of ivory a year in making handles for cutlery. In the Latin countries ivory was used in many articles such as delicate ivory fans ... the fingerboards of Spanish guitars ... and finely carved boudoir articles ... statuettes, crucifixes.... Ivory was used for false teeth until porcelain came into use for that purpose... In the United States... ivory was used for piano and organ keys, musical instruments, billiard and bagatelle balls, not to mention the ivory inlaid butts of six-shooters.... America was the market for 80% of the soft ivory exported from Zanzibar in 1894. (Beachey 1967: 288).

Over the same period, however, hunting in Africa became increasingly restricted: game laws first applied in the Cape were extended to other British colonies, while international conservation legislation began with the 1900 Convention for the Preservation of Wild Animals, Birds and Fish in Africa. Rights to hunt became vested in the colonial authorities and were increasingly restricted to particular areas (ibid.: 201–4).

In the Lado, however, things were different. The application of international game laws was always sporadic and the Congo authorities were never among its strongest proponents, nor did they ever effectively control the Enclave outside the immediate areas of their settlements. The area was just over the river from what was by the turn of the century the northern part of the Uganda Protectorate, easily reached from the east coast. Also nearby was the Sudan frontier, and poachers could move easily across borders, avoiding the laws, which differed between the three countries. In Uganda, for example, a licence was required, only male elephants could be killed and all ivory below 10 lb in weight could be seized by the authorities (Beachey 1967: 286), but these regulations did not apply to 'green' ivory, i.e. old tusks from African sources. The appearance of 'greenness' was easily faked by a few weeks burial in elephant dung, while female tusks could be swapped with Sudanese Arab traders, who sold them in Ethiopia, where they faced no such regulations (Collins 1960a: 219).

For the Congo, on the other hand, it was impossible to get hold of licences in the Lado itself; one had to make the three and a half month trip to Boma (Bell 1923: 97). At the same time, unlicensed ivory was liable to confiscation (Collins 1960a: 217), or was at least subject to the rules governing African ivory hunters, i.e. the state took 50 per cent.[5] If Congo ivory was shipped through Uganda, the British took their cut. As one hunter put it: 'the British government became a sort of partner in the hard-earned gains of the elephant poachers.... Long before the death of Leopold the [British] Government ... charged 15% in cash on all ivory imported into British territory and later another 10% on the removal of it for export' (Boyes 1928: 75).

---

[5] An explanation of these laws is in Sir A. Hardinge to Sir Edward Grey, Brussels, 3 January 1910, 22 January 1910, PRO:FO 403/417, items 7 and 10.

All this was happening even before the 1906 agreement but, as the Belgians began to pull out of the Enclave,[6] the commercial ivory hunters increasingly took over. In Collins's phrase, the Belgian authorities, 'let the Enclave go to ruin' (Collins 1968: 306).

> Poaching rapidly changed from a hazardous sport to a prosperous profession. By 1908 there were already about eight or ten hunters making a lucrative occupation from ivory poaching.... At first these poachers, deterred from going inland by the ferocious reputation of the Lugbara, kept near the Nile, but after a time they grew bolder and by 1909 had overrun the whole of the southern Enclave.... No one discouraged the hunters. Uganda officials put few obstacles in their way, while the indigenous tribes helped them in return for the elephant meat. (Collins 1960a: 218)

Some of the later hostility of local people to Weatherhead's forced labour may stem from this period, though it was not the first time they had been forced into hard labour as porters, carrying heavy loads over long distances. Ivory had always had its links with slavery, and this was still the case: 'Porters were seized from the riverain tribes. Frequently, if a poacher was unsuccessful, he would intimidate a local chief to supply him with ivory, threatening to shoot him and burn his village if turned away empty handed' (ibid.: 219).

Moreover, ivory was also intrinsically linked with the small-arms trade, as the Stokes affair taught the British government at an early stage. In 1895, the Congo authorities executed a British ivory trader named Charles Stokes for illegally importing arms from German territory into the Congo for sale to the locals, contrary to the Brussels Act which forbade the arming of Africans. The British complained, on the grounds that (as a German witness testified):

> The most experienced African travellers consider that it is impossible to separate the trade in ivory from the trade in arms; when an ivory trader starts on an expedition, he must take with him trade arms (and also arms for his defence).... without the trade in powder the trade in ivory would come to an end.... [Moreover] every African knows that it happens on every expedition that arms and powder are sold by detached men and deserters without the knowledge of the head of the expedition. This constantly happened to Stanley. (Testimony of Dr Stuhlmann, Inclosure No. 3 in No. 308, PRO:FO 403/218)

The hunters were well aware of the ironies of the trade. One former ivory trader, quoted by another, commented:

> How the refined possessor ... of a delicately carved ivory would recoil in horror, were it possible to see the blood-stained panorama of destruction to human life, relentless cruelty, and remorseless barbarism daily and hourly enacted to obtain the precious substance....
> The man of civilization condemns with indignation the barbarisms of the Arab slaver, but let the white man pause and think but for one moment and he will realize how deeply he himself is implicated. By whom are the guns and ammunition supplied with which this persecution is carried on, and who is the purchaser of the costly elephant tusk? (Glave, quoted in Moore 1931: 164)

Glave was a pioneer English trader, whose business slogan had been 'A tusk for

[6] By 1907, according to Collins, 'they held only five stations scattered along the road running from the Congo–Nile watershed through the centre of the Enclave to the Nile' (1960a: 217). Under the 1906 agreement, the enclave ran from the Nile/Congo watershed (the present Congo/Uganda border) on the west to the 'thalweg' (deepest channel) of the Nile on the east.

a man' (ibid.: 163). Aside from the links with slavery and the arms trade, moreover:

> Poachers were in general an undesirable lot. Many of them created serious disturbances among the indigenous tribes of the Enclave through which they passed in their quest for elephants. Burning villages and commandeering porters were part of their normal procedure. Not only did they seriously deplete the great elephant herds, but they prevented any peace, security or stability in the Lado Enclave. (Collins 1960a: 222)

After Leopold's death in 1909, for some months no authority whatsoever (effective or otherwise) existed in the Lado; it was not until June 1910 that the Enclave was formally transferred to the Sudan. The effect of this complete collapse of authority, at a time when lawlessness and violence on the part of the poachers was in any case rife, was disastrous. The former Mombasa ivory trader E.D. Moore wrote:

> [T]he abandoned territory was left wide open. Into it poured all the adventurers and riffraff of British East [Africa], Uganda, and the near-by Sudan, all bent on getting rich quick in a few months of unrestricted elephant-shooting for ivory, or to find the hoard of ivory that Emin Pasha was supposed to have left there. All restraint was thrown aside; the raiders were in a country absolutely without the presence of constituted authority; and crime, even murder, could be committed without fear of legal consequences, for the British could not touch the country until the time was up, and the Belgians had abandoned it. (Moore 1931: 174)

Even the none too delicate sensibilities of the older-established elephant hunters were upset by the newcomers. The famous hunter W.D.M. ('Karamoja') Bell wrote:

> All sorts of men came. Government employees threw up their jobs. Masons, contractors, marine engineers, army men, hotel keepers and others came, attracted by the tales of fabulous quantities of ivory. More than one party was fired with the resolve to find Emin Pasha's buried store. It might almost have been a gold 'rush'. Into the Enclave then came this horde. At first they were for the most part orderly law abiding citizens, but soon this restraint was thrown off. Finding themselves in a country where even murder went unpunished, every man became a law unto himself.... Some of the men went utterly bad and behaved atrociously to the natives, but the majority were too decent to do anything but hunt elephants. But the few bad men made it uncommonly uncomfortable for the decent ones. The natives became disturbed, suspicious, shy and treacherous. The game was shot at, missed, wounded or killed by all sorts of people who had not the rudiments of hunter-craft. (Bell 1923: 98)

Another famous hunter, John Boyes, was one of those who went to the Enclave during the interregnum. As a young man on the make he was in Kenya when there came: 'news that gold had been found across the Nile, near the Belgian Congo frontier ... when I heard further that a number of white adventurers were shooting elephant in the Lado Enclave, it seemed to me that if the gold strike did not turn out to be rich I might make up in hunting any losses in prospecting' (Boyes 1928: 1). Arriving in 1909, he found that: '[t]he Natives in this part of the world seemed to be continually on the war-path; in fact, most of their time was spent in fighting with the people of the neighbouring villages, and some of them were killed every day' (ibid.: 9). In 1902, Joseph Conrad had sited Mr Kurtz's heart of darkness, 'in the true ivory country', where he 'sends in as much ivory as all the others put together' (Kimbrough [ed.] 1988: 22). Now nature was imitating art.

Some, however, romanticised these criminals as *Boy's Own* heroes. One such was Theodore Roosevelt, who was taken on a guided shooting tour of the Enclave during the interregnum. Roosevelt wrote:

> They are a hard-bitten set, these elephant poachers; there are few careers more adventurous, or fraught with more peril, or which make heavier demands on the daring, the endurance, and the physical hardihood of those who follow them. Elephant-hunters face death at every turn, from fever, from the assaults of warlike native tribes, from their conflicts with their giant quarry; and the unending strain on their health and strength is tremendous. (Roosevelt 1926: 330)

He was introduced to a selection of the more respectable ones, toasting them at dinner as 'the Gentleman Adventurers of Central Africa, for that is the title by which you would have been known in Queen Elizabeth's time' (Boyes 1928: 92–3, see also Collins 1960: 220).

In local accounts, the ivory hunters tend to blur into a series of incursions over the period covered in this chapter. Their impact on local people was not unlike that of the earlier slavers: homes were burned, people abducted as porters or held to ransom for ivory, cattle killed or taken away for food, random killing or wounding of anyone who got in the way. But some accounts suggest that they had a specific effect on attitudes to the British after 1914: 'On the side of the Lugbara, they thought the British had come to finish off their elephants. They looked at the White men as a "glorified band of ivory poachers"'[7] (Lulua 1996: 36).

However, the key influence on later attitudes to colonial administration arose not so much from the ivory hunters but from the earlier period of Belgian occupation. The Enclave was always a sad disappointment to the Belgians, especially economically.[8] Their concessionaires found 'little ivory and less rubber' (Collins 1968: 125). The real problem was one of communications: no crop, and probably not even ivory, was worth the prohibitive transportation costs down the Uele and Congo rivers to the west coast. Throughout the period of European disputes over the upper reaches of the Nile, the importance of 'facts on the ground' in the Scramble meant a gradually increasing number of Belgian troops had to be sent to the Lado, which by 1902 was costing Leopold at least £60,000 per year (Collins 1968: 135).

As the Belgians realised the lack of commercial possibilities in the Lado, and as their chances of taking over the Bahr el Ghazal evaporated, the troops made no real attempts to govern the area, especially in the southern district of the Enclave, known as Mount Wati, which was later to become West Nile District. As a later British administrator put it:

> It appears that the Belgians were impressed by the fierceness of the Lugbara and therefore no steps were taken to provide an overall administration. The stations were

---

[7] The quote is from Weatherhead's first Annual Report, RH mss Afr.s.586.

[8] Which may explain why a book such as Adam Hochschild's popular account *King Leopold's Ghost* (Hochschild 1999), which argues that Leopold's motivations were exclusively commercial, does not mention the Enclave at all.

kept secure by armed askaris called [by the Lugbara] 'Tukutuku' after the sound of their guns, and the Belgians were content to acquire the support of surrounding chiefs without going any further afield. Many parts of the district were left to elephant hunters and tribal raiding parties. The Belgian stations were unfortified (except at Wadelai and Dufile where they were built within the old Egyptian fortifications), and simply consisted of dwelling houses, guardroom and storehouses built in burnt brick on the sides of a cleared area or open square.[9]

John Middleton suggested that 'The administration was little more than nominal; only the Kakwa and the Alur submitted easily to the Belgians, the Lugbara maintaining a sullen independence' (Middleton 1971b: 14–15). It is interesting that the Lugbara had a fearsome reputation even to these early incomers. It seems quite likely that they will have heard about the Lugbara from those neighbouring people with whom they had earlier contact, and who served them as guides and assistants, ie the Alur, Nubi and Madi people who lived nearer the river (cf. Johnson 1981, on how the Nuer acquired their warlike reputation from their neighbours).

Middleton's informants remembered the Belgians themselves as spending 'most of their time drinking gin and tea' (Middleton 1992: 4). They were seen as, 'pleasant enough men who did little but talk and drink; but the Tukutuku are remembered as evil people' (Middleton 1971b: 15). After King Leopold's death, the British diplomat Sir Arthur Hardinge wrote that, 'the raiding propensities of the large force maintained ... [in the Enclave] by the king in connection with his claims and designs on the Bahr al-Ghazal were rather a terror to its shy and savage aboriginals'.[10] My own informants agreed. Those who collaborated with the Belgians and accepted chiefly offices seem to have been particularly at risk. One elder told me about his great grandfather:

> During that time when the Belgians were here ... these people created a lot of brutality in the area. With their agents, they looted peoples animals, they killed people, they raped women. The relation between these authorities with our local people was hostile. I can remember one of my great-grandfathers, who was the first Sub-County Chief of Belgium. He was shot by the Belgian authority. When he was called to come to the muzungu, I think he told to the messenger that he was still preparing himself to come. This messenger went immediately and reported that the man says he is a Chief, he doesn't want to be bothered by people here, by foreigners here. So when he came he was just shot dead straight away. He was called Ajukua. And then from that time I think the issue of joining the administration and so on was alien completely. I think the elders even cursed whoever wanted to associate himself with the foreigners here. She will affect him, he will fail, he will get his fate. So there has always been suspicion between the people and a new administration and so on since that time.[11]

The curse on those who collaborate with government was not lifted until 1992. Its effects will be discussed in Chapter Seven.

Aside from their own casual violence, and that of the 'Tukutuku', the Europeans unwittingly brought with them new diseases and infections for the local

---

[9] RH mss Afr.s.1350, 'Notes on the early history of West Nile District' by David Harris (ADC West Nile 1957–9). This may be the item listed in Dalfovo's bibliography of the Lugbara as No. 111. Harris, D.L. 'Early Days in the West Nile District of Uganda' (Dalfovo 1988: 26).

[10] Quoted in Collins (1968: 305).

[11] Interview, Mr Nahor Oyaa, 6 February 1997.

people and their herds, bad enough to be clearly remembered more than fifty years later by Middleton's informants:

> the Lugbara were ... seriously affected by ... the appearance between 1890 and 1895 of cerebrospinal meningitis, smallpox and rinderpest. There seem always to have been recurrent famines, but there was a particularly severe one around 1895. I have also heard Lugbara say that there were outbreaks of plague and smallpox around this time. These disasters resulted in serious changes in both the human and animal populations, and in considerable movement of people from one area to another. (Middleton 1971b: 13)

If Belgian rule faded away gradually after 1906, it had been established equally gradually, in response to political pressures generated by the scramble for Africa. By the early 1890s, the Lado Enclave had become seen as, as one historian put it, 'the most annexable part of the interior' (Smith 1972: 53). Britain, France, Germany and Belgium competed over it, seeking to establish both legal claims and 'facts on the ground'. The main aim was to control the upper reaches of the Nile, a political position which acquired the status of a mythical quest in the minds of certain Europeans, including King Leopold of the Belgians.

To cut a very long story[12] short, Belgian troops became the first European forces on the ground. In 1892, they arrived in the southern Enclave and came to an agreement with Fadl el Mula, the leader of the Nubi, who were the major armed power in the area other than the Mahdist forces.[13] By 1898 the Belgians were the sole organised military force in the Lado.[14] However, their supply lines to the West African coast were stretched, and the British combined immense diplomatic pressure with increasing control over the Nile route. The Belgian troops became more and more dependent on their rivals for supplies. In 1900, they set up bases in the town of Lado and elsewhere in the Enclave. A British officer of the Egyptian army, Kaimakam [Lieutenant] Malcolm Peake, reported that:

> The total strength of the Belgian force now on the Nile is about 1,500 men, distributed at Kirro, Lado, Regaf and Adiffo, the latter place being about 20 minutes from the river and opposite Dufile. There are six European officers at Kirro, two at Lado, two at Regaf and two at Aduffo. Kirro is at present the head-quarters, but I understand they are going to make it at Lado in the future. The Belgians are in every place very busy building and making themselves comfortable, and I could see no sign of any movement of troops to occupy any other territory.

---

[12] The role of the Lado during the period of the European 'scramble for Africa' is discussed in several works of diplomatic history, see especially Taylor (1950), Collins (1958, 1962a, 1968), Sanderson (1965, 1971), Cookey (1968), Robinson and Gallagher with Denny (1981), and Stengers and Vansina (1985).

[13] See correspondence between Leopold's emissary Van Eetvelde and the British Ambassador in Brussels, Sir Francis Plunkett, June 1894, in PRO:FO 403/201 Inclosure in No. 135. According to Van Eetvelde, Baert's force in both the Lado and the Bahr el Ghazal at the time consisted of 70 European officers and NCOs, 1,500 Congolese troops, 4,000 'Semio' auxiliaries and 12 Nordenfelt guns. (Sir F. Plunkett to the Earl of Kimberley 7 June 1894, ibid., No. 136). From 1893 to around 1906 forts were set up around the Enclave. The major push against the Mahdists began in 1896, and Rejaf was taken by Commandant Chaltin in February 1987.

[14] The process is described in detail, as stories reached Wingate's intelligence service, in the Sudan Intelligence Reports (SIR, a part set of which is in Rhodes House Library). A useful brief outline of events is in pp. 181–4 of the 1904 'Military Report on the Congo Free State', which is in PRO:WO 33/316.

Chaltin told us that he himself considered the occupation of the Nile valley a mistake; the length of their lines of communication may be judged by the fact that it is 3½ months journey from Kirro to Boma, their port on the sea. Both the Belgians and the English are very anxious for regular communication, via the Nile.

Inspector Chaltin appears most anxious to encourage the natives to cultivate the land, and generally wishes to improve everything; there is no doubt, however, that the natives dislike the Belgian rule; this may be accounted for I think, by the fact that Belgians, living in the country, live on the country as a rule, taking food from the natives and not paying for it. I had a personal experience of their mode of travelling on the night I spent in their boats.[15]

The British tried hard to control supplies to the Congo troops in the Enclave,[16] and did nothing to discourage the anti-Congo agitation of various humanitarian and commercial groups. At the same time, a complex series of negotiations took place, during which the British Foreign Office sophisticates were much amused by Leopold's suggestion that the area be partitioned according to tribal boundaries:

On November 3 [1901] ... Eetvelde [Leopold's negotiator] came equipped with an elaborate tribal map of the southern Sudan....

The map itself was a fantastic combination of the King's imagination and Junker's explorations made some twenty years before. Neither Phipps nor Eetvelde had heard of such tribes as the Kakwa or the Kuku, and Lansdowne confessed in exasperation that he had no idea who the 'Quak Quak' or the 'Ku Kus' were.... By the time Salisbury saw the King's 'exploit in cartography' the Kakwa and Kuku had become a standing joke at the Foreign Office. (Collins 1968: 122)

In 1905, having asserted de facto military control in the Bahr el Ghazal, the British lost patience, and a blockade was imposed against Congo supplies travelling down the Nile. Eventually the exhaustive negotiations culminated, as we have seen, in the Anglo-Congolese Agreement of 1906, which spelled the end of any realistic prospect of Belgian rule.[17]

Emin Pasha & the birth of the Nubi (1892–1880)

What brought the Lado Enclave so prominently to the attention of the European powers in the 1890s was a single event, even a single man: a German doctor known as 'Emin Pasha'.[18] No figure is more iconic in the history of the area covered by this book. It was thanks to Emin that (as Stigand put it) 'this little territory [Lado district] has perhaps passed through more vicissitudes and has at

[15] SIR 69 (10 April 1900–9 May 1900), Appendix A, p. 5.
[16] The various stages of this transparent manoeuvre are outlined in SIR 73 (6 August 1900–7 September 1900) p. 2; No. 78 (9 January 1901–8 February 1901), p. 2. It culminates with SIR 85 1–31 August 1901, p. 2, 'M. Chaltin said he was in no need of supplies and was at a loss to know why a quantity of rice had been sent to him.' These issues of SIR were consulted in Rhodes House Library.
[17] Among those not best pleased by these events was Cecil Rhodes, who spent some time in Brussels in 1907–9, trying to revive the corridor for his railway. He was never reconciled to having to run it through Congo territory west of the Lakes. Leopold, true to form, managed to tangle the Cape to Cairo project up with an idea for a Congo to Nile railway through the Lado, a project which Winston Churchill helped to scupper (Collins 1968: 289–305).
[18] A full, if now dated, bibliography of Emin Pasha is Simpson 1960. Stigand (1923: Ch. XIV) gives perhaps the best account for my present purposes.

one time, had more interest centred around it than any part of Central Africa' (1923: 4–5). Even today his name conjures up images of exotic treasure, violence, and the Heart of Darkness (see, for example, Youngs 1994, Chs 4–6). We have already seen how frequently commentators on Idi Amin refer to his namesake, Emin (the most gratuitous example being perhaps Mazrui 1977c), but it is equally true that, since the 1970s, mention of Emin evokes the spectre of Amin (see, for example, Twaddle 1993: 71). Emin brought the Nubis to 'West Nile', but it is perhaps even more significant that he generated an immense interest in the area, particularly in Britain, but also elsewhere in Europe and in the USA. The Western gaze was turned on this hitherto obscure piece of land to an extent it is now difficult to imagine, a concern which was to have incalculable consequences for the people of the area and their later history.

Ironically, Emin would have been the last European explorer to seek such attention. Among those arrogant and forceful adventurers he stands out as a mild, rather scholarly and modest man. When Gordon was promoted by the Egyptian authorities to Governor-General of the Sudan in 1876, he had a series of short-term successors as Governor of Equatoria, before Emin took over in 1878. Emin was a German doctor whose original name was Eduard Schnitzer, and his main interests were in natural history. He adopted a fairly common Arabic name meaning 'faithful' (the full style should be Muhammad al-Amin, see Collins 1968: 14). and professed the Islamic faith, though some commentators, such as Stigand (1923: 166), have doubted his belief. Emin's parents were Silesian Jews who had converted to Protestantism; he may have found religious conversion less unimaginable than Stigand, the descendant of a Saxon Archbishop of Canterbury.

As the Mahdi's Islamic uprising surged over the Sudan in the early 1880s, pinning down and eventually wiping out Gordon at Khartoum, it also spread south, forcing Emin and his troops down into the tip of Equatoria (see Collins 1962b: 42–51). By 1885, the Lado was a European-run enclave more or less surrounded by hostile African forces. While his German friend Wilhelm Junker managed with some difficulty to escape through Bunyoro to meet up with the British in Buganda, Emin remained behind with several hundred Egyptian and Sudanese troops and their dependents, and shortly afterwards opposition to Europeans in Buganda made that route impassable. Many of the soldiers had served with the slave- and ivory traders throughout the region, often having been recruited from the civil populations which moved with the soldiers (Johnson 1989: 78). Stigand distinguishes between three sorts of armed groups: 'bands of undisciplined soldiery consisting of (i) Kutiria, who were Dongolan irregulars, recruited from the disbanded Nubian forces of the old ivory and slave raiders. These were armed with percussion guns. (ii) Dragomans, local natives armed like the Kutiria.... (iii) Jehadia, or Egyptian regulars, armed with Remingtons. Of these there were comparatively few' (1923: 170–71).

Although Emin grew a few vegetables, the troops lived largely by pillaging the local population.[19] Even Middleton, despite his usual emphasis on the isolation of

---

[19] See Harris, RH mss Afr.s.1350.

the Lugbara, concedes that 'although he himself [Emin] never entered their country, he employed some Lugbara as servants and his troops raided them' (Middleton 1971b: 13). Harris says that:

> Emin did not confine himself to the river but went inland and made contact with Alur chiefs, Arera of Nyapea and Aredja of Angal, and in November 1880 a small station was built at Okoro, probably at Paidha. The lands of the Lendu were raided for cattle by Emin's soldiers but it is unlikely that the Lugbara suffered except for minor raids near Mount Wati by soldiers from Ganda station in Keliko. Though Emin made detailed notes on the language and customs of the Alur people, his only comment on the Lugbara is that they were 'six or seven days march from Wadelai'. It appears that his soldiers had a route from Wadelai via Yumbe to Keliko and Zandeland for bringing ivory to Wadelai and in this way made contact with the Lugbara.[20]

In 1887 Emin made the decision to remain at his headquarters in Wadelai, ignoring explicit orders from the Egyptian Prime Minister, Nubar Pasha, to withdraw.[21] The Mahdi's successor, Khalifa Abd Allahi, however, was interested in removing the taint of European occupation from this last bit of the Sudan, and also perhaps in the Lado as a source of ivory and, particularly, slaves (Collins 1962b: 57–8). In 1888 he ordered the invasion of the Enclave.

The Khalifa was not the only one interested in ivory. The fact that Emin was said to be sitting on at least £60,000 worth of tusks may, as Youngs (1994: 114) and others have suggested, have motivated some of the group of people who formed the Emin Pasha Relief Expedition Committee in London. Others, such as Emin's friends Felkin and Junker, had personal reasons for wanting to help the beleaguered German. But for many there was a richer prize to be had. The scramble for Africa was getting under way, and the abandonment of Equatoria by the Egyptians meant that it became, in legal terms, open to annexation by anybody: 'Emin's isolation, his immediate need, and his offer of his province presented an opportunity to enlist Emin himself and to annex his province. Through Emin in Equatoria the whole Lake region might be controlled and its resources exploited' (Smith 1972: 53).

Emin's own preference was for British annexation (see Sanderson 1965: 37). Others had different ideas; King Leopold of the Belgians was anxious to add the area to his own Congo territories, while not everyone in the British establishment agreed with Sir William Mackinnon of the Imperial British East Africa Company (IBEAC) that it would be a useful addition to the British empire.[22] It was decided to send Henry Stanley (who was secretly working for Leopold) with a massive party of men, up the Congo from the west coast of Africa, to rescue Emin and bring him out through East Africa. The adventure succeeded in this aim, but at a dreadful cost:

> [O]ut of 570 refugees from the Equatorial Province ... only 260 reached Bagamoyo [on the east coast]. Two of Stanley's ten white companions died on this expedition. One of

---

[20] RH mss Afr.s.1350.

[21] Stigand gives three reasons for this: 'Firstly, the difficulty of making the Egyptians believe that their only way out was to the eastwards, secondly, the difficulty of moving the immense number of dependents, thirdly, an unwillingness to abandon his life's work' (1923: 178).

[22] The analysis of the setting up of the Emin Pasha Relief Expedition and the motives of its participants, are standard themes in imperial historiography. A classic account is Sanderson (1965: Ch. II). The best analysis is probably that in Smith (1972). On the IBEAC see Moyse-Bartlett (1956: Ch. 1).

them, Major Barttelot, who was much criticised for the severity of his conduct and for his racism, was shot dead by an African porter. The other, Jameson, died, apparently from fever, after rumours that he had solicited, witnessed and sketched, and possibly even participated in, the cannibalistic killing of a young girl. Half of the seven hundred Africans failed, because of desertion or death, to return from the journey. (Youngs 1994: 116)

On top of all this, on arrival at the coast Emin, who had come to hate Stanley, fell out of a window and nearly died. Stanley had to return to Europe without him, to a mounting pressure of condemnation as his officers published competing accounts of the horrors of the expedition.[23] One, whose story was not published at the time, left a diary account of the progress of the expedition through the upper Congo and into present-day Uganda, which shows the similarities between Stanley's methods and those of other visitors to the region, before and since:

> I often wonder what English people would say if they knew of the way in which we go for these natives; friendship we don't want as then we should get very little meat and probably have to pay for the bananas. Every male native capable of using the bow is shot. This, of course, we must do. All the children and women are taken as slaves by our men to do work in the camps. Of course, they are well treated and rarely beaten as we whites soon stop that. After three or four weeks with the men they get to be as happy as clams. (Konczacki 1994: 159–60)

Emin went off with Stanley, but he left an immense legacy both materially and in the developing discourse on the Lado area. Most of his soldiers remained, under the control of Fadl el Mula Bey, convinced that his departure constituted rebellion against Egypt (see, for example, Soghayroun 1981: 23–5). Stories abounded in Europe of the vast wealth he had been forced to leave behind. More important still, the events of 1888 left an enduring image, especially as the gorier tales of the expedition emerged, of white men gone to seed in the jungle. It was the Emin Pasha Relief Expedition that is said to have triggered memories of his own earlier trip to the Congo in the mind of Joseph Conrad, producing his modernist masterpiece *Heart of Darkness*.[24] A recent historian of the Expedition concludes that it 'occupies an important place in the decline and disappearance of the romantic Victorian conception of exploring expeditions led by determined Europeans [*sic*] through "unknown" continents' (Smith 1972:299).

Few accounts exist of the period after Emin left the Lado. The remaining soldiers presumably exploited their superior fire-power over the local people, while at the same time becoming increasingly integrated into the host population. They were split into two groups. The main one, under the command of Fadl el Mula Bey, was based at Wadelai, and consisted of those who had refused to go with Stanley: they were regarded as rebels by most Europeans, and it was (wrongly) believed at the time that they had thrown in their lot with the

---

[23] See Youngs 1994: Ch. 4, for an account of the different versions of the story published on the expedition's return.

[24] On the relationship between Conrad and the Relief Expedition see especially Youngs (1994: Ch. 6). On Conrad and contemporary anthropological ideas of race and degeneration, see Griffith (1995). The most useful edition of *Heart of Darkness*, which includes important literary-critical evaluations, including the famous critique by Achebe, is Kimbrough (1988). See also Brantlinger (1985), Lindqvist (1997).

**AFENDI SALIM BEY - 1890'S
THE NUBIAN LEADER WHO MADE
AGREEMENT WITH CAPTAIN LUGARD IN
1895 AT BUTIABA.**

Figure 6.1 A local representation of Salim Bey (picture presented to the author)

Mahdists. A smaller group under Salim Bey was left behind by Stanley to the south of the Enclave, at Kavallis near the banks of Lake Albert: they were later joined by a large number of deserters from Fadl el Mula.[25]

---

[25] On Salim Bey see Furley (1959: 311–3), Collins (1962b: 70–71), Soghayroun (1981: 27). On Fadl el Mula's force and its relations with the Mahdists see Collins (1962b: 80–117). He seems to have oscillated between attempting to surrender to the Mahdists and firing on them when approached. He and his men are said to have killed 700 Mahdists at Wadelai in 1891, after which the latter were more or less pinned down in Rejaf, which became a place to which the Khalifa sent his political enemies. According to Collins (ibid.), around 800 of Fadl el Mula's men went south to join Salim Bey at Kavallis in 1891, and when the Congolese forces under Captain Van Kerckhoven arrived in 1892 at Fadl el Mula's camp, he had only some 500 men left. Soghayroun (1981: 27–9) says that Salim Bey established himself at Kavalis with only 90 soldiers (plus many women and children) but Lugard took over seven thousand people into Uganda, including more than two thousand adult men. Fadl el Mula's support further fragmented when a force under Ahmad Agha went to join Salim at Kavalli, only to find that he had already left with Lugard. They were eventually picked up at Mahagi by Major Thruston (Soghayroun 1981: 29). Among these men was probably the Fadl al Mula Murjan who later became Sultan of Aringa (see previous chapter).

It was Salim's people who were approached by Captain Frederick Lugard of the IBEAC in 1891. By then the Kabaka Mwanga's kingdom of Buganda had become a prize for which European nations were fighting tooth and nail through trade, arms and religious rivalry.[26] Emin, on recovering from his fall, was involved in German attempts to secure Buganda for Bismarck's East African empire, while Mackinnon's IBEAC were batting for Britain, though with only sporadic support from Lord Salisbury at the Foreign Office. Lugard arrived in Buganda at the end of 1890 with:

> Just under 300 porters – a third of them good men, a third indifferent and a third useless ... about 50 Somali and Sudanese soldiers, with whom he could only communicate through an interpreter; about eleven rounds of ammunition per man; the Maxim gun which Stanley's Emin Pasha Relief Expedition had dragged across Africa and was now showing signs of wear; extremely little food by the time Buganda was reached; and an ornate pair of pyjamas which doubled as his dress uniform. (Twaddle 1993: 71)

In Buganda, Lugard threw himself forcefully into the religious politics in which European adventurism and the Kabaka's regional aspirations were cloaked. In May 1891, at the head of a Baganda force, he defeated the army of the Bunyoro kingdom, which had allied itself with the Buganda Muslims, and proceeded towards the western lakes in search of Emin's former soldiers:

> Emin Pasha's troops, now under the command of Selim Bey, had the reputation of being 'the best material for soldiery in Africa', and Lugard thought that with their aid the Company might hold both Buganda and Bunyoro. He accordingly marched through Buddu to Ankole, where he made a treaty with the king, Ntale; reached Lake Edward; built a stockade which he called Fort George; marched up the eastern flank of Ruwenzori and built another, Fort Edward; and continued to Lake Albert, where at last he found Selim Bey and his Sudanese at Kavalli's. (Moyse-Bartlett 1956: 50)[27]

Salim, the kind of disciplined officer who appealed to the British,[28] had maintained his loyalty to the Khedive, and at first refused to go with Lugard, who wrote to Egypt to request that they be allowed to join British service with the IBEAC. At this, Salim relented, and the massive force of more than 7,000 men,

---

[26] The deep involvement of religious factions in Ugandan politics dates from this period, in which British Anglicans vied for influence over Kabaka Mwanga's court with the French White Fathers, and both with the Muslims. After defeating the latter, Lugard armed the Protestants, causing a massacre of Catholics at the Battle of Mengo which was so devastating that it was compared to the worst excesses of industrialisation in Britain; a British missionary wrote that 'Every RC house and garden is a mass of ashes and charred bananas & some Protestant places too. The place reminds one of entering Birmingham from Wolverhampton by night' (quoted in Twaddle 1993:72)

[27] Furley (1959:313-14) suggests that Lugard's actions were determined by his ambitions in the Toro kingdom, which he saw as rich in natural resources and with a biddable young King, rather than by Bugandan politics.

[28] Soghayroun says: 'Felkin described him as "a very quite man, and very devout".... Jephson [an officer of Stanley's on the Relief Expedition] describes him as a "great easy-going" Sudanese, well over six feet tall and "enormously fat and broad". He was described in congenial terms by all the Europeans who met him. As to Captain Lugard, he described Selim as "a man of very considerable character.... [He] touched no kind of liquor, nor did he smoke. He was a man, too, of much determination"' (Soghayroun 1981: 26). Stanley was the exception to this universal admiration. Furley says that 'the prevarications and evasive habits of Selim drove him to exasperation, and his parting judgement was that he was "One of those men with whom it is impossible to reason... He was therefore abandoned as a man whom it was impossible to persuade, still less to compel"' (Furley 1959: 312). Compared with Stanley, of course, almost anyone would seem to prevaricate.

women and children moved east towards Baganda. As the official military historian of the King's African Rifles described the situation:

> Lugard realised from the first that he ran some risk in enlisting the help of such a body of men.... Though they had loyally served their government for several years without pay, the fact that they had perforce grown self-supporting made them eager for followers and slaves. Lugard looked forward to the day when they would become entirely dependent on him for ammunition. (Moyse-Bartlett, 1956: 51)

Furley points out that:

> Lugard was unable to offer the Sudanese any establishment in the service of the Company, and could only offer them regular pay at such time as the Company and the Khedive might agree, and Lugard was fully aware that such agreement might take a year to materialise. Lugard's idea was that the troops and their followers should meanwhile live off the land....
>
> The troops had had no pay for ten years, living on plunder meanwhile, while the newer recruits had never been under proper military control. In some companies self-promotions had been prolific and majors, captains, sergeants and corporals abounded, to the confusion of a handful of luckless privates. This was the task facing Lugard then: he not only had to impose discipline and order on a motley army, but had to lead a whole community into fresh territory and settle them there, knowing full well that their habit was to plunder and loot wherever they went. (Furley 1959: 315–16)

This, then, was the birth of the Nubi, and it is perhaps no wonder their reputation for violence spread quickly through both the future Uganda and back to Britain. By the time of the 1897 mutiny, the British press knew all about them and responded in ways typical to each journal; the *Spectator* waxed worldly-wise:

> The Sudanese soldiers are extremely brave, but they require special methods of treatment. Though they love fighting and are not afraid of hard work, they are very domestic in their habits. It is never safe to separate them for too long from their wives. This sounds as if they would not be very useful soldiers, but this is not really the case... The women are excellent porters, can cook and make the men comfortable, and if need be are quite able to take a hand in a fight.

The Times offered a more materialist (if unlikely) theory:

> The troops have cultivated land for themselves and the large families dependent on them, thus providing for most of their wants and dispensing with the necessity for high pay. The arrangement has been economical, and has been held to have worked, on the whole, satisfactorily ... but a force which was trained to depend largely for the means of existence upon the cultivation of the ground was evidently not well fitted to carry out distant expeditions.

while the *Manchester Guardian* concluded in true liberal fashion that 'the best troops in the world might have mutinied under such provocation' (all quoted in Furley 1959: 325–6).

There is no space here to recount the details of the Sudanese troops' role in creating a British Uganda out of an expanded Buganda, or of their rebellion in 1897 and its consequences.[29] These events took place outside the area of my primary concern, though they, too, added to its reputation as a place from which violence came. What is worth emphasising, in the light of their later image as an alien, Sudanese or even Egyptian group, is that the bulk of the Nubi were from

---

[29] Moyse-Bartlett (1956: 53–94) gives a blow-by-blow account of these events.

people local to what became Uganda, or their near relatives in the Sudan. The original soldiers Emin brought south were, according to Stanley's assistant Jephson, 'for the most part men belonging to the Dinka, Madi, Boru, Shafalu, Maru Maru, Bongo, Makraka, Mongbutee or Moru tribes'. Soghayroun comments on 'the close relationship and connection between these Sudanese groups and the Nile tribes of Northern Uganda, such as Bari, Madi, Lur, Lendu and Acholi. A considerable number of their followers came from such tribes' (Soghayroun 1981: 29).

As we have seen, they also already included second-generation 'Nubi' with Lugbara, Madi or Alur mothers, such as Fadl el Mula Ali and Fadl el Mula Murjan. They regarded the West Nile area as their home: only thirty-one Nubians eventually volunteered to 'return' to Egypt (Soghayroun 1981:33) while many, like the Fadl el Mulas, went back to the Lado once they left the army. Nevertheless, their Islamic faith meant that they were always regarded, especially by Christian missionaries, as dangerous aliens from the Sudan, and hence possibly Mahdists (despite their long history of struggle against the forces of the Khalifa). The Rev. Ashe wrote that:

> It was therefore a serious undertaking to introduce a large number of fanatical Muhammedans into Uganda, since the danger was always threatening of a coalition between those of the same religion against native Christians and Europeans alike. The knowledge of the vast hordes of Muhammedans in the Sudan had always hung as a dark cloud on the northern horizon... sooner or later, these hordes of Muhammedans would... sweep away whatever of Christianity or civilization had been established on the shores of the great lake. (In Soghayroun 1981: 41–2)

This was also the vision that reappeared in the minds of many Britons and Baganda when, some seventy-five years later, the unmistakably Nubi figure of Idi Amin emerged from the postcolonial struggles between northern and southern Uganda. Ashe also wrote, in terms very reminiscent of early British descriptions of Amin:

> [T]he Sudanese, much as I disliked them, and deeply as I regretted their introduction into Uganda, were yet not without sterling qualities, which, in some respects, made them superior to the pleasanter and more versatile inhabitants of Uganda [i.e. Buganda]. They were what the Scotch call dour bodies, scowling and sullen, but they were brave and industrious and possessed a certain amount of dignity which commanded respect. (Soghayroun 1981: 42, fn57)

Travellers & slavers (1879–c.1850)

Although Emin became an iconic figure in the discourse of West Nile history, he was by no means the first outsider whose troops ravaged the district. The convention, in European accounts of this early period of 'contact', is to define different kinds of interloper, on the basis of their intent in making the trip. Thus, writers will distinguish between 'slavers'[30] and 'explorers', between 'hunters', 'mission-

[30] There is, of course, a racial element in this particular designation. Much of the earlier writing on the area assumes a primary dichotomy between the Arabs, who were assumed to be motivated by the desire to exploit and enslave the blacks, and the Europeans and Americans, who apparently sought merely to befriend, convert, trade with or study them.

aries', 'soldiers' and 'administrators'. These categories may be less analytically useful than they seem. In the first place, these groups of people often travelled with and assisted each other, as David Livingstone relied on Tippu Tib (Moorehead 1960: 159, 349–50) and the explorer Wilhelm Junker on the slaver Ahmed Atrush (see below). Secondly, the occupier of one role frequently turned into another – as Lugard and Stigand, for example, were both hunters before becoming administrators (Collins 1962a; MacKenzie 1988: 151). Thirdly, from the point of view of local people, what perhaps counted most was the interlopers' actions rather than their motivations, and in such terms it was often impossible to distinguish between one set of plunderers and another. In most cases, as we shall see, the methods used to get what the outsiders wanted (ivory often, food sometimes, labour usually) were remarkably similar, even when the ostensible reason for travelling differed.

The early outsiders all came from the north, down the River Nile. Soghayroun suggests that 'Islamic influence first reached the northern districts of modern Uganda around the 1830s' (Soghayroun 1981: 1), but in the north-west it seems to have happened a couple of decades later. According to Middleton, at this period:

> Arab slavers and traders ... had taken slaves from the Kakwa, Kuku, Madi and the other peoples of the north, but not from among the Lugbara ... [until] after the turn of the century.
>
> The Egyptian slavers and government officers, most of whom were little more than slavers, set up posts in Kakwa country.... All these posts were only a few miles from Lugbaraland. (Middleton 1971b: 12–13)

However, Samson Geria, who interviewed Lugbara elders in Maracha County in the 1970s, found that 'Many informants ... maintain that the first group of Arabs, the Tukuria, came in their grandparents' generation' (Geria 1973: 79), which he estimated as being around the early 1850s. A second group, known as the Jahadia, Jandia, or Wolo-Wolo came later, in the 1870s or early 1880s. According to Geria:

> The activities of both the *Tukuria* and *Wolo-Wolo* ... were identical. Both groups came principally for slaves and cattle. Each group brought with it black attendants who were most probably Nubians and Bari.
>
> The Arabs usually made surprise attacks on villages at day-break. They would first shoot their guns into the air to frighten the villagers, who would panic and run off into hiding, leaving behind their cattle and children. The Arabs would kill all the children of tender age but would take away the older children as slaves. They would capture all able-bodied men who were not able to run away in good time or were discovered in their hiding places. They killed all senile people. They drove away all the abandoned cattle, and either ate or took away a lot of the abandoned food and foodstuffs. Lastly, they set houses and granaries on fire leaving the place completely desolate.
>
> The captured slaves were tied together by their necks and were taken into the Sudan. To help them to identify their run-away slaves, the Arabs marked their captives cheeks by making three deep vertical cuts on each cheek. The slaves walked the whole distance to the Sudan and were forced to carry heavy loads including ivory. However, children were allowed to ride cattle as they were too young to walk such a long distance. Any slave who became too weak to continue the journey was either left in the wilderness to die a slow death or was shot down.

The main slave route passed through the following stations: Rubu, Gbegbe, Bangule, Pilima ... Yei, Juba and Khartoum. However, some of the slaves stopped at Yei which was the main slave market for the southern regions of the Sudan. (Ibid.: 83–4).

This experience began what we have seen is a persisting historical pattern for the West Nilers, in which armed groups appear from the north, looting, burning and carrying off children. But the long-term effects were more subtle than this: many of the abducted children later returned to West Nile, having converted to Islam, and brought their new religion with them.[31]

The first European to enter the region seems to have been the Italian ivory trader Giovanni Miani in March 1860.[32] Perhaps the first to set foot on what became Ugandan territory was a Maltese trader named Andrea de Bono or Amabile (Thomas and Scott 1935: 8; Langlands 1962: 57), who established an ivory station on the east bank of the Nile at Faloro, opposite what was to become the small town of Rhino Camp. According to the British explorer Grant, it was already a cosmopolitan place: 'At Faloro there were upwards of a hundred men of every Egyptian caste and colour.... There were only one or two European countenances. Curly locks were exceptional and wool predominated. They were adventurers without a home' (quoted in Beachey 1967: 280). Another British explorer, Samuel Baker, who had travelled up the Nile to Lake Albert in 1864, returned ten years later as Egypt's first Governor-General of (what would become) the Sudan.[33] Beachey describes how the Sudan ivory trade worked in Baker's day:

> Parties of 100–300 men, the scum of Khartoum, many of them criminals sent south from Egypt, would be collected and sent up the Nile in December in several vessels. On reaching the desired region, villages would be attacked, and ivory, slaves and cattle captured. This plunder would be exchanged for more ivory, which was brought daily into the camp. The rate of exchange, a cow for a tusk of ivory, offered a very profitable transaction, since the cows cost nothing. Baker speaks of expeditions capturing as many as 2,000 cattle. Slaves captured by the ivory traders were ransomed back to their people at the price of more ivory tusks. A good season for a party of 150 men would produce about 20,000 lb of ivory, valued in Khartoum at about £4,000. The men were usually paid off in slaves and cotton-pieces, and after payment had been made there was usually a surplus of 400–500 slaves which would bring in an average profit of £5–£6 each for the ivory trader. (Beachey 1967: 279)

In 1874, General Gordon, who had the previous year succeeded Baker as Governor of Equatoria Province of the Egyptian Sudan, annexed the area as Lado District. One of his officers, Kemp, reached Dufile in 1874 and heard complaints of the slave raids.[34]

---

[31] See Doka Ali Kujo's unpublished history 'The coming of Islam in Uganda 1830–1843' (copy in my possession), also Soghayroun (1981: Ch. 1).

[32] Miani reached somewhere called 'Affudo', which has been identified as Galuffi, on the north bank of the Unyama River just on the Sudan side of the present northern border (Langlands 1962: 57), or possibly even Dufile, on the east bank of the Nile inside Uganda (Harris, RH mss Afr.s.1350).

[33] A brief bibliography of Baker is given in Hall 1980. Allen 1991c considers Baker in a 'Madi' historical context. Baker does not seem to have landed on the West bank of the Nile (see the map attached to Langlands 1962).

[34] Harris in RH mss Afr.s.1350.

The first European to enter Lugbara territory was the Russo-German explorer Wilhelm Junker, who travelled in 1877 with a slaving and ivory expedition led by Ahmed Atrush. Unusually, they entered 'Lubari Land' (Junker 1890: 466) from the north west rather than from the Nile, but their methods were the familiar ones. Junker has left a vivid picture of their progress:

> To me it was given to penetrate into regions hitherto untrodden by any white man, and to extend our knowledge of Africa. Yet I could not take pleasure in my successful journey. The constant recurring scenes of savage brutality, the floggings liberally dispensed every day to the slaves and servants, the sick and wounded, the dread of fire, for hardly a day passed without one or two huts being burnt; my indignation at the robbers, the Nubians being the worst, pity for the poor plundered negroes, all this added to the possibility of an attack in the dark, and the heavy storms every night with deafening thunderpeals and deluges of rain, made it impossible to feel peace or comfort or satisfaction. (Ibid.: 464)

A few pages later, he notes that:

> To the losses of the natives in oxen, goats, and sheep, to the wasting of their fields, and the destruction of their huts, was added the theft of women and children. In the hunt for slaves neither age nor sex is spared. Whatever fell into the hands of the robbers was driven from the camp; and of course the men were able to get away much more easily than the women and children. The Makarakas were not above taking even the old women from their homes, so long as they were capable of working in the fields.... Many of these Kalika women were ransomed by their husbands with ivory.... The full-grown men alone were set apart as recruits for the government, and all the rest remained to the officers, Dongolans and soldiers engaged in the expedition. (Ibid.: 468)

The missionaries C.T. Wilson and R.W. Felkin, who visited the district in the late 1870s, emphasised the potential commercial importance of the slave trade. The Rev. Wilson, with a fine grasp of the links between commerce, Christianity and civilisation, wrote:

> The question of opening up commerce with the tribes inhabiting central Africa is becoming every year of greater importance to Great Britain.... But one great obstacle has to be encountered at the very outset of the enterprise, viz the difficulty of transport from the great lakes to the sea....
>
> That it is possible to create wants, and thus stimulate trade, may be seen in the case of the Waganda, who have had a variety of wants created through contact with Arabs, Egyptians and Europeans... In the case of Uganda, ivory and slaves are the only products obtainable, as nothing else at present pays for transport to Zanzibar.... When the negro has had a fresh want created he will be found ready enough to exert himself to supply it. Slaves and ivory come most readily to hand at first, but trade in the former being prohibited and the supply of the latter being not only limited, but even on the decrease, he will soon turn his attention to other articles which may be exchanged for cloth or whatever else he might need. (Wilson and Felkin 1882:337, 340-41)

It is difficult, reading this, to understand how European commentators have, until the present day, persistently maintained their tone of moral superiority over the 'Arab slavers'. In local terms, their effects were much the same: indeed, a boy taken off as a slave by Ahmed Atrush probably had a greater chance of survival than one pressed into Stanley's service as a porter.

Conclusion

In this chapter, I have examined the period before the area later known as West Nile became part of Uganda. I defined four 'substrata' to this history and dug back through each of them, ending with the first contacts between local people and outsiders. In each layer, I have shown elements of what later crystallised into a discourse of West Nile and its inhabitants as wild, violent and lawless. The echoes of this post-Contact, pre-Colonial period in the later history of the area are many and various: in this conclusion I want to draw out a few of them.

In November 1996, I spoke to a refugee aid worker, a European who had been abducted by West Nile Bank Front forces six months earlier. Her car was held up at gunpoint by a band of a dozen or so rebels, and she was marched off into the bush for several hours before being released, shaken but unharmed. She told me the WNBF had given her a 'political lecture': they spoke about a place she had never heard of, something called the 'Lado Republic', which they intended to establish once the Ugandan government and the SPLA had been vanquished. The WNBF are not alone in this. Leaflets circulate underground in Arua and Kampala, and openly among the West Nile diaspora in Europe and the US, produced by exiles who advocate the resurrection of the Lado Enclave as an independent nation. According to newspaper articles in Uganda, this group has even lobbied the UN for recognition of a Lado state.[35] Absurd though it seems as a political project, the idea that West Nilers should express nostalgia for such a violent and disturbed period in their history is in itself an indictment of both colonial and postcolonial regimes in Uganda.

The West Nile Bank Front, knowingly or not, operates in a manner familiar to West Nilers for a century and a half, since the slave armies first came down from the north, burning homesteads, killing, robbing and abducting young people. The Nubi origins of the rebels and the rootedness of Nubi tradition in West Nile are apparent from this and previous chapters. At the same time, the rebels' opponents in the NRM government, along with southern Ugandans in general, echo stereotypes about West Nile people that were formed in the era of the slavers, travellers and hunters. The very names of and distinctions between the 'tribes' often appear for the first time in this period, such as the earlier variants of 'Lugbara' ('this name was given by foreigners, most probably the Arabs who came to this land about a hundred years ago' (Lulua 1996: 23). This issue is discussed further in the next chapter.

Some echoes of life in the pre-colony apparently disappeared from history, only to reappear in transformed ways. As I mentioned in the first chapter, the three vertical stripes scored by the Arab traders on the faces of their slaves reappeared as a mark of Nubi identity in the army of the Protectorate. In the 1970s, it became a badge of allegiance to the Amin regime: even the President's British henchman, 'Major' Bob Astles, carved the three vertical lines in his cheeks, as a sign of loyalty (see the photograph from *Drum* magazine in Seftel 1994: 213).

---

[35] See reports in the government-owned *New Vision* newspaper, 8 October 1995 and 23 November 1997.

This is an unusually literal case of inscribed as well as embodied social memory (Connerton 1989).

It is scarcely surprising that 'Western', or 'Northern' (or, in the Ugandan context 'Southern'), knowledge about the people of West Nile, developed as it was in the disturbed frontier society of the pre-colony, portrays them as intrinsically violent. Indeed, it is true that violence has been at the heart of their historical experience: notably the violence of states which have marginalised and manipulated them into the roles of slaves and soldiers, the effect of which was to produce agents of state violence whose 'nature' could be ideologically disowned by the 'superior' civilisation, which nevertheless depended on their coercive force. West Nile history is a wilderness of mirrors, full of such historical reversals and ironies. In this it resembles the structure of Conrad's *Heart of Darkness*, the phenomenological lesson of which is that attempts to locate the source of evil in the Other will always fail to mask its true origin in the Self.[36]

In the next chapter, I begin by considering the nature of West Nile society before it was caught up in the violent ironies of Western culture. In particular, I examine the nature and role of 'violence' in a stateless society, in relation to what little we know about pre-contact West Nile, and contrast Middleton's model of Lugbara thought as essentially ahistorical, with local historical narratives of various kinds. This leads on to a return to the present of my ethnographic research, with an account of how such local historical narratives were central to the attempts of certain elders in the 1990s to build and maintain peace in the district.

---

[36] This view is *contra* Achebe's account (Kimbrough [ed.] 1988: 251–85).

7
Lifting the Curse
Writing history & making peace

The Lugbara past & the uses of history

In this chapter, I begin by going beyond recorded history, to look at the time before the people of (what was to become) West Nile made contact with radically different outsiders. I focus on two interrelated themes in pre-contact society, violence and history: the same conceptual pair that have dominated this book throughout. Functionalist anthropologists, notably John Middleton, presented 'traditional' Lugbara society as a 'segmentary lineage system', characterised by ahistoricity and structured around the central function of violence in maintaining social order in a stateless society. Here, I attempt to reopen the issue of history in such societies, arguing for the importance of historical concepts and narratives in 'traditional' Lugbara culture and society, albeit not histories that use conventional Euro-American narrative forms. The chapter then moves from the distant past to the ethnographic present, in order to reconsider further the relationship between violence and historicity. I examine how both 'traditional' historical forms and more conventional written historical narratives were deployed by certain elder men in Arua town, in the late 1990s, in the attempt to make peace within the district, between the Lugbara and their neighbours and between the West Nilers and the Ugandan state. The functionalist concept of the relationship between violence and historicity 'among the Lugbara' is thus inverted, as local ideas of history are used to counteract the legacies of past violence, the consequences of present violence and the fears of future violence I have outlined in the previous chapters.

Middleton on the pre-contact Lugbara

> Virtually nothing is known of them, in a documentary sense, before the arrival of the first Arabs and Europeans.... We may surmise an everlasting succession of epidemics, droughts, famines and population movements going back for centuries. But we have no detailed knowledge of how these events affected the people.... Our knowledge goes back to only the remembered knowledge of some five or six generations from the time I worked there, to perhaps the 1870s at the earliest. (Middleton 1992: 2–3)

Middleton portrays the pre-contact Lugbara as isolated from the rest of the world and living an unchanging traditional lifestyle pretty much like that described by his informants in the 1950s:

In the 1950s, Lugbara still carried on their traditional way of life much as they had always done... for most of the adult population the government, whether European or that of an independent Uganda, was still extraneous and strange, existing for some purpose of its own. All old men remembered the pre-European period from their youth, and had taken part in feuding and warfare. (Ibid.: 6)

The previous chapters have described the disrupted social environment in which Middleton's old men must have 'taken part' in such violent behaviour but, for Middleton, this violence is rooted, not in the historical circumstances prevailing when his informants were youths, but in the very nature of their traditional social and cultural system. In his analysis, both the ahistoricity of the Lugbara and the place of violence in their lives stem from the nature of the segmentary lineage system, a concept which Middleton took pretty much entire from his teacher Evans-Pritchard's early work on the Nuer.[1]

Middleton (unlike the Lugbara themselves) distinguishes between groups defined by locality (which he terms, in descending order of size 'tribes', 'major sections', 'minor sections' and 'minimal sections') and descent groups ('clans', 'sub-clans', 'major', 'minor' and 'minimal' lineages). In traditional Lugbara society, only the smaller segments had any practical relevance; social cohesion was maintained solely at the level of a three- to five-generation agnatic descent group, consisting of several households living in proximity. There were no councils of elders or wider authority. Because of the complex, low-level nature of segmentation, genealogies are unreliable: 'Genealogies usually have from eight to thirteen generations from the present day to the clan founders. It would be possible to trace the supposed genealogical relationship of any two members of a sub-clan and even a clan, but this is never done: the range of recognition of kinship ties between individuals is at a much lower range of segmentation' (Middleton 1960a: 8). There is, therefore, no Lugbara history as such, simply versions of myth, which serve to validate contemporary (and sometimes short-lived) social relationships between small groups:

> In mythical and genealogical distance, any actual or comparative time-scale is irrelevant. In the myths of origin and that of the coming of the coming of the Europeans the same thematic pattern emerges. Similarly, an actual or comparative scale of topographical distance is irrelevant to the spatial categories.... In both schemes the essential distinction is between the close people – members of one's own field of social relations, validated by genealogical tradition, and the distant inverted people who are outside the range of social relations and outside genealogical tradition. (Ibid.: 237)

This same social short-sightedness which makes history impossible at the same time makes violence necessary. Within the small, related, residential group, sanctions against social transgression and conflict are based essentially on the threat of being cursed by shared ancestral ghosts (indeed, such curses are still almost universally feared). Where there is no external authority and there are no recognised shared ancestors (ie, outside the 'minor' or 'major' lineage segment),

---

[1] See, for example, 'I found that the word *suru* was used for several kinds of grouping. Some of these were true clans and lineages according to the usual anthropological usage, others were territorial areas and groupings; I could deal with this one easily since I had read *The Nuer* several times as a student' (Middleton 1970a: 41).

only force, or the threat of force, can mediate behaviour: 'Fighting, *a'di*, occurs between groups which do not share the same or sufficiently closely related ghosts'. (Middleton 1958: 219).

Thus, in Middleton's account, the principal narrative representations through which the Lugbara talk about their past – genealogies, myths, spoken and sung accounts of clan migrations and past relations with their neighbours – are, where they are not just entertainment, simply ideological justifications for present states of affairs. He writes (Middleton 1967) of 'social aspects' of Lugbara myth, but sees the historical aspects as simply metaphorical ways of talking about present social relations, with no historical value:

> It is realized that genealogy is notoriously unreliable as a source of historical data, since genealogies are used by the people to validate social relations as they are today: as these change, so do the genealogies which provide charters for them. Historical accuracy as we know it today is irrelevant in the context of genealogies of clans and other descent groups of societies that lack centralised political authority. And the same is true, of course, of the mythology of such people. An example is that of the Lugbara myths of the origins of their society and the relationship between themselves and their neighbours. (Middleton 1955c)

There is, of course, something in this, but one has to counter that European historical narratives are also concerned, as I have argued, with asking questions of the past from the standpoint of the present, and, very often, with justifying or criticising (some aspect of) the present state of affairs. In the next section I examine both genealogies and origin myths, giving an example of each and discussing their value as historical narratives.

Lugbara histories

One of the first things that strike the present-day researcher asking about pre-contact Lugbara history is that most people begin by explaining that 'the Lugbara' did not exist, either as a social or conceptual unit, prior to the invention of that name and 'tribal' concept in the contact period. The Chairman of both the Lugbara Literature Association and the Arua Council of Elders, Mr Jason Avutia, told me that he had never heard the term until he was fourteen or fifteen years old: he only knew of his clan.[2] The word normally translated as 'clan' is '*suru*', a term which applies to both lineage and locality-based groups at all of Middleton's levels of segmentation: indeed, it really means little more than 'group' or 'category'. As Middleton puts it,

> *Suru* had the meaning of a group of people who considered themselves and were considered by others to form a group because they shared a territory and had ties between them based on common ancestry.... Thus *suru* referred to major lineages and sections, clans, subclans and subtribes. The term was also used in a wider sense as the *suru* (people) of Madi or Europeans, and as species or category, as in a *suru* of birds or trees. (Middleton 1992: 45–6)[3]

[2] Interview, Mr Jason Avutia, 20 March 1997.

[3] The other group designation in Lugbara is *Ori'ba*, people who have the same ancestry or, literally, those who share ghosts (see Middleton 1992: 45). This term, too, can be used for groups of any size, at any of Middleton's levels of segmentation.

Lulua's history of the Lugbara says:

> the name 'Lugbara' was given by foreigners, most probably the Arabs ... [he discusses several local explanations of where the name came from].... However, Father Crazzolara's view appears to command more respect, that the Arabs took the name 'Lugbari', a clan in Udipi Division, to refer to all the other people by mistake. The name was adopted by the Belgians and later on by the British. As there was no traditional government or committee, the name remained unchanged. The name is artificial and baseless. The historical truth is that the Lugbara belonged to the Madi nation. They were called *Madi Dyang* (cattle Madi) by the Alur of Okoro. The Alur called the Madi of Okello as *Madi-Dyel* (goat Madi). In the Aru district of Zaire, many people of the older generation still refer to the bygone days as *Andra drio Madi-si* (the old Madi days). (Lulua 1996: 23–5)

The various clans[4] all have their own stories of the pre-contact past, 'the old Madi days', and there are other tales with a wider currency, such as the origin myths dismissed by Middleton as ahistorical. Traditional[5] 'Lugbara' accounts of the past may be divided into broadly three kinds:

(a) widely told stories of the past, such as origin myths.
(b) more narrowly clan-based histories of migration and settlement (which may be either told as stories or sung as songs, particularly at funerals) and
(c) individual genealogies, which link related individuals to each other and to their mutual ancestors in the pre-contact past.

I shall give examples of all three and outline the senses in which these narrative forms may be considered as 'historical':

(a) A Lugbara 'origin myth'

This narrative is taken from S.A. Geria's undergraduate dissertation (Geria 1973), produced as part of Makerere University's History of Uganda project. It was synthesised from accounts told to him by several elders from Maracha district. This is a version of a widespread story, which was also discussed by Middleton,[6] and is known today in various forms. I think it is worth quoting at length, as it is rich in both imaginative detail and historical metaphor:

> The first two beings, which the traditions describe as super human beings, were Gboro-Gboro, a male and Meme, a female. However, some traditions only speak of one of the beings, namely, Meme. The traditions which speak of Meme only say that God filled her womb with all the living things in the world. All the traditions agree that except for man, the rest of the creatures came out through an opening in Meme's belly which the gazelle ruptured with its hoof from Meme's womb; and that these creatures came out into the world before man. The first human beings were twins, Arube and Oduu. Arube was a male and Oduu a female. The twins, unlike their parents are described as the first ordinary human beings.

---

[4] Middleton says at various times that there were: 'about 45 tribes in the Uganda part of Lugbara' (1960b: 328); 'about sixty... maximal sections' (1967: 47); 'some sixty jural communities, which I call subtribes' (1970b: 55); and 'at least sixty clans' (1992: 57). According to Lulua (1996: 16), there are '100–150 Lugbara clans (*suru*)'.

[5] I am dealing here with what local people took to be traditional forms and genres, dating ultimately from the pre-contact past. I discuss local deployment of written historical narratives below.

[6] See especially Middleton (1967) (1992: 24–5).

It is said that Arube and Oduu were born in the natural human way.... Meme is said to have died immediately after giving birth to Arube and Oduu. Then, the traditions say, there developed some tension between the rest of the creatures and the two siblings. The cause of the tension is believed to be the fact that the siblings were born in a different way from that of the rest of the creatures who are said to have regarded this difference in birth as a bad omen.[7] Thus, it is believed, the rest of the creatures plotted to kill the siblings in order to prevent being befallen by the imminent mishap. The jackal, on behalf of the rest of the creatures, is said to have seduced the elephant to kill the siblings by trampling on them. But the siblings are said to have been saved by the dog who, by the use of certain tricks, outmanoeuvred the elephant and therefore saved the siblings. This kind act of the dog to man, the traditions say, explain why from time immemorial man has always kept the dog at home. It is believed that the dog looked after Arube and Oduu in an Adrogoa's house.[8]

... When Arube and Oduu grew up, as there were no other human beings in the world to make cross-breeding possible for them, they committed incest and begot four children: *Jokodra, Lebenyere, Mutelema* and *Telebenyere*. The first and third were males and the other two were females. In time the four siblings also committed incest. Jokodra and Lebenyere became the ancestors of black people and Mutelema and Telebenyere became the ancestors of white people.

When the children grew up, one day the Adrogoa asked them to leave his house so that they could go and settle in any part of the world of their choosing. But before he allowed them to leave his house, some traditions say, he set them two tasks. The first task was to test each of the boys' competence in gun-shooting. The second task was to test their competence in archery. Jokodra being the eldest son was offered the first opportunity to demonstrate his ability in gun shooting. Unfortunately, he shot so wildly that he could not qualify for a gun prize. When Mutelema took his turn he shot so well that he received a gun prize from the Adrogoa. In the second task Jokodra did much better than Mutelema and the Adrogoa gave him a bow and arrows. The prizes the two brothers received, the traditions say, explain why Europeans have superior arms to Africans.

After these tasks, the Adrogoa gave each of the boys some lifetime possessions such as:- cattle, sheep, goats, chicken, millet, beans, pigeon peas, simsim, black simsim, etc. In short, he gave the siblings all the necessary domestic animals and foodstuffs and seeds which would enable them to start a new and independent life.

The dog and the four siblings came to settle on Mount Liru, where Mutelema squandered all his property and turned to depend too much on his brother, Jokodra. A quarrel ensued which finally led to their separation. Mutelema and his sister, Telebenyere, went off to Europe, but Jokodra and his sister, Lebenyere, remained on Mount Liru.

In time, Jokodra and Lebenyere committed incest and begot *Yeki*. In Europe, Mutelema and his sister also committed incest and begot *Agbau* (or *Gbau*). Some years later, the traditions say, Mutelema's descendants sent a bird (Koli-Kolia) from Europe to come to Mount Liru to place its claws in some cowdung in Jokodra's kraal, to see if the latter still had cattle. Following the bird's return to Europe with some cow-dung on its claws, Mutelema's descendants (i.e. the Europeans) came to Africa to cheat us of our cattle.

When Yeki grew up, he got married to *Gbele* from Yataa clan and begot children who became the ancestors of Terego, Acholi, Lango, Southern Luo, Alur, Bunyoro, etc. In time, Yeki's wife, Gbele, became too old to bear any more children but she was still interested in seeing her husband begetting more children. So she seduced a young girl

---

[7] Middleton, in his version of this story, says that the names 'Arube' and 'O'du' both mean 'miraculous omen' (1967: 52). Geria, however, translates them as 'bad omen' (as does a recent Lugbara–English dictionary, Ichile [1995]).

[8] An *Adrogoa* is a kind of water spirit – Geria translates it as a 'fairy'.

called *Nyadaa* who had an incurable wound on one of her legs to sleep with Yeki.[9] In time, Yeki and Nyadaa begot Jaki ... [who] begot many children who became the ancestors of most of the clans in North-Western Lugbaraland (modern Maracha).... [the clans are listed]. Some of the traditions, particularly those of the Paranga cluster of clans, say that when his children grew up, Jaki partitioned the territory then under his 'sphere of influence' to them. Each son acquired land by throwing a spear to the land of his choice; where the spear landed became his territory. All the sons threw spears to the various territories that are today inhabited by their descendants. (Geria 1973: 21–3)

This story is obviously more than a myth of origin. It explains where human beings come from, and particularly where the people of Maracha County come from, but also the historical circumstances in which they found themselves a century before Geria collected the story. It is a tale of imperial dominance, in which the contest between Jokodra and Mutelema explains why and how the descendants of Mutelema and Telebenyere, the Europeans, were able to conquer the district, and provides an unsavoury motive for them doing so – to steal cattle. The myth does not simply express short-lasting, present-day social relations, but analyses the results of the coming of the white men in the previous century. It is more like one of Cunnison's 'universal' histories, shared by many *suru* and told, not to aggrandise a particular lineage group, but to express the relatedness of the groups, and their relationships with their neighbours, as well as with the whites. This produces a history in which, as Paul Dresch says of Cunnison's material, 'collective identity is defined precisely by reference to the actions of individual persons or particular groups' (Dresch 1989: 357).

(b) Clan histories

Here I give two examples: first, a traditional Lugbara funeral song (baiko) collected and translated by Mr John Alokore of Muni National Teachers' College. It comes from Ayivu county, near Arua town.

Amukua buti njile	Open the grave, Amukua
Ombaciale Yole fibua	Buried is Yole in Ombaci
Osumani njolia	Rendered useless are my bows
Masi ndundu rua?	Should I retreat?
Aria Drako be cere	Aria Drako's voice yonder
Imvetrea le miminaru	In Imvetre valley is heard with sadness
Asea di udhuru	Asea unavenged inside
Aba joti kua	With doors open he lies
Irekoa ye idi oale omvusi	Irekoa in grief wails
Owayi angua le	In Owayi land
Ama uma ngu donia	How we rot and stink
Ayivu izi ma tiku	Don't tantalise us, Ayivu
Ojo lima do	Utterly in despair, we succumb
Izatiru mia	Know well, Izatiru
Ama kariko nibo	To oblivion reduced
Amukua buti njile	Now is our home[10]

[9] In a footnote, Geria says that Yeki was so old and sexually inactive that he had to be circumcised in order to rejuvenate him. Circumcision is not performed by the Lugbara or neighbouring West Nile groups (except, of course, by Muslims).

[10] From 'Songs in West Nile', an unpublished typescript in my possession. It forms a chapter of Mr Alokore's unpublished work on the oral history of West Nile.

This is what Cunnison (1951) terms a 'personal' history, one relating to and related by members of a particular *suru*, grieving over a deceased senior member and comparing him with the great dead of the past, a past which is recalled (as it is in all the *Baiko* I have encountered) as the scene of failure and bitterness. *Baiko* are very sad, emotional songs (the atmosphere of bitter nostalgia is, perhaps, not unlike that of Portuguese *fado* music). They are sung before other kinds of song at funerals to accompany the first funeral dances. Middleton does not discuss the lyrics of the funeral dances, but, as this example shows, they are also partly about expressions of clan history.[11]

My next example of a clan history is an account of migration and settlement told to me by a local historian and elder from Aringa County:

The people of Aringa come from southern Sudan. We were few in number, and we came individually or in small groups, because of hunger and tribal wars, and also in search of pasture. Then others came to join their brothers and relatives. They began to marry among themselves and some married Kakwa women. There are three different groups, Lugbaras, Madis and Kakwas. In Sudan we interacted with the Pajelu, Moro, Mundari, Abkaya, Nko, Madi, Kuku.

Our family came from Korokota. Kakwa and Bari and Pajelu are the same language, really. Also Ligi, Nyambara, Moro and Kaliko, they are all like Lugbara and Bari.

The clans were the most important thing that the people used. The first group to come to Aringa came via Midigo, a hill there in Aringa. They settled there. The hill was not there then. Then Midigo hill came up. It killed some of the people, from the Yambora, Nyai, Wande and Adiba clans. Others came. Those people disappeared. Others who had been away came and found their people not there.

A second group came via Lobe hill. Inigo was a person who came through there. He brought his father with him and settled on that hill, then his father died. He decided to cross the river Kochi to go to his uncle, Forbe. He reached the middle of Aringa and there he was under a tree with his cows and animals. There were already some people in that place: the Uroba, Morobo, Nchoko, Monoja and Yomoni clans. There Inigo met a man named Ira, from the Rogbo clan. Ira's daughters went out and they saw some cattle, they came back running telling their father, 'We have seen things with very long tails.' Then Ira sent for Inigo to come to his home. He asked him 'Where are you going?', 'I am following my uncles, Forbe's people.' Ira said, 'There are no Forbe people here. Don't wander for nothing with these animals. Settle near me here.' Then our ancestor accepted.

From there, they continued to stay with Ira until April. Then Ira said 'You can take part of my fields and dig them.' So Inigo did it. Ira wanted him to sow millet, but he refused and instead sowed beans. Ira was surprised, he said 'It would be better if you followed what I told you.' But Inigo said 'This one is better.' 'In June', Ira said, 'sunshine usually comes. It takes time to rain, so you may be at a disadvantage.' Inigo said, 'Let me try and we shall see,' and he continued digging more. When sunshine came, he found Ira's millet was flowering. Then there was no rain again. The millet all got burned in the garden. Inigo's beans yielded better, and he continued. By July there was another rain, and then he sowed his millet and it did very well and he harvested it. He told his wives to give some to Ira's wives. So Ira got that one from him.

In the second year, he repeated his way of cultivation and Ira thought that perhaps man was becoming something different, and he decided that he should leave that place

---

[11] Middleton, typically, sees funeral dances as expressive of the structure of the 'segmentary lineage system. The dances have two main functions. One is to re-form the relationships between lineages, both those related patrilineally and those related affinally, that have been temporarily broken by the death of the person.... The other, on a more mystical plane, is to re-establish the continuity of the lineage' (1982: 148; see also Middleton 1985).

for Inigo and go away. Before he left, he asked Inigo to give him something. Inigo said, 'What do you want?' He sent his young men to Inigo and Inigo gave him a cow, which he refused. He tried to give him other things, which he didn't like, except for some chickens. He said he wanted something with a mouth like this [he makes pecking motions with his hand]. When the chickens were given, he killed four: one for the Rogbo people, one for Monobo, one for Echoko, one for Monoja. Then Ira left the place for Inigo. Ira said, 'You can settle here' and he went south to Rhino Camp or someplace.

So Inigo settled with his two sons. They brought wives from southern Sudan with them when he came. The first son was called Ikabe and the second Kuliji Jamero. They grew up and married, and Ikabe's family was now called Loyenya. Kuliji Jamero's children were called Bora. These two united as the Loyenya Bora clan. From Loyenya came four clans – Nyori, Moju, Lokora and Odav. From Kuliji Jamero came Miroba, Moli, Uluba, Logule, Terem, Nyepi, Nomva, Ger and Renda clans. These multiplied widely in Aringa and occupied two and a half divisions there; one was Kol division and the other Odrave division. These are the biggest clans in Aringa.

Another group from Sudan came via Kei mountain. These are the Gimera people, the Mbala, Kifoli and smaller clans. Another group also came, who reached the Kakwa area first. They went to Lira mountain and then went down to Aringa. These are the Mbachi and Rigbona. They are now Aringa people, not Kakwa.

These are the four streams through which people came. They stayed without external government. They had no other name, they were just clans.... Later they communicated with the people of Kakwa who came from the Sudan at about the same time. Also the Madi. They intermarried with both these groups.[12]

The next day, my informant returned, wanting to add two further groups to his previous account.

There are two other groups who came to Aringa, making six groups in all. The fifth group came to Aringa from the south side, from Terego, from the family of Banyele. They were two groups, Angudri and Funyaro, and they were three clans, Gopile, Ilike and Lainga. They came from Mount Wati, they went to Aringa late and the other people were already there.

The sixth group was the people of Yumbe. By the time they reached Aringa they were known by the clan name Yiba. They were received by the Bora people who were already there. The name Yumbe is the local name from Aringa. The man who went there was called Olubi. He settled there and founded these clans: Modicha, Akubara, Uluba Odravoria, Orunji and Pena. They are presently in Aringa, in Yumbe.[13]

It is notable that far more detail is provided for one group of clans, the speaker's own. They are shown to have a legitimate claim to their land as first arrivals, who were given their territory by an autochthonous people who then went away. Their claim was sustained (and the original people left) because they had agricultural techniques that suited the land and climate better than those used previously. Like Cunnison's personal histories of the Luapula peoples, it concerns how groups came to occupy the particular piece of land on which they live.[14] Unlike the more 'universal' myth given above, it is clear that other groups would be likely to have different versions of when and how they came to occupy their land.

---

[12] Interview, Mr Adoka Ali Kujo, 5 February 1997. Transcribed from notes.

[13] Interview, Mr Adoka Ali Kujo, 6 February 1997. Transcribed from notes.

[14] As Middleton shows, *suru* above the minimal level do not in practice tend to be territorially coherent groups, but they are so in theory.

(c) Individual genealogies

On 16 March 1997, I travelled with local historian Mr Lulua Odu to meet Mr Yoramu Badrayi at his home in Muni village, a few kilometres south of Arua. Mr Yoramu was born in 1918 and studied up to Primary Six level at Mvara school. Today he is Deputy Chair of his LC2 Committee. Mr Lulua is a lawyer by training; he was born in 1947. Both are members of the Ombokoro clan. Mr Lulua introduced Mr Yoramu, translating from Lugbara as follows: 'Now, he says he is from the Ombokoro clan, which is the one also I belong to. He says he can quote the family tree, up to the man who came from the East of the Nile, who was called, what? 'Banyele. 'Banyele begot Angundru.'[15] Together, taking turns, they then recited the genealogy below. The two men's lineages are not very close (segmentation having occurred seven generations previously) and yet they were readily able to agree on the genealogy. Mr Lulua, though the younger of the two men, is of a senior generation in the combined lineages, but Mr Yoramu is of the senior branch of the clan (Anzu being the elder brother, Yia the younger).

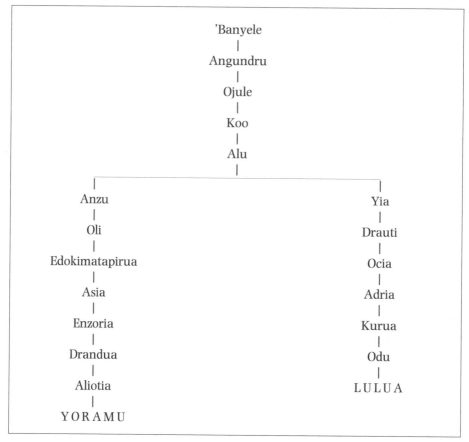

Figure 7.1 A Genealogy of the Ombokoro Clan

[15] Interview, Mr Lulua and Mr Yoramu, 16 March 1997. Transcribed from tape and field notes.

I suspect that Middleton is correct when he writes that:

> The form of Lugbara genealogies is not fixed, but easily changeable. It depends merely on the consensus of the more senior men, at a given time. The genealogies given by the senior men of a lineage may often be at variance with each other, since genealogical validation is the only accepted criterion for *de jure* as distinct from *de facto* eldership. (Middleton 1960a: 12)

However, my example partially contradicts his statement (quoted above, p 175) that the tracing of genealogical relationships between two members of a sub-clan is 'never done' (Middleton 1960a: 8). It should also be noted that Mr Lulua himself has a close and detailed knowledge of Middleton's work. However, their 'quoting the family tree' was not simply a performance for my benefit (though in context it was that, too). I have heard other (albeit briefer) accounts of the genealogical relationship between two Lugbara people being recited for the benefit of others in a bar, to tell them how two of those present are related. The very fact that Mr Yoramu and Mr Lulua were able to agree so speedily on the genealogy is evidence that they are relatively used to reciting their own descent lines.

Stories of the past

How are we to evaluate these various forms of discussion of the past? In the first place, it should be clear that these are narratives: they do not outline a chronological 'linear account of events' (Comaroff and Comaroff 1991: 34) but this is not, *pace* the Comaroffs, the only kind of historical narrative.[16] Chronology is, as I argued in my introductory chapter, an extremely powerful narrative trope (see White 1987 [1980]). Attempts to compare non-chronological 'ethno-histories' with Westernised chronological accounts will usually end up showing the greater power of the latter.[17] That this is a question of rhetorical force, and not of truth versus fiction, is exemplified by the conventional historical accounts of Yakan discussed in Chapter Five. These, as I showed, are in their content chronologically inaccurate: it is the convincing nature of the *form* – event E happened on day D, month M, year Y, preceded and followed by other dated events – which has sustained their power as the hegemonic narratives of the events concerned.

The local historical narratives given here lack this power. But that does not render them ahistorical. Nor does the fact that they are in part concerned with present-day questions such as 'why do we occupy this piece of land and what should our relations be with our neighbours?'. All meaningful histories, as Collingwood argued, are concerned with a past encapsulated in a context of

---

[16] See Peel 1995. While Middleton denied the historicity of such narratives, the Comaroffs deny their narrativity.

[17] For example, I find highly unconvincing Morphy and Morphy's (eg 1984) attempt to valorise unchronological Australian Aboriginal historical narratives, over the chronological accounts of the settlers. Even on the evidence of the texts they provide, the settler story seems to me richer and more convincing, due at least in part to the use of chronological narrative.

present thought. Our own canonical schools of history – from the Whig interpretations of the nineteenth century to various Marxist schools of the twentieth – were written to justify and explain present states of affairs (or, in the latter case, future states). In my view, then, Middleton is wrong to see such a justificatory function as evidence for the ahistoricity of Lugbara accounts of the past.

The opposite mistake would be to try to read traditional histories of the kind instanced here as simply factual chronological accounts. This was one of the problems with the History of Uganda Project in the 1970s. Geria, for example, tries to date migrations of centuries ago by using traditional chronologies going back (as does the one instanced above) to mythical hero-ancestors such as Banyele. He writes that: 'It can be assumed that the remembered history of the Northwestern Lugbara begins with the creation story, which takes us back in time to between 14 and 15 generations ago, therefore 1517–1571.... The next two generations in which Arube and Oduu must have lived might be dated to 1544–1598' (Geria 1973: 24). Perhaps the most extreme example of this approach can be found in the work of Makerere historian O.J.E. Shiroya (a Kenyan), who wrote, on the basis of the oral evidence gathered by Geria and others for the History of Uganda Project, of a Lugbara state or states existing in the eighteenth and nineteenth centuries (Shiroya 1984: 205). In the Uganda of the 1970s, where the most powerful groups in society were (as they are today) from the Bantu kingdoms of the south, it is easy to see why the West Nilers would want to have had states, too, but Shiroya's evidence does not bear out his contentions (see Shiroya 1972, 1984).

One narrative strand in many traditional Lugbara histories is the importance of hills, an importance which has been noted by Middleton and others. These are the features of the West Nile landscape which most often define social groups, both locality-based groups (as in the role of hills in the Aringa clan history quoted above) and descent groups (as with the hills mentioned in the account of settlements in Aringa). All the Lugbara origin myths, like the one I have quoted, site the birthplace of humanity on one of the two great mountains of the district, Mount Liru and Mount Eti or Wati. Even Europeans have been affected by this trope; R.N. Posnett, a colonial officer, wrote an account of the relationship between 'West Nile hills and history' in the *Uganda Journal* (Posnett 1951). Geria explains the importance of hills instrumentally: 'The hills and mountains, as important landmarks, must have guided the early migrants to their destinations. No wonder Mount Liru and hills like Ajebe and Aba stand out in the traditions of the northwestern Lugbara as the first homes of the people's hero-ancestors' (Geria 1973: 13). Whatever the plausibility of such an explanation, it is clear that a historical/political emphasis on hills is by no means unique to the West Nile, but a way of talking about past and present society found throughout Africa – perhaps even part of a continental 'political tradition', in Vansina's (1990) phrase.[18]

---

[18] To take two examples from an African country far from West Nile, Zimbabwe, David Maxwell in his social history of the Hwesa people, writes that: 'The Katerere polity's political history, from the outset, is a history of its hills. The relation of factions to mountains was a form of local politics in

A central aspect of all the historical genres I have instanced is that they are not simply texts but have a performative aspect (not necessarily in Austin's sense, quoted in Chapter One, but in the basic sense of performing). Origin myths, clan histories (spoken or sung) and individual genealogies are all recited or sung for an audience (who may also be co-performers) in specific contexts. Some histories will only be told (sung, danced) at funerals. Others are tales told to the young, perhaps around the fire in the evening, by their parents and grandparents. Still others (the genealogies, for example) are recited for the benefit of other adults. Different genres belong in different contexts (contexts from which my, and others', transcriptions wrench them).

Performed histories, whether or not they have the narrative force of chronology, have a different kind of rhetorical power, one perhaps derived ultimately from the body. This is particularly obvious in the case of funeral dances, but applies to other genres, too, in so far as they are performed. As Connerton put it, 'if there is such a thing as social memory ... we are likely to find it in commemorative ceremonies; but commemorative ceremonies prove to be commemorative only in so far as they are performative' (Connerton 1989: 4–5). James suggests something very similar in her definition of 'cultural archives', which: 'Like an archive, may constitute a lasting base of past reference and future validation. They may at times rest dormant but on occasion be drawn upon for the formation of new discourse. The elements of this cultural archive, revealed as much in the repertoire of habitual ritual action as in language, constitute the foundations of a moral world' (James 1988: 6). Performative narratives which involve such 'habitual ritual action' are particularly suited to transmit historical knowledge which has been repressed, through the process of what R.G. Collingwood called 'incapsulation' (1970 [1939]: 140), the perpetuation and later re-emergence of historical memory. Collingwood's own explanation of the transmission process uses an example which, like the stories in this chapter, is both performance and text: a father telling stories to his children:

> Suppose a very warlike people, at a certain crisis in its history, turned completely peaceful. In the first generation, warlike impulses would survive; but let us suppose them sternly repressed, so that everybody behaved in an entirely peaceful manner. When the people of this generation set to work on the moral education of their children, the children would be carefully told that they must on no account indulge in the forbidden pleasures of war. 'But what is war, Daddy?', then Daddy gives a description of war, emphasizing its wrongness but (doubtless altogether against his will) making it plain to his innocent offspring that war was a grand thing while it lasted and that he would love to fight his neighbours again if only he did not know that he ought not to. The children are quick to understand all that. They not only learn what war is, or was, but they learn also that it is, or was, a grand thing, though of

---

18 (cont.) the vernacular which found expression in Hwesa praise songs sung in honour of mountains and their associated chiefs.... The nineteenth century reality was that their territory was an extension from hills at the centre.... [M]ountains were sources of political legitimacy. It is hardly surprising that dominant families seized the highest and most visually impressive of peaks. Other less powerful factions lived on smaller mountains'. (Maxwell 1999:26). At the other end of the country, Ranger (1999: e.g. 16-26) has discussed the historical-religious-political importance of the Matopos hills in Matabeleland. No doubt other examples exist elsewhere in Africa.

course wrong; and they carefully pass all this on to their own children when the time comes. (Collingwood 1939: 142–3)[19]

Myths, like bedtime stories or their equivalents, are both performative and linguistic. These tales are told at family and clan gatherings, such as weddings and funerals, when sad songs are sung of the loss of former power and the death of old heroes. They transmit aspects of a cultural archive through many generations, social memories which from time to time may become salient again after years of repression, as stories of Sudanese origins became during the West Nilers' exile in southern Sudan in the 1980s.

But as Collingwood's example reminds ūs, such social memories may include traces from the past which are by no means pleasant. The 'very warlike people' he was thinking of in 1939 were presumably the Germans, but one has to ask whether, as the colonial (and postcolonial) authorities all thought and as Middleton's analysis of the traditional role of violence in maintaining social stability suggests, Lugbara culture too is inherently 'warlike'. Could the violence and marginality traced throughout this book stem originally, not from the oppression of others, but from the very nature of traditional Lugbara (or Madi, or Kakwa) society?

Violence and social order

Middleton portrays violence as central to the segmentary lineage system, which he sees as characterising Lugbara social relationships. In the functionalist style, he portrays fighting and warfare as the central part of a system of social sanctions designed to strengthen the social structure:

> In the traditional system relations between groups beyond immediate neighbours are in terms of fighting. The nature of fighting and the means to end it and the type of reparation to settle the dispute vary with the social distance between the parties, expressed in lineage distance. Fighting, *a'dị*, occurs between groups which do not share the same or sufficiently closely related, ghosts. (Middleton 1958: 219)

Violence was so important to the Lugbara that it persisted (at the level of local discourse at least) to Middleton's own day, despite the colonial legal system: 'The more formal ways of settling disputes include, traditionally, feud and warfare and, today, court actions. Feud and warfare were prohibited by the British and Belgian colonial governments in the 1920s; but intergroup fights still break out and Lugbara still discuss intergroup relations largely in terms of organized force' (Middleton 1969a: 156). Violence was the main sanction deployed in disputes outside the 'family cluster' (the 'minimal', or occasionally 'maximal', lineage): 'Relations within the family cluster are controlled by the cult of the dead, and relations between clusters other than those closely related by agnatic kinship were traditionally sanctioned by the operation of the feud and warfare' (Middleton

---

[19] It is interesting that Middleton wrote: 'I read, very belatedly, Collingwood's *The Idea of History* at the very end of my fieldwork while trying to make sense of Lugbara ritual. I wish that I had read it two years earlier' (Middleton 1970a: 3).

1963: 80–82). As explained in many of his works,[20] the ways fighting operated and the means by which it could be ended depend crucially on the degree of relatedness of the disputants. Each of his accounts outlines the precise genealogical points at which different kinds of violence operated:

> Within what I call the inner section and inner lineage, close lineage ties inhibit prolonged fighting, but beyond it feud and warfare were traditionally frequent.... Within the inner segment almost all disputes are settled by the elders of the parties concerned, and open violence, except for duelling, is rare. But beyond it, elders regard themselves as too remotely related. Fighting within the subtribe could be stopped by the elders meeting and cursing the fighters or by calling in a rainmaker or a 'man whose name is known' to do the same. Fighting between subtribes was not stopped in this way and merely continued until both sides grew tired of the inconvenience of fighting and of losing their men in battle. (Middleton 1969: 156)

As we have seen different papers by Middleton use different names for the social units between which cursing, feuding or warfare is the dominant mode of negotiating social conflict,[21] though the Lugbara themselves do not recognise the distinctions. Middleton is, of course, fully aware of this; in his most reflexive work he says:

> I found that all Lugbara men who had been more than about fifteen years old in the 1930s could tell me about the operation of feud and warfare. I had hoped at first that they would tell me about them in terms of the lineage paradigm that I had constructed ... but that simply did not work....
>
> I soon found that I was asking questions that, although they could be answered in terms of particular lineages taking part in a particular feud, were answered among the Lugbara themselves in quite other terms. They did not use the words for clan and lineage nor did they always use the name of these groupings, but instead referred to categories of kin and clusters of groupings that were defined according to a particular situation. (1970a: 42–3)

Moreover, the empirical, oral, evidence did not suggest that fighting was very widespread, or that the level of violence was very intense:

> The only way was to ask for details of actual cases of feud and warfare that the men concerned had taken part in, or at least could recall with fair accuracy. I found, not unnaturally that they tended to exaggerate the glories of the deeds of prowess of themselves or their lineage kin – Lugbara can never be accused of false modesty. What was at first told to me as a glorious war which seemed to involve the entire countryside for months at a time usually turned out after detailed questioning to have involved a dozen men on each side who had fought sporadically for a week or two. But this

---

[20] Eg Middleton (1953: 8–9; 1958: 216–18; 1960b: 328; 1963: 80–82; 1969: 153–6; 1970a: 42–3; 1971b: 10; 1992: 53–8).

[21] For example, the description of fighting quoted above can be compared with the following: 'Before the [colonial] prohibition of intergroup fighting, disputes were settled within the major section (and certainly within the minor section) by arbitration by respective [sic] elders or by duelling; beyond the major section and within the subtribe by feud; and beyond the subtribe by warfare. The distinction between feud and warfare was simply that there was a recognised obligation that feuds should quickly be settled by agreement, but warfare could not permanently by settled.... Arbitration within the subtribe was typically by rainmakers. Each subclan had its own rainmaker, the senior man of the senior descent line of the subclan. He had powers of cursing men engaged in feud, and his person was regarded as a sanctuary for an evildoer. But rainmakers could not act beyond the subtribe.... Fighting was the concern of men only (although women had the task of collecting corpses). Women could travel with reasonable safety between hostile groups and often acted as go-betweens' (Middleton 1971b: 10).

exaggeration showed me something of the importance of fighting for the Lugbara and of the central part it played in the traditional political system. (Ibid.: 43)

It is perhaps unsurprising that martial prowess was seen as important to the Lugbara of Middleton's day, after thirty-five years of systematic army recruitment and even longer being associated with 'the best material for soldiery in Africa'. It is no more surprising that I failed to find much evidence of Lugbara pride in their military past. Post-Amin, West Nilers in general are not inclined to boast of their fighting skills. The one reasonably extensive interview I was able to conduct on the issue of traditional warfare, with an elder born in Weatherhead's time, emphasised the limited occasions on which it was appropriate (he agreed with Middleton that the cause was usually a quarrel over women or cattle) and the ways in which it could be averted or ended.[22] Other elders spoke of the need for ritual cleansing after killing someone (discussed below).

Middleton is, of course, not alone in seeing violence as intrinsic and central to stateless societies. This has been an enduring theme both in the anthropological literature and in the earlier reactions of colonial officials to such societies. It is interesting that British imperial officials took two opposite kinds of African society as paradigmatic of the violence of the continent: the highly centralised state system typified by Shaka's Zulus, and stateless societies such as the Nuer or Lugbara (see Mazrui's comparisons between Amin and Shaka discussed in Chapter Three). Of course, the colonial discourses of both state and stateless violence on the continent were affected both by Western political (and racial) ideologies and by local accounts, which affected how officials on the ground saw particular groups (as Hamilton 1998 demonstrates in the case of Shaka's Zulus, and Johnson 1981 shows for the Nuer).

The implied comparison is always with a view of Western political systems as rational systems based on contract and consensus, as depicted by the canonical theorists of the liberal state – from Locke to Weber. Indeed, Middleton's account of Lugbara violence is at root a Lockean one. Without traditional chiefs, or any authority recognised outside the immediate residential lineage group,[23] they are portrayed as having lived in a constant 'state of war', defined in Locke's *Second Treatise of Government* as a situation of 'force, or a declared design of force upon the Person of another, where there is no common Superior on Earth to appeal to for relief' (Locke 1988: 280). This is not quite the Hobbesian state of war, in which 'every man is an enemy to every man' (Hobbes 1957: 82),[24] because group solidarity persists at the level of the local community, but it comes close. As Turton has argued, the Durkheimian tradition in social anthropology (of which Middleton was such an exemplary practitioner) modified but did not change Hobbes's analysis of the relationship between violence and the state, 'Thus has anthropology bolstered the Hobbesian project: the legitimisation of the state form of political organisation' (Turton 1994: 21).

[22] Interview, Mr Yoramu Badrayi, 16 March 1997.
[23] Middleton makes a partial exception here of the northern Lugbara, who, influenced, he says, by the Kakwa, have a rain-chief who settles disputes beyond the minimal lineage (see the appendix to his thesis – Middleton 1953: 329–35).
[24] Hobbes cites stateless American Indian societies as examples of actually existing 'conditions of war', where the only social cohesion is at the level of 'small families' (1957: 83).

Perhaps the most explicit recent formulation of a Hobbesian political anthropology of statelessness is that of Pierre Clastres. He argued that Hobbes was right, in the sense that warfare is inevitably at the heart of stateless societies; indeed, it is the only means they have to maintain their existence as stateless:

> What is primitive society? It is a multiplicity of undivided communities which all obey the same centrifugal logic. What institution at once expresses and guarantees the permanence of this logic? It is war, as the truth of relations between communities, as the principal sociological means of promoting the centrifugal force of dispersion against the centripetal force of unification. The war machine is the motor of the social machine: the primitive social being relies entirely on war, primitive society cannot survive without war. The more war there is, the less unification there is, and the best enemy of the state is war. Primitive society is society against the State in that it is society-for-war.
>
> ... Hobbes ... was able to see that war and the State are contradictory terms, that they cannot exist together, that each implies the negation of the other: war prevents the State, the State prevents war. (Clastres 1994: 166)[25]

If 'warfare' in this sense is indeed intrinsic to stateless societies, it should be pointed out that violence of another kind is central to the concept of the state. Indeed, in the Weberian formulation, a claimed monopoly over violence is at the heart of the very definition of the state. As the philosopher Paul Ricoeur pointed out:

> the state has another face, rationality has its other side: the residue of founding violence ... basically there is probably no state that was not born out of violence, whether by conquest, usurpation, forced marriage or the wartime exploits of some great assembler of territories. One might believe that this is a heritage that will be gradually eliminated, reduced to a minimum by constitutional rationality, but the constitution itself restores this irrational in the form, precisely, of the capacity of decision of the prince.... We discover here the residual violence that Max Weber had in mind when he said that the state is the recourse to legitimate force as a final resort.... We are obliged to come to terms with this, and it imposes on the citizen a duty of vigilance – vigilance with respect to the outbreaks of violence that are inscribed in the very structure of the political. (Ricoeur 1998: 98)

Political theory aside, in reality one thing is clear: the kind of 'warfare' practised by groups such as the pre-contact Lugbara was different in both its content and scale from the 'violence' practised upon the people of West Nile by successive state formations – the Turco-Egyptian Sudan, the Belgian empire, the British Protectorate, postcolonial Uganda. The feuds and wars over women and cattle described by Middleton and others were fought with spears, knives, bows and arrows between roughly equal forces. They were constrained by conventions (for example, over the treatment of non-combatants, such as old men, women and children) that recognised the essential humanity of the opposition: the combatants may not have shared the same ghosts, but each side recognised the other as full people (*'ba oriba*). The post-contact violence experienced by the people of West Nile, on the other hand, has been both technologically unequal and based on assumed racial characteristics, which rendered the enemy (the violent, warlike Lugbara) less than human. It seems almost inappropriate to use

---

[25] Cf also Clastres (1987), esp.189–218.

the same words ('war', 'violence' or whatever) to describe such different social processes.

So far in this chapter, I have examined two aspects of pre-contact West Nile society, history and violence, in relation to John Middleton's account of the Lugbara. I have argued that local historical narratives have greater interest and value than Middleton assumed, and have questioned his views about both the ahistoricity of the Lugbara and the role of violence in their society. Once again, I have focused on the interconnections between discourse and reality and between knowledge and power. But my argument here has to be tentative: it is simply not, I believe, possible to reconstruct the details of pre-contact life for the West Nile peoples with any accuracy. The catastrophic impact of the contact period, whose major events were outlined in the previous chapter, and the subsequent violent incorporation of the people of the district into marginal roles in the colonial system have broken decisively the traditions of the past. The disasters of the postcolony have only reinforced this alienation. It seems likely that Middleton's picture is the best we shall ever have – it is certainly today the main point of reference for many Lugbara people when they ask themselves questions about their past and their traditions. Such questions have come increasingly to be asked, as West Nilers have recovered from the events of the 1980s and sought to define their relationship with the new Ugandan state. In the next section, I look at these processes of social reconstruction in West Nile, and at the role played in them by history.

Writing history & making peace

We now return to the late twentieth century for the rest of this chapter. Beginning with an examination of the complex relationship between West Nilers and the state, I go on to outline the various attempts of local elders, since the mid-1980s, to broker a different kind of relationship between local people and the state, to de-marginalise their society and culture and to make peace with their neighbours. I focus on the relationship between history and reconstruction, and the role of history and historiography in peacemaking and cultural renovation. The past weighs heavily on the shoulders of the West Nile people and, perhaps inevitably, my historical chapters have concentrated on the ways in which they have become trapped by the past, and its evolving discourse about them. Here, I aim to reintroduce them as active agents, trying to understand their history and to reinterpret their traditions in order to shape a future that will not repeat the mistakes of the past. This is at the core of my understanding of 'social reconstruction', in the West Nile context.

Despite its increasing currency as a buzz-word, 'reconstruction' seems to have no agreed definition. A number of different economic and political discourses are involved. On the one hand, reconstruction can be seen as more or less synonymous with the similarly vague and contested notion of 'development'. It may also involve, especially in a politically marginalised area like West Nile, an emphasis on local relationships with the state, such as involvement in the 'normal' politics of the nation, rather than support for rebel activity. At the local level, which is my primary focus here, attitudes towards reconstruction differ. To use again the crude and overlapping categories introduced in Chapter Two, the worlds of the state, the market, the land and the agencies all have their own perspectives on social reconstruction.

For the state's men, the political agenda is foremost; 'reconstruction' involves mainly the ending of rebel activity in the area and its integration into the Ugandan polity, particularly through the Local Council (LC) system and support for the NRM. For the world of the market, the economic issues of jobs and trading opportunities predominate. For the elders, the representatives of the land, reconstruction involves above all a return to what they consider to be traditional norms and ways of life. For the people of the agencies, it is a question of moving along a continuum from relief to development, where the latter is understood as a miscellaneous bundle that includes both economic improvements and social changes, such as greater power for women. Most people, of course, combine elements of more than one of these attitudes, but the different approaches may also generate conflict, for example between younger and older men, between men and women, or between the market and the state.[26]

More theoretical analyses of reconstruction tend to approach the issue very differently. The most influential anthropological account of reconstruction in West Nile is the work of Tim Allen, whose research in the Madi village of Laropi in the late 1980s was discussed in Chapter Three. In a number of articles (especially Allen 1989a, b, 1991b, 1992, 1997) he has developed a medicalised discourse of reconstruction, in which local adjustments to the social changes that followed the return of the Madi refugees from southern Sudan are described in terms taken from biomedicine – phrases such as 'social trauma' (1989a: 45), 'collective therapies' (1997: 126), or 'social wounds' and their 'healing' (1997: 101). Characteristically, Allen (1989a, 1997) draws on Middleton's (and Barnes-Dean's 1986) work on Lugbara medicine, rather than his 'political anthropology' paper on peacemaking (Middleton 1966).

Notwithstanding the inherently functionalist implications of using the metaphor of an individual organism as the model for social processes, there are advantages to Allen's approach. In the first place, it is justifiable in local terms. As elsewhere in Africa, West Nilers tend to use the same phrases for both individual and social sicknesses: in African languages, as in the language of the World Health Organisation, the socio-economic and the biomedical may be synonymous.[27] A second strength in Allen's analysis is that the biomedical analogy allows him to understand, or at any rate to explain, the close relationship between social reconstruction and violence. Allen shows how even extremely violent episodes such as the torturing to death of witches may be understood as aspects of social healing, just as violence and healing are frequently associated in Western biomedicine. In fact, Allen goes further than this, to suggest that: 'It seems likely that one of the

---

[26] As I suggested in Chapter Two, the normalisation of relations with the central state may involve reductions in economic opportunities, especially those in the informal sectors.

[27] The WHO's constitution defines health as 'a state of complete physical, mental and social wellbeing'. A recent collection focusing on peacemaking, peacekeeping and social reconstruction in Africa is entitled *Traditional Cures for Modern Conflicts: African Conflict 'Medicine'* (Zartman 2000).

reasons why aspects of biomedicine, Christianity and nationalism have become so important to African populations caught up in appalling social upheavals is precisely because they are modes of thinking which seem to make sense of violence, particularly violence associated with other introductions from indus-trialised countries' (Allen 1997: 108).

Alongside these heuristic advantages, however, Allen's approach has its weak-nesses, particularly for my present purposes: first, it does not provide a useful language for talking about the political and economic aspects of social recon-struction, which local people themselves see as central. Secondly, while it shows how local people draw on ancient 'cultural archives' (see James 1988) in under-standing and responding to contemporary problems, it restricts their relationship with the past to such unconscious traditions or to incorporated social memories expressed through bodily practices (Connerton 1989).

Without denying the importance of the unconscious and incorporated, it is also important to emphasise the role of conscious, explicit, knowledge of the past ('inscribed' rather than 'incorporated' memories, in Connerton's terms) in coming to terms with the present and trying to shape a more acceptable future. The people I spoke with had their own ideas of how they had got into their present state and what needed to be done to improve matters. As with other aspects of local life, discussed in Chapter Two, reconstruction involved a blending of, rather than a stark dichotomy between, the 'traditional' and the 'modern'. These local ideas involved both the creative use of 'traditional' forms of knowledge and the deployment of modernist discourses of language, history and culture. The same people who were involved in the performance of healing rituals also agitated for local-language teaching in schools and the writing of local history. All these activities had a political focus: they all involved redefining the relationship between the West Nilers and the central Ugandan state.

West Nilers, peacekeeping and the state

As earlier chapters have shown, the West Nilers developed a complicated relationship with the state, ever since their first contacts with emissaries of such forms of society. On the one hand, as I showed in Chapter Six, from an early stage traditional lineage heads largely avoided co-option as government chiefs and, among at least some groups of elders, such forms of collaboration with the state were heavily cursed from Belgian times onwards. This should perhaps be distinguished from the different kind of collaboration discussed in Chapters Three and Four, which involved working at a relatively low level (as a soldier, a prison officer, an informer, or whatever) for the most repressive organs of the colonial and postcolonial state. The expansion of this process through the colonial and postcolonial era might be seen as the 'Nubification' of the district as a whole.

This uneasy relationship between West Nilers and the nation they lived in was blown apart, from the latter's viewpoint by the events of the Amin period, and for the former by the effects of the exile that ensued. Allen characterises the results of this on traditional forms of social authority among the Madi as follows:

In the past, it would seem that the people responsible for divining why a serious problem had arisen were ritually important elders of the various patri-lineages. Healing appears to have occurred in much the same way as described by Middleton for the linguistically related Lugbara....

However, the elders' status had already been much weakened before the population had fled. The appointment of ritually insignificant men as government chiefs, the opportunities for younger men to find employment in southern Uganda, cash cropping and various other factors had conspired to erode their capacity to distribute resources among their relatives and arbitrate in disputes. The refugee experience further undermined their influence, as they were not even in a position to negotiate bride-wealth payments. The result was that, while they might be turned to for an explanation of the awful things that had happened, their responses did not usually carry much weight. The situation was compounded in the late 1980s by the fact that the kinds of men who had partly replaced the ritual elders as local patrons, such as government chiefs and other men earning salaries, were in an equally weak position. Like the elders they had manifestly failed to protect their clients and were now as impoverished as everyone else. For most people, social life ought to be regulated by 'big men' and by customs associated with patrilineages. But this was not the case. (Allen 1997: 117)

In contrast to Allen, I would emphasise the similarities, rather than the differences, between the roles of 'ritually important elders' and those of the ritually insignificant 'new men' of the state and the market, especially where relations between the people of the area and the central state are concerned. As Middleton himself explains, in the stateless society of traditional Lugbaraland, it was not only senior lineage heads (and in places rain-makers) who exercised forms of authority, but also *'ba rukuza*, translated by Middleton as 'men whose names are known' (e.g. Middleton 1958: 224; 1970b: 3). These were:

Men who are important because of their character, influence and usually their wealth; they attract dependants and are 'like the great trees in the forest' against which lesser trees lean for support. They may also curse combatants in the feud, act as sanctuary and as mediator. They may carry white staves as a mark of status. They are not attached to the lineage system and the status is not formally hereditary. Their distribution is more haphazard than that of rainmakers, but there are rarely more than one to a tribe. Some have a wide influence over several tribes. Today, much of their authority has been usurped by Government chiefs. (Middleton 1958: 224–5)

Elsewhere, he says that: "ba rukuza ("men whose names are known") ... were men of wealth and influence and had powers of persuasion, and thus rudimentary political authority. They could occasionally act as arbiters in inter-subtribe disputes. Both rainmakers and 'ba rukusa acted only when asked to do so by the participants in feud or warfare' (Middleton 1971b: 10). I suggest that the existence in traditional Lugbara society of this, apparently semi-meritocratic, status gave that society a degree of flexibility in responding to the incursions of the state. Government chiefs, if they ruled fairly and brought benefits to their clients, could be understood as a kind of *'ba rukuza*. Through this, the state could be understood as at least potentially a source of legitimate authority (though one naturally weakened by the curse on collaborators).

Thus the elders who were in a position to respond, to some extent at least, to the social consequences of exile, and to negotiate a new relationship with the Ugandan state which would allow the return of the West Nilers, included both traditional lineage heads and other prominent people, who were at the same time 'men whose names were known' in the district, and people with a wider status in postcolonial Ugandan society, either as state's men (such as military officers, local politicians and senior civil servants) or in other 'modern' roles, such as businessmen, academics or religious leaders.

Middleton's account of 'The resolution of conflict among the Lugbara of Uganda' mentions towards the beginning that the *'ba rukusa* 'sometimes stop fighting by their powers of persuasion' (Middleton 1966: 143) but omits them from the subsequent analysis, which is summarised in the following diagram:

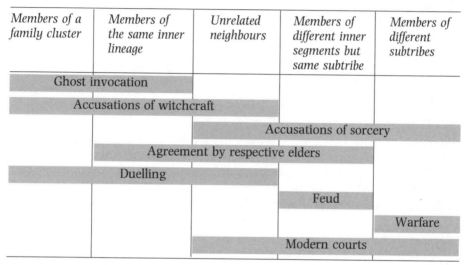

Figure 7.2 Lugbara Methods of Conflict Resolution
(from Middleton 1966: 152)

This is self-explanatory but, whatever its accuracy in relation to pre-contact life, it does not assist much in an analysis of the relationship between 'the Lugbara', or the West Nilers in general, and the Ugandan state, which is my present focus. This requires a historical approach. Once the history of attempts to make and maintain peace in West Nile since the mid-1980s is outlined, it becomes apparent that neither Allen's analysis of the decreased role of the elders nor the distinction he shares with Middleton between traditional lineage heads and 'big men' or *'ba rukuza* fully fit the circumstances.

Peace-keeping, reconstruction and historiography in the 1990s

The initial enthusiasm for the NRM in West Nile, following their negotiated entry into the district in March 1986 (described in Chapter Three), was, perhaps unsurprisingly, not maintained for long. Widespread resentments quickly grew up over the treatment of ex-soldiers and the general economic marginalisation of the district. The troops who were persuaded not to oppose the NRM/A believed they would be absorbed into the new Ugandan army, but many of those who initially were were subsequently sacked under a World Bank-sponsored retrenchment exercise. As the US analyst Gersony remarked: 'to the degree that educational qualification was a factor in de-selection, Muslims from northern Arua tended to be disproportionally retrenched.... Thus, a fair number of former soldiers were unemployed and disaffected' (Gersony 1997: 77). Similar reasons led to the compulsory retirement of hundreds of West Nile teachers. Another source of grievance was the behaviour of the increasingly obvious, and government-supported, SPLA troops in the district.

Despite this growing degree of disillusionment with the government, local attempts at peacemaking, peace-keeping and social reconstruction continued. As Gersony recounted:

> Some incipient low-intensity anti-government conflict began in the early 1990s in northwest Arua's 'Oraba finger', which juts into northeastern Zaïre and southwestern Sudan.... As these incidents began to gather momentum, and later when WNBF recruitment patterns were noticed, the elders of Arua, who had helped to keep the peace until that time, alerted the government to these occurrences but, apparently, received little government response. (Gersony 1997: 78)

Central to these attempts to preserve peace by reconstructing relationships with the central state were the production and dissemination of historical narratives: it was felt that other Ugandans misunderstood the history of West Nile and needed to be told the truth (as the elders saw it). As Lulua Odu tells it, in the Preface to his *Short History of the Lugbara (Madi)*:

> When President Yoweri Museveni visited Arua District in March 1993, he wanted to be briefed on the history of the Lugbara. Nobody volunteered to answer the request. The Chairman, District Resistance Council, Mr Donato Amabua, had to instruct Mr Nahor Oyaa to quickly form an adhoc committee, which included Doka Ali Kujo and myself.[28] Thus, thirty years after independence, the Lugbara still had no written history, not even Colonial History. (Lulua 1996: iii–iv)

As the security situation worsened, the elders redoubled their attempts to teach the government. An ad hoc Committee for Peace and Stability in Arua District (CPSAD) was formed to express the views of the West Nilers on the rebel situation in the district and to inform central government of local attitudes. Its membership, as we saw in Chapter One, consisted, not of traditionalist elders, but of former state's men: the CPSAD was chaired by Brigadier Gad Wilson Toko, the district's peacemaker with the Acholi regime of the Okellos, and its membership consisted of a retired senior civil servant, a local NRM politician, another retired military officer and one of Arua's leading businessmen. The Committee produced a working paper, quoted several times in this book, which was sent to the President's office, explaining how West Nile history had been seen 'upside down' since Amin's coup, and listing the scars of colonialism, as well as summarising local views of the rebels (and of the role of the SPLA) and a series of recommendations for improving local attitudes towards central government.

---

[28] Mr Oyaa is Coordinator of the Lugbara Literature Association (see below) and the Arua Council of Elders. He is a frequent translator into Lugbara at public and political occasions, such as visits from dignitaries from outside the district. Mr Doka Ali Kujo is a former District Education Officer and author of an unpublished history, 'The coming of Islam in Uganda, 1830–1843'.

The 1996 Report of the CPSAD demonstrates that the process of reconciliation between West Nilers and the state necessarily involves the (re-) writing of history. Indeed, the report begins with a three page 'historical background', emphasising the social distortions produced by colonial policies and attitudes. The next section, 'The problem stated', focuses on postcolonial Ugandan history, seeking to dissociate the West Nilers from the Amin regime, and blaming its worst excesses on 'citizens of Sudan and Zaïre ... who later became a source of tremendous insecurity in West Nile and Uganda as a whole'. The report goes on to claim that the West Nile:

> has continued to suffer untold hatred from the various tribes of Uganda who cannot bring themselves to accept that the atrocities committed during Idi Amin's regime were not really propped up by the people of West Nile as such, but rather by people of diverse origin and background who were believed to be from West Nile and yet their tribes ranged from Bantu and Nilotic tribes other than those in West Nile.

It goes on to outline the history of relations between the people of the area and the NRM, and the role of the SPLA in souring these relations. The origins of the West Nile Bank Front are analysed and its support assessed as minimal. In all, the greater part of the seventeen-page report is historical narrative.

Reconstruction and ritual

Alongside these efforts to explain local history and motivations to central government and to alert the NRM to local problems before they turned into support for armed opposition, another set of local attempts to come to terms with the legacy of the past were more inward-directed, towards the community itself and its immediate neighbours, rather than the state. Some of these initiatives involved the performance of traditional rituals, undertaken to heal the land and make peace with neighbouring people, as well as lifting the long-standing curse on participation in government.

From the first attempts to make peace in West Nile, ritual formed a vital component of the reconciliation and reconstruction process. As the 1996 Report of the Committee for Peace and Stability in Arua District reported:

> The West Nile Peace Initiative by the elders and soldiers of the region in January 1986, after the fall of the Tito [Okello] government was a positive move to limit damage that could have been caused had the people of West Nile resisted the entry of NRA forces into West Nile. The same initiative was also used to patch up our differences with the Acholi and Langi, but it only became possible for the elders of Arua and Acholi to meet and perform some traditional ceremonial pact of non-aggression towards each other.

The US analyst Robert Gersony somewhat underplays the ritual aspects, writing:

> In January 1986 ... General Okello dispatched representatives to Arua. On 29 January, according to eyewitnesses, they met with the elders of Arua and asked them to join them in a united armed northern resistance to the NRA. [The elders refused]....
> Nonetheless, it appears that both sides took the opportunity of this dialogue to reconcile their past differences (Amin's slaughter of Langi and Acholi military in 1971 and the UNLA's reprisals in the West Nile in 1980–81). They agreed to engage in no further conflicts with each other. Shortly after these meetings in Arua, a delegation of Arua

elders travelled to meet a similar Acholi delegation in Gulu District's Patiko Trading Center. In a traditional ceremony (which was reputedly interrupted by the imminent arrival of NRA forces) they celebrated a mutual non-aggression pact. (Gersony 1997: 75)

Another traditional healing ceremony occurred six years later, this time to lift the curse on working with the government. Once again, it was the elders who initiated and performed the ritual. As recounted in Chapter Six, from the time of the Belgian administration onwards, because of the blood they spilt, collaborators with government were cursed by the Lugbara elders. In 1996, I interviewed a local elder, the grandson of the government chief at the time of the Belgians, whose death at their hands precipitated the original curse. Mr Oyaa told me how the curse was lifted (the following interview is transcribed from tape):

> From that time [the period of Belgian rule] I think the issue of joining the administration and so on was alien completely. I think the elders even cursed whoever wanted to associate himself with the foreigners here. She will affect him. He will fail. He will get his fate. So there has always been suspicion between the people and a new administration and so on since that time. But I think sometime in 1992 I summoned the Council of Elders who were able to perform some rituals to put that one right. The elders came and they talked at length as to why they said these things and what problems they faced, who were killed by the foreigners and so on. And then they were able to forgive, and to forgive whoever wants to participate now in any government, because the foreigners have already left. So their kingdom as a matter of fact has not been handed over to them. It should be possible to participate now in all political, social, economic activities of all governments. It is post-independence governments now, because of the ritual. I think we did perform it around 1992. It was my own idea, but we had got a lot from them out of it. It also prompted some unity, and people have been doing well, until recently. I think politically now there has started to be a little confusion out here. But otherwise, traditionally, people now know they are the same people.... I remember, I think it was the 8th of August 1992 that I summoned all the elders.

I asked 'and that was to clear all the business of the past, both the colonial period and the postcolonial?'

> To forgive and then so it is possible for any of us now, or in future generations, to participate in this, without any suspicion of being biased, or we are getting problems here because our fathers did this, this and that. I said no. I said, now let us close that chapter. It was because of the problems at that time, but the situation has now changed. Now there is a need to think again and to perform some rituals and to cleanse it.

'And that worked well?' I asked:

> Yes, I think so because now, in any forum we can talk freely now, we used to say you work hard, you participate and so on but you get nowhere because of this curse and so on. There should be no question now of saying 'we are cursed' and so on. Because many people were taking it for granted. So, you work; if you don't work you fail. So there is no particular curse here any more.[29]

I was not given all the details of the ritual, but I was told that it involved reciting the names of all those killed in the district, to lift the curse of their spilt blood from the land. Senior representatives of many clans attended. I was told that the

[29] Interview, Mr Nahor Oyaa, 6 February 1996. Transcribed from tape.

rituals carried out were based on certain death rituals. It seems likely that they were those carried out in cases of deaths that are *onzi*, translated by Middleton as 'wrong', 'evil' or 'dangerous'. According to Middleton 'Essentially a bad death takes place when the psychical elements of the person do not disperse properly and at the same time, or they do so at a wrong time or in a wrong place' (Middleton 1982: 143). These kinds of death, Middleton says, are followed by rites of purification (which he does not describe in detail) known as *rua eduza* ('to cleanse the body') and *angu edezu* ('to cleanse the territory') (ibid.: 145).

Culture and tradition

At the same time as these traditional rites were being carried out, and involving many of the same people, there was a sustained campaign by local elders to reinvigorate local tradition through quintessentially modern means: campaigning for local-language teaching in schools, holding traditional dances at non-traditional public occasions and writing local histories. These activities involved a different group of individuals from the CPSAD, local elders (including some who were involved in the peacemaking rituals described above) rather than retired state's men, and they grouped themselves, not into a committee, but in a cultural association. In November 1994, the Lugbara Literature Association (LULA) was formed by this group of Arua-based West Nile elders (Figure 7.3). As I have noted previously, unusually for a tribally based cultural association, they take the position that 'the Lugbara' as a tribe are a colonial invention and see themselves as having traditionally been part of the Madi people. According to the Preamble to LULA's Constitution:

> since the coming of independence, the Lugbara language and culture have been on the decline and in gradual erosion due to neglect and the impact of foreign cultural and political manipulations, which are injurious to our African heritage ... the Lugbara oral and written literature is fast disappearing from the scene before being recorded and/or preserved for our posterity.... Determined to reverse and remedy this lamentable situation and to prevent the Lugbara from drifting towards a socio-cultural extinction, now therefore we the members of the LUGBARA LITERATURE ASSOCIATION have resolved to form an Association in the name of our people, ourselves and our generations yet unborn...

The central aims and objects of LULA are 'to carry out research and to promote the production of books and other reading materials in Lugbara with a view to facilitating the language in Primary, Secondary and Tertiary institutions'.

This is to be achieved by a range of activities, including:

(a) Promoting the standardisation of orthography.
(b) Carrying out research into current problems as well as into dialects and forms of the language which, while possibly not in common use, are nevertheless inseparable from the literary traditions of the language.
(c) Securing as far as possible, uniformity in the use of existing and new words by the exercise of control over the publication of school books.
(d) Securing a high standard of grammar through the publication of standard books on the subject.
(e) Giving encouragement and assistance to authors and translators in Lugbara.

Figure 7.3 From *A Short History of the Lugbara (Madi)*, by Lulua Odu (published by the Lugbara Literature Association)

The emphasis on standardisation is important: LULA is well aware that the diversity of mutually incomprehensible forms of the Lugbara language (mentioned in Chapter One) is one of their main problems. The language they seek to have taught is an artificial, simplified version based on the dialect spoken around Arua town. But the association is concerned with more than purely linguistic cultural activities. Its wider aims include such aspects as:

(k) Promoting the study, practice and knowledge of instrumental and vocal music in Lugbara and to give or arrange concerts and musical entertainments.

LULA also published Lulua's *Short History* (Lulua 1996), widely cited throughout this book, as well as a series of four basic primary school textbooks in Lugbara (which I used in my attempts to learn the language) (Figures 7.4 and 5). Following the fall of Mobuto in 1997, the elders of LULA were able to visit Lugbara elders on the Congo side of the border, and these latter have been encouraged to form their own cultural association.

Writing of the Holy Spirit Movement of Alice Lakwena, the predecessors of the Lords Resistance Army rebels of Gulu and Kitgum in the 1990s, Heike Behrend suggests that:

The HSM documented itself and produced its own texts in answer to the mass media. Composing these writings was an act of self-assertion, an attempt to have their truth, their version of the story prevail against others. In a certain sense it was also a magical act with which they fixed a reality that became more real through the very act of writing. (Behrend 1999: 4)

Behrend associates this 'magical' effect with the performative effects of language in traditional Acholi society:

One should recall that in Acholi, from the local viewpoint, speaking words is the equivalent of an action. Just as the words of an elder or an ajwaka [spirit medium] in the form of a curse or blessing, would sooner or later have an effect... the writing of sayings and proverbs must also be interpreted as a kind of act. For like the power of speech, the power to write also affected the world. It is possible that the Holy Spirit soldiers imagined that the effect of writing was even greater than that of speaking words. (Ibid.: 159)

There may be something in this analysis, but I do not see the need to evoke 'magic' to explain the effects of writing on reality. As this book as a whole has argued, discourse and reality (or, to put it another way, knowledge and power) are intimately linked. In Arua, the local elders and officers of LULA are well aware of this. As one of them explained to me, shortly before I left the district after my final fieldwork period, writing can change the world. 'Who knows where it will end, if we can write our own history,' he said. 'After all, the French revolution happened because of writers like Voltaire and Rousseau.'[30]

History, healing and narrative

In the second half of this chapter, I have discussed social reconstruction in the late 1990s both in terms of the renegotiation of relationships between the West Nilers and the Ugandan state and in terms of healing (in Allen's metaphor) the internal social wounds of local society. In both cases, I have focused on the role of historical narratives in reconstruction – whether these are reports explaining local interpretations of Ugandan history to the central government, or the ritual listing of the historical dead, in the attempt to lay their ghosts and lift the curse

[30] Interview with member of LULA (anonymity preserved), 28 June 1998.

Figure 7.4 Lugbara language textbooks produced by the Lugbara Literature Association

on cooperating with the state. While this focus on history in the present is unusual in the literature, I have argued that it fits with local conceptions, understandings and preoccupations concerning reconstruction.

It could very reasonably be argued that I have overemphasised the role of a small (albeit influential) number of elder males, who are bound to have their own agendas of social stability, the containment of youth and the maintenance of control over women. All this is true. However, as I have suggested, both traditional lineage heads and 'men whose names are known' (*'ba rukuza*) do have a traditional role in peacemaking and the maintenance (or reconstruction) of social structures. Both Allen and Middleton concede this, while seeking to downplay the latter in favour of an emphasis on the ritual role of the former. In discussing history and reconstruction in Arua in the 1990s, I have attempted to explain the roles of both groups of male elders. To focus, as I have done in this chapter, on the actions and attitudes of the elders in peacemaking and reconstruction is to recognise the continuing local importance of these people, both those who are 'ritually important' and the 'men whose names are known'.

But this is not to suggest that there are no other narratives of history and social reconstruction in the area. One which is obviously important, and which can be seen in part as a response to the peacemaking of the elders, is the view of the state. Over the late 1990s this fluctuated with the course of the rebel war and of the electoral fortunes of the NRM in the district. Broadly speaking, between the

Figure 7.5 Lugbara language textbooks produced by the Lugbara Literature Association

failure of Museveni to win the West Nile districts in the presidential elections of 1995 and the victory of 'pro-Movement' candidates in the LC elections of 1998 (following the virtual destruction of the rebel forces the previous year), relations with the central government improved steadily, an improvement symbolised by the presidential visit in June 1998 (mentioned in Chapter One). But the key practical issues for local people, from the construction of a tarmac road joining the district to the rest of the country to local-language teaching in schools, remained to be addressed when I left Arua in July 1998, as indeed did the more intangible and intractable problem of the hostile attitude of most southern Ugandans to the West Nilers.

The attitudes of the international (and some national) assistance and development agencies to reconstruction were also important. By 1998, most refugees having repatriated, the refugee agencies were much less visible in the district than they had been in previous years. They had been replaced, however, not by development NGOs but by agencies operating over the border into SPLA-held 'New Sudan'. In Arua district itself, 'development' remained noticeable by its absence. An important exception was an organisation which itself demonstrates the unreliability of the conventional categorisations of 'governmental' and 'non-governmental', 'local' and 'international'. This was the Community Action Programme (CAP): theoretically a 'local NGO', it in fact operated largely through the state structures of the LCs while being funded and (to a considerable extent) managed by the Dutch government agency SNV (which also had a separate programme in the district). CAP funded a variety of local-level development initiatives, from literacy groups to rural income-generating projects (and, indeed, the publishing programme of LULA). In 1997, a spin-off agency was created named the Women's Empowerment Programme (WEP), which focused on literacy classes for women. Both CAP and WEP were closely associated with the state (indeed, in 1998 WEP banners were carried in parades supporting the pro-NRM candidate for the fiercely contested women's seat on the LC5 District Council). For most people in Arua, however, the agenda of development, to which virtually all are committed, though they define it in different ways, depends crucially on the kind of infrastructure projects (roads, telecommunications links, power supplies) that are usually outside the remit of NGOs. The latter are widely seen as merely scratching the surface of Arua's economic problems.

In concluding, I return to the contested notion of 'social reconstruction', a concept which raises the question of just what is being reconstructed. In one sense, the answer is simple; it is the relationship between local people and the state (or, one might say, with the southern Ugandans) that existed before Amin and Obote II ruptured it. For many people in Arua this is seen as being intimately linked with the possibilities of economic development. However, as I have shown, the troubled relationship between the traditionally stateless West Nilers and the central authorities long predates the postcolonial era. In lifting the old curse on collaboration with the government, cleansing the area of the effects of both colonial and postcolonial killings and attempting to rewrite their role in the history of Uganda, the elders are in fact trying to construct something new, rather than restoring a past condition. In this sense, 'reconstruction' is a misnomer. For my present purposes, however, the 're-' serves the function of emphasising the crucial role of understandings of the past in constructing a better future for the people of Arua.

8
Violence, History & Representation
An afterword

The last chapter ended where this book as a whole began; with the situation of the West Nilers in Arua town during my fieldwork in the late 1990s. In the interim, I have attempted to trace back the course of the Vicovian spiral that led to the state of affairs I found there. I have examined the relationship between the very real violence that has characterised the region's history, and the symbolic and imaginary 'histories' which have projected on to the victims themselves the violence to which the West Nilers have repeatedly been subject. In this way, each change of rulers and each new regime of violence brought with it a new wave of outsiders who already 'knew' that the people of West Nile were inherently violent and dangerous and dealt with them accordingly. Throughout the book, I have stressed the role of narrative representations in creating, rather than simply reflecting, realities, the most detailed example being the account in Chapter Five of the falsification of the Yakan uprising.

Chapter Seven showed the elders of Arua attempting to respond to the situation in the district by deploying a variety of forms of historical representation, from the conventional historical account in a report to President Museveni to the performance of 'traditional' healing ceremonies designed to lay the ghosts of past enmities. In a similar way, I have used several different kinds of narrative forms and sources. As the various layers of the West Nile past have been unearthed, the different chapters have used different kinds of sources and narrative techniques to describe what I found there. The picture of contemporary Arua at the beginning and end of the book was based on my fieldwork, and uses such conventional tropes of ethnographic writing as the 'reflexive' auto-biographical account and the transcription of life histories, genealogies and the like. Chapter Three, on the West Nilers in post-independence Uganda, deployed a mixture of oral, archival and secondary material, including the analysis of academic discourses on Amin. Chapters Four and Five, on the colonial era, were largely based on archival historical material, and used conventional historical techniques to assess the reliability and implications of such material. In such terms, the conventional historical record is shown to have been falsified. Chapter Six focused on a range of secondary sources, some (such as the ivory poachers' memoirs) of doubtful reliability, but these too have added much to the discourse of West Nile violence and marginality. Here, the historical accuracy is less important than the historical impact of such texts. Chapter Seven brought

161

together all these various sources and methods to examine the role of violence and that of historical narratives in traditional West Nile society, before going on to show how such forms of historical representation, together with more conventionally 'modern' historical narratives, were being used in the 1990s by some of the West Nilers to respond to contemporary violence and to explore and improve the area's relationship with the central state. A central part of this was the attempt to depict themselves as the witnesses and victims of violence (as they certainly were), rather than as its performers or perpetrators (which some of them also were).

This patchwork quilt (or, to use a less tidy but more pretentious metaphor, this *bricolage*) of evidence reflects the untidiness both of the situation I found in Arua in the late 1990s and of the relationship between discourse and reality I found in the district's past. It might be argued that it also reflects the inevitable inadequacies of the fieldwork I was able to undertake. While, in dark moments, I can see the strength of this argument, I would argue that a more conventional ethnographic approach (if, in other words, I had been able to stay with a local family, to learn the language properly, to conduct rural as well as urban fieldwork, etc., etc.) might well not have improved this book or changed its approach and conclusions as much as conventional anthropological or Africanist understandings might suggest (though it would certainly have raised a different set of questions).

In the first place, such techniques are just not possible in some circumstances, such as those of Arua in the last years of the twentieth century. Nor are they necessarily even appropriate for places that have had such a disturbed and violent history. My account of the linguistic complexity of the town and its people, together with the obvious 'unreliability' (in a conventional sense) of much of the oral historical material I gathered (including some I have used here), raises serious doubts about the possibility of displaying some final 'truth' about the 'traditional' culture and society of the region by revealing an 'authentic' African voice. Nor am I at all convinced that this should be the aim of the anthropologist.

Indeed, perhaps this is not just a peculiarity of 'ethnography in unstable places ... in contexts of dramatic political change' (to quote the title of Greenhouse et al.'s 2002 edited collection), or even of anthropology. Oral historians of Africa have also recently begun to question the traditional pieties of the field. As Cohen, Miescher and White argue, in their introduction to Luise White et al. (2001):

> what has been called historical memory is valuable precisely because it is not necessarily an accurate memory – that is, it is not the historical veracity of a statement or memory that gives that statement or memory constitutive power. The thing that happened, and the ideas transmitted by its distorted reporting, silencing, or even and most especially invention, reveal a space of colonial and postcolonial conflict. (Ibid.: 15–16)

This is precisely the approach that seems to fit the complex history and discourse of West Nile, and is the one I have taken in this book.

Much contemporary writing on the anthropology and history of violence (e.g., LaCapra 2001; Stewart and Strathern 2002; Douglass and Vogler 2003), has been concerned to distinguish between victim, witness and performer, and to individualise guilt and responsibility. This echoes the international legal framework that has grown up since the Nazi Holocaust, and also reflects the centrality of that quintessentially European experience in how Europeans and Americans understand and deal with violence in the post-Second World War era. In Africa, the Truth and Reconciliation Commission in South Africa and the different courts (international for the leaders, national for the minor perpetrators) for the Rwanda genocide both reflect this European, individualist tradition, and were, indeed modelled on the Nuremberg trials of Nazi war criminals. Sometimes (as in one of the most widely cited contemporary edited series on violence: Kleinman et al. 1997; Das et al. 2000, 2001) this model is combined with an equally individual-istic pseudo-Freudian (or perhaps semi-Catholic) notion of social reconstruction and rehabilitation through individual confession and admission of guilt, so that rebuilding society depends on bringing the social unconscious up to the surface, so to speak. Neither of these approaches seems to me to fit the complex historical background or present circumstances of West Nile. Unlike South Africa or Rwanda, the violence here is not based on long-standing 'ethnic hatreds' between groups defined ultimately on physical or pseudo-biological grounds, and the culpability of individuals is not an issue in present-day Uganda (not is it at all clear that matters would be improved if it were).

Another contemporary focus in political anthropology, especially since Wilson and Donnan (1998), has been on the importance of borders and frontiers in creating political cultures around them. This is certainly important in under-standing West Nile, which, as I have shown, is a border area in several different senses of the term. The different state powers that at various times have controlled the district have all had their concerns about threats from 'over the border', such as the Muslim threat from the Sudanese soldiers which determined so much of British policy in the colonial era. But the importance of state borders can be exaggerated; the Uganda–Zaïre border, for example, remained undemarcated along its length until the late 1950s when, in the run-up to independence, the colonial authorities decided to mark the boundary. A young British colonial officer was given the task, and was told (the border being defined as the Nile–Congo watershed) to mark where the streams ran west as the Congo side, and where they ran east as the Uganda side. He asked what to do where there were no streams and was told to urinate on the ground and see which way the liquid went.[1] This presents a splendid metaphor for the impact of colonial rule and of colonial borders on postcolonial Africa but, as I have argued, the problems of West Nile and its characteristic image of violence and marginality went back well beyond the period of British rule.

In order to question this image, I have found it necessary to reverse the normal chronological approach to writing history, beginning with the present, rather than a point in the past chosen to demonstrate the source of the problem. This has produced problems both for the writer and for readers, but it has served the purpose of avoiding the assumptions behind conventional readings of West Nile history, and of questioning the relationship between acts and discourses and that between past and present. In doing this, I have presented a case-study of how violence and knowledge, past and present, local and global forces all interacted to produce the situation I found in Arua in the last years of the twentieth century.

[1] I interviewed this gentleman in 2001. Anonymity is preserved.

Bibliography

This book cites written material from a variety of sources. Here I list archival and published sources. 'Grey' material, such as agency reports and student theses, are cited, as appropriate, under the archive in which they were consulted and/or under 'published works'.

Archival Sources

i. Uganda National Archives (UNA)

A46 Secretariat Minute Papers (SMP) 1910–1929 Second Series.
OS (open shelf) files.
Uganda Protectorate Annual Reports.
Unclassified Files (awaiting reclassification)
ADMI/4/M Madi Annual reports 1954–1960.
ADM/21/Mpt.II Madi District Council Minutes.
LAN/4 Boundaries – Interterritorial.
Northern Province Monthly Reports.

ii. UK Public Record Office (PRO)

FO 2/215   Corresp. with Belgian Authorities 1899.
FO 403   Further corresp. respecting French and British negotiations with the Congo state, January–June 1894.
FO 407   Further corresp. concerning the affairs of Egypt and Soudan. 1910.
WO 32/8417   Uganda Mutiny papers 1897–1899.
WO 33/316   Military report on the Congo Free State 1904.
WO 106/249   Precis of corresp. relating to Uganda/Congo boundary.
WO 106/253   Uganda Protectorate – General.

iii. Rhodes House Library, University of Oxford

RH mss Afr.s.586   Annual Report on West Nile District Uganda, 1914–15.
RH mss Afr.s.1220   J. Middleton, Report for Colonial Office 1949.
RH mss Afr.s.1350   Notes on the early history of West Nile.

RH mss Afr.s.1638   Diaries of A.E. Weatherhead 1905–1936.
Sudan Intelligence Reports (SIR).

iv. Refugee Studies Centre, University of Oxford

RSC LU-46   Reports of EEC Fact Finding Mission to Uganda 1986.
RSC LU-65.I.OLO   Community Action Programme (CAP) *Arua District, a Profile.*
                  1993.
RSC Conf.Alt 1984 Conference report: Assistance to refugees, alternative viewpoints.

v. Makerere University Library

Undergraduate dissertations, Dept. of History:
Baba, J.B.   The coming of the Kakwa and the development of their institutions, 1971.
Geria, S.A. A traditional history of the Northwestern Lugbara of Uganda, 1973.
Loro, M.   Pre-colonial history of the Kakwa of Northern Uganda, 1971.

Published works

Ahluwalia, D.P.S. 1995. *Plantations and the Politics of Sugar in Uganda.* Kampala, Fountain
   Press.
Allen, T. 1989a. 'Violence and moral knowledge: observing social trauma in Sudan and
   Uganda', *Cambridge Anthropology* 13 (2): 45–66.
Allen, T. 1989b. 'Closed minds, open systems: affliction and healing in West Nile, Uganda'.
   Paper presented to the Fifth Satterthwaite Colloquium.
Allen, T. 1991a. 'Understanding Alice: Uganda's Holy Spirit Movement in context', *Africa*
   61 (3): 371–99.
Allen, T. 1991b. 'The quest for therapy in Moyo district', in H.B. Hansen and M. Twaddle
   (eds), *Changing Uganda*, London: James Currey.
Allen, T. 1991c. 'Histories and contexts: using pasts in the present on the Sudan/Uganda
   border.' *Bulletin of the John Rylands University Library of Manchester* 73 (3): 63–91.
Allen, T. 1992. 'Upheaval, affliction and health: a Ugandan case study', in H. Bernstein, B.
   Crow and H. Johnson (eds), *Rural Livelihoods: Crises and Responses.* Oxford: Oxford
   University Press.
Allen, T. 1993. *Social and Economic Aspects of the Mass 'Voluntary' Return of Refugees from
   Sudan to Uganda between 1986 and 1992.* Report for UNRISD. Milton Keynes: Open
   University Group for Development Policy and Practice.
Allen, T. 1994. 'Ethnicity and tribalism on the Sudan–Uganda border', in K. Fukui and J.
   Markakis (eds), *Ethnicity and Conflict in the Horn of Africa.* London: James Currey.
Allen, T. 1996a. 'Making the Madi: the invention of a Ugandan tribe'. Unpublished paper.
Allen, T. 1996b. 'A flight from refuge: the return of refugees from Southern Sudan to
   Northwest Uganda in the late 1980s', in T Allen (ed.), *In Search of Cool Ground: War,
   Flight and Homecoming in Northeast Africa.* Oxford: UNRISD/James Currey.
Allen, T. 1997. 'The violence of healing', *Sociologus*, 47 (2): 101–28.
Allen, T. 1998. 'From "informal sectors" to "real economies", changing conceptions of
   Africa's hidden livelihoods', *Contemporary Politics* 4 (4): 357–73.
Amaza, O.o. 1998. *Museveni's Long March from Guerilla to Dtatesman.* Kampala: Fountain
   Publishers.

Amis, M. 1991. *Time's Arrow or the Nature of the Offence*. London: Jonathan Cape.

Amselle, J.-L. 1998 [1990]. *Mestizo Logics: Anthropology of Identity in Africa and Elsewhere*. Stanford, California: Stanford University Press.

Anderson, D.M. and R. Rathbone (eds) 2000. *Africa's Urban Past*. Oxford: James Currey.

Austin, J.L. 1970 [1961]. *Philosophical Papers*, ed. J.O. Urmson and G.J. Warnock. Oxford: Oxford University Press.

Baba, J.B. 1971. 'Adiyo: the coming of the Kakwa and the development of their institutions'. Undergraduate dissertation, Makerere University, Kampala.

Ballard, J.G. 2001. *Complete Short Stories*. London: Flamingo.

Barnes-Dean, V.L. 1986. 'Lugbara illness beliefs and social change', *Africa* 56 (3): 334–51.

Baxter, P.T.W. and A. Butt. 1953. *The Azande, and related peoples of the Anglo-Egyptian Sudan and Belgian Congo*. London, International African Institute.

Bayart, J.-F. 1993. *The State in Africa: the Politics of the Belly*. London: Longman.

Beachey, R.W. 1967. 'The East African ivory trade in the nineteenth century', *Journal of African History* 8 (2) 269–90.

Behrend, H. 1999. *Alice Lakwena and the Holy Spirits: War in Northern Uganda, 1986–97*. Oxford: James Currey.

Bell, W.D.M. 1923. *The Wanderings of an Elephant Hunter*. London: Country Life.

Bell, W.D.M. 1960. *Bell of Africa*. London, Neville Spearman and the Holland Press.

Bender, L.M. 2000. 'Nilo-Saharan', in B. Heine and D. Nurse (eds), *African Languages: An Introduction*. Cambridge: Cambridge University Press.

Berger, I. 1995. 'Fertility as power: spirit mediums, priestesses and the precolonial state in Interlacustrine East Africa', in D.M. Anderson and D.H. Johnson (eds), *Revealing Prophets: Prophecy in Eastern African History*. London: James Currey.

Boyes, John. 1928. *The Company of Adventurers*. London: East Africa Limited.

Brantlinger, P. 1985. 'Victorians and Africans: the genealogy of the myth of the dark continent', *Critical Inquiry* 12: 166–203.

Brett, E.A. 1975. 'The political economy of General Amin', *IDS Bulletin* 17 (1): 15–22.

Callaway, H. 1987. *Gender, Culture and Empire: European Women in Colonial Nigeria*. London: Macmillan Press.

Clastres, P. 1987 [1974]. *Society Against the State*. New York: Zone Books.

Clastres P. 1994 [1980]. *Archaeology of Violence*. New York: Semiotext(e).

Collingwood, R.G. 1970 [1939]. *An Autobiography*. Oxford: Oxford University Press.

Collingwood, R.G. 1993 [1946]. *The Idea of History*. Oxford: Oxford University Press.

Collins, R.O. 1958. 'Anglo-Congolese negotiations 1900–1906', *Zaïre* 12 (5–6): 479–512, 619–54.

Collins, R.O. 1960. 'Ivory poaching in the Lado Enclave', *Uganda Journal* 24 (2): 217–28.

Collins, R.O. 1962a. 'Sudan–Uganda boundary rectification and the Sudanese Occupation of Madial, 1914', *Uganda Journal* 26 (2) 140–53.

Collins, R.O. 1962b. *The Southern Sudan, 1883–1898: a Struggle for Control*. New Haven and London: Yale University Press.

Collins, R.O. 1968. *King Leopold, England and the Upper Nile, 1899–1909*. New Haven and London, Yale University Press.

Collins, R.O. 1971. *Land Beyond the Rivers: the Southern Sudan 1898–1918*. New Haven and London: Yale University Press.

Collins, R.O. 1983. *Shadows in the Grass: Britain in the Southern Sudan, 1918–1956*. New Haven and London: Yale University Press.

Comaroff, J. and J. Comaroff. 1991. *Of Revelation and Revolution*. Chicago: University of Chicago Press.

Community Action Programme (CAP) 1993. *Arua District, a Profile*. Arua: Community

Action Programme.

Connerton, P. 1989. *How Societies Remember*. Cambridge: Cambridge University Press.

Cookey, S.J.S. 1968. *Britain and the Congo Question 1885–1913* London: Longmans Green and Co.

Crazzolara, J.P. 1950–54. *The Lwoo* (3 vols. Part 1, *Lwoo Migrations*; Part 2, *Lwoo traditions*; Part 3, *Clans*). Verona: Istituto Missioni Africane.

Crazzolara, J.P. 1960. *A Study of the Logbara (Ma'di) Language: Grammar and Vocabulary*. London, New York, Toronto: Oxford University Press for International African Institute.

Crisp, J. 1986. 'Ugandan refugees in Sudan and Zaire: the problem of repatriation', *African Affairs* 85: 163–80.

Cunnison, I.G. 1951. *History on the Luapula. Rhodes Livingstone Papers 21*. Cape Town, London, New York: Oxford University Press.

Dalfovo, A.T. 1988. *A Bibliography of Lugbara Studies and Literature*. Kampala: Makerere University.

Das, V., A. Kleinman, M. Ramphele, and P. Reynolds (eds) 2000. *Violence and subjectivity*. Berkeley and London: California University Press.

Das, V., A. Kleinman, M. Lock, M. Ramphele, M. and P. Reynolds (eds.) 2001. *Remaking a World: Violence, Social Suffering and Recovery*. Berkeley and London: California University Press.

Davis, J. 1992b. *Exchange*. Buckingham: Open University Press.

De Waal, A. 1989. *Famine that Kills: Darfur, Sudan, 1984–1985*. Oxford: Clarendon Press.

Douglass, A. and T.A. Vogler, (eds) 2003. *Witness and Memory; the Discourses of Trauma*. New York and London: Routledge.

Dresch, P. 1989. *Tribes, Government and History in Yemen*. Oxford: Oxford University Press.

Dresch, P. 2000. 'Wilderness of mirrors: truth and vulnerability in Middle Eastern fieldwork', in P. Dresch, W. James and D. Parkin (eds), *Anthropologists in a Wider World*. Oxford: Berghahn.

Driberg, J.H. 1931. 'Yakañ', *JRAI* 61: 413–20.

Driberg, T. 1978. *Ruling Passions: the Autobiography of Tom Driberg*. London: Quartet Books.

Dumont, L. 1970. *Homo hierarchicus*. Chicago and London: University of Chicago Press.

Ehret, C. 1998. *An African Classical Age: Eastern and Southern Africa in World History, 1000 BC to AD 400*. Charlottesville: University of Virginia Press.

Eliade, M. 1955. *The Myth of the Eternal Return*. London: Routledge & Kegan Paul.

Evans-Pritchard, E.E. 1940. *The Nuer; a Description of the Modes of Livelihood and Political Institutions of a Nilotic People*. Oxford: Clarendon Press.

Evans-Pritchard, E.E. 1947. 'Obituary: Jack Herbert Driberg 1888–1946', *Man* 47 (2–4): 11–13.

Evans-Pritchard, E.E. 1962. *Essays in Social Anthropology*. London: Faber & Faber.

Evans-Pritchard, E.E. 1990 [1951]. *Kinship and Marriage Among the Nuer*. Oxford, Clarendon Press

Fardon, R. (ed) 1990. *Localizing Strategies: Regional Traditions of Ethnographic Writing*. Edinburgh. Edinburgh University Press.

Fenton, W.N. 1962. 'Ethnohistory and its problems', *Ethnohistory* 9 (1): 1–23.

Ferguson, J. 1999. *Expectations of Modernity: Myths and Meanings of Urban Life on the Zambian Copperbelt*, Berkeley, University of California Press.

Ferguson, R.B. and N.L. Whitehead (eds) 2000 [1992]. *War in the Tribal Zone: Expanding States and Indigenous Warfare*. Santa Fe: School of American Research Press, Oxford: James Currey.

Fetterman, M.H. 1994. 'The British are red!: Jack Driberg and the Didinga 1922–1926',

Unpublished conference paper (Brown University).

Fitzgerald, P. and M. Leopold 1987. *Stranger on the Line: the Secret History of Phone Tapping*. London: Bodley Head.

Fukui, K. and J. Markakis (eds) 1994. *Ethnicity and Conflict in the Horn of Africa*. London: James Currey.

Furley, O.W. 1959. 'The Sudanese troops in Uganda', *African Affairs* 58 (233): 311–28.

Geria, S.A. 1973. 'A traditional history of the Northwestern Lugbara of Uganda', Undergraduate dissertation, Dept. of History, Makerere University, Kampala.

Gersony, R. 1997. *The anguish of Northern Uganda: Results of a Field-based assessment of the civil conflicts in Northern Uganda*. Report submitted to US Embassy, Kampala and USAID Mission, Kampala, April.

Gingyera-Pinycwa, A.G. 1978. *Apolo Milton Obote and His Times*. New York, London and Lagos: NOK Publishers.

Gingyera-Pinycwa, A.G. 1989. 'Is there a Northern question?' in K. Rupesinge (ed.), *Conflict resolution in Uganda*. Oslo: International Peace Research Institute; London: James Currey, Athens: Ohio University Press.

Gingyera-Pinycwa, A.G. 1991. 'Towards Constitutional Renovation; Some Political Considerations' in H.B. Hansen & M. Twaddle (eds), *Changing Uganda*, London: James Currey.

Gingyera-Pinycwa, A.G. 1992. *Northern Uganda in National Politics*. Kampala: Fountain Publishers.

Government of Uganda 1995. *Constitution of the Republic of Uganda*. Kampala: Government of Uganda.

Grahame, I. 1980. *Amin and Uganda: a Personal Memoir*: London, Granada Publishing.

Green, R.H. 1981. *Magendo in the Political Economy of Uganda: Pathology, Parallel System or Dominant Sub-mode of Production?* Discussion Paper 164. Brighton: Institute of Development Studies, University of Sussex.

Greenhouse, C. 2002. 'Introduction: altered states; altered lives', in C. Greenhouse, M. Mertz and K.B. Warren (eds), *Ethnography in Unsuitable Places: Everyday Lives in Circumstances of Dramatic Political Change*. Durham and London: Duke University Press.

Greenhouse, C., M. Mertz, and K.B. Warren (eds) 2002. *Ethnography in Unstable Places: Everyday Lves in Circumstances of Dramatic Political Change*. Durham and London: Duke University Press.

Griffith, J.W. 1995. *Joseph Conrad and the Anthropological Dilemma: Bewildered Traveller*. Oxford: Clarendon Press.

Hailey, Ld. 1950. *Native Administration in the British African Territories: Part 1. East Africa: Uganda, Kenya, Tanganyika.*. London: Colonial Office, HMSO.

Hall, R. 1980. *Lovers on the Nile*. London, Collins.

Hamilton, C. 1998. *Terrific Majesty: the Powers of Shaka Zulu and the Limits of Historical Imagination*. Cambridge Massachusetts: Harvard University Press.

Hansen, H.B. 1991. 'Pre-colonial immigrants and colonial servants. The Nubians in Uganda revisited', *African Affairs* 90 (2) 559–80.

Hansen, H.B. 1995. 'The colonial control of spirit cults in Uganda.' in D.M. Anderson and D.H. Johnson (eds), *Revealing Prophets: Prophecy in Eastern African History*. London: James Currey.

Hansen, H.B. and M. Twaddle (eds) 1988. *Uganda Now*. London: James Currey.

Hansen, H.B. and M. Twaddle (eds) 1991. *Changing Uganda*. London: James Currey.

Hansen, H.B. and M. Twaddle (eds) 1995. *From Chaos to Order: the Politics of Constitution-making in Uganda*. London: James Currey.

Hansen, H.B. and M. Twaddle (eds) 1998. *Developing Uganda*. Oxford: James Currey.

Harrell-Bond, B.E. 1986. *Imposing Aid, Emergency Assistance to Refugees.* Oxford: Oxford University Press.

Hastrup, K. 1992. 'Writing ethnography: state of the art.' In J. Okely and H. Callaway (eds), *Anthropology and Autobiography.* ASA Monographs 29. London and New York: Routledge.

Hobbes, T. 1957. *Leviathan* (ed. R. Oakeshott). Oxford: Basil Blackwell.

Hochschild, A. 1999. *King Leopold's Ghost: a Story of Greed, Terror and Heroism in Central Africa.* London: Macmillan.

Huntingford, G.W.B. 1953. *The Northern Nilo-Hamites.* London: International African Institute.

Ichile, L.L. n.d. [1995] *Ichile's First Lugbara-English Dictionary.* Self-published in St Joseph, Minnesota.

James, W. 1988. *The Listening Ebony: Moral Knowledge, Religion and Power Among the Uduk of Sudan.* Oxford: Clarendon Press.

James, W. 2000. 'Beyond the first encounter: transformations of "the field" in North East Africa', in P. Dresch, W. James and D. Parkin (eds), *Anthropologists in a Wider World.* Oxford: Berghahn.

Jamison, M. 1992. *Amin and Uganda: an Annotated Bibliography.* Westport, Connecticut and London: Greenwood Press.

Johnson, D.H. 1981. 'The fighting Nuer: primary sources and the origins of a stereotype', *Africa* 51 (1): 508–27.

Johnson, D.H. 1985. 'C.A. Willis and the "Cult of Deng": a falsification of the ethnographic record', *History in Africa* 12: 131–50.

Johnson, D.H. 1988. 'Sudanese military slavery from the eighteenth to the twentieth century.' In L. Archer (ed.), *Slavery and Other Forms of Unfree Labour.* London: Routledge.

Johnson, D.H. 1989. 'The structure of a legacy: military slavery in Northeast Africa', *Ethnohistory* 36 (1): 72–88.

Johnson D.H. 1991. 'Criminal secrecy: the case of the Zande secret societies', *Past and Present* 130: 170–200.

Johnson, D.H. 1994. *Nuer Prophets: a History of Prophecy from the Upper Nile in the Nineteenth and Twentieth Centuries.* Oxford: Clarendon Press.

Johnson, D.H. and D.M. Anderson 1995. 'Revealing prophets (introduction)', in D.M. Anderson and D.H. Johnson (eds), *Revealing Prophets: Prophecy in East African History.* London: James Currey.

Jorgensen, J.J. 1981. *Uganda, a Modern History.* London, Croom Helm.

Jung, C.G. 1983 [1963]. *Memories, Dreams, Reflections.* London: Fontana Paperbacks.

Junker, W. 1890. *Travels in Africa during the Years 1875–1878,* 3 vols. Trans. A.H. Keane. London: Chapman & Hall.

Kabera J.B. and C. Muyanja 1994. 'Homecoming in the Luwero Triangle', in T. Allen and H. Morsink (eds), *When Refugees Go Home.* London: UNRISD/James Currey.

Kimbrough, R. (ed.) 1988. *Heart of Darkness: Joseph Conrad* (Third Norton Critical Edition). New York: W.W. Norton.

King, A. 1970. 'The Yakan cult and Lugbara response to colonial rule', *Azania: Journal of the British Institute of History and Archaeology in East Africa* 5: 1–25 .

Kiwanuka, Semakula. 1979. *Amin and the Tragedy of Uganda.* Munich and London: Weltforum Verlag.

Kleinman, A., V. Das and M. Lock (eds) 1997. *Social Suffering.* Berkeley and London: California University Press.

Kokole, O.H. 1995. 'Idi Amin, "the Nubi" and Islam in Ugandan politics, 1971–1979', in

H.B. Hansen and M. Twaddle (eds), *Religion and Politics in East Africa*. London: James Currey.

Konczacki, J.M. (ed.) 1994. *Victorian Explorer: the African Diaries of Captain William G. Stairs 1887–1892*. Halifax, Nova Scotia: Nimbus Publishing.

Kopytoff, I. (ed.) 1989 [1987]. *The African Frontier: the Reproduction of Traditional African Societies*. Bloomington and Indianapolis: Indiana University Press.

Kujo, Doka Ali (n.d.) 'The coming of Islam', unpublished typescript.

Kyemba, H. 1977. *State of Blood: the Inside Story of Idi Amin*. London: Corgi Books.

LaCapra, D. 2001. *Writing History, Writing Trauma*. Baltimore and London: Johns Hopkins University Press.

Langlands, R.W. 1962. 'Early travellers in Uganda: 1860–1914', *Uganda Journal* 26 (1): 55–71.

Lanning, E.C. 1954. 'Sultan Fademulla Murjan of Aringa', *Uganda Journal* 18 (2): 178–80.

Leopold, M. 1999. '"The war in the North": ethnicity in Ugandan press explanations of conflict, 1996–97.' In T. Allen and J. Seaton (eds), *The Media of Conflict: War Reporting and Representations of Ethnic Violence*. London and New York: Zed Books.

Leopold, M. 2001. '"Trying to hold things together": international NGOs caught up in an emergency in North-Western Uganda, 1996–97', in O. Barrow and M. Jennings (eds), *The Charitable Impulse: NGOs and Development in East and North East Africa*. Oxford: James Currey.

Leopold, M. 2003. 'Slavery in Sudan, past and present', *African Affairs* 102 (409): 653–61.

Lindqvist, S. 1997 [1992]. *Exterminate all the Brutes*. London: Granta Books.

Listowel, Judith. 1973. *Amin*. Dublin and London: IUP Books.

Locke, J. 1988. *Two Treatises of Government* (ed. P. Laslett). Cambridge: Cambridge University Press.

Loro, M. 1971. 'Pre-colonial history of the Kakwa of Northern Uganda'. Undergraduate dissertation, Dept. of History, Makerere University, Kampala.

Low, D.A. 1988. 'The dislocated polity', in H.B. Hansen and M. Twaddle (eds), *Uganda Now*. London: James Currey.

Lulua, Odu. 1996. *A Short History of the Lugbara (Madi)*. Arua: Lugbara Literature Association.

McConnell, R.E. 1925. 'Notes on the Lugwari tribe of Central Africa', *JRAI*. 55: 439–67.

McCracken, J. 1997. 'Terence Ranger, a personal appreciation', *Journal of Southern African Studies* 23 (2): 175–85.

MacGaffey, J. 1991. *The Real Economy of Zaïre: the Contribution of Smuggling and Other Unofficial Ativities to National Wealth*. London: James Currey.

McGregor, J. 1985. 'Marketing in Yei River District', in K. Wilson, J. Mcgregor and J. Wright, *The Lutaya Expedition; a Report on Research in Yei River District*. Occasional Paper No. 1, Refugee Studies Programme, University of Oxford.

MacKenzie, J.M. 1988. *The Empire of Nature: Hunting, Conservation and British Imperialism*. Manchester: Manchester University Press.

McNeill, W.H. 1995. *Keeping Together in Time: Dance and Drill in Human History*. Cambridge, Massachusetts: Harvard University Press.

Malkki, L.H. 1995. *Purity and Exile: Violence, Memory and National Cosmology Among Hutu Refugees in Tanzania*. Chicago and London: University of Chicago Press.

Mamdani, M. 1976 *Politics and Class Formation in Uganda*. New York and London: Monthly Review Press.

Mamdani, M. 1983. *Imperialism and Fascism in Uganda*. London: Heinneman Educational Books.

Martin, D. 1974. *General Amin*. London: Faber & Faber.

Matatu, G. 1974. 'Amin', *Africa Magazine* No. 37, September, p. 70.

Maxwell, D. 1999. *Christians and Chiefs in Zimbabwe: a Social History of the Hwesa People, c1870s–1990s.* Edinburgh: Edinburgh University Press for International African Institute.

Mazrui, A.A. 1975a. 'The resurrection of the warrior tradition in African political culture', *Journal of Modern African Studies* 13 (1): 67–84.

Mazrui, A.A. 1975b. *Soldiers and Kinsmen in Uganda: the Making of a Military Ethnocracy.* Beverly Hills/London: Sage Publications.

Mazrui, A.A. (ed.) 1977a. *The Warrior Tradition in Modern Africa.* Leiden: E.J.Brill.

Mazrui, A,A. 1977b. 'The warrior tradition and the masculinity of war', in A.A. Mazrui, (ed.), *The Warrior Tradition in Modern Africa.* Leiden: E.J. Brill.

Mazrui, A.A. 1977c. 'Religious strangers in Uganda: from Emin Pasha to Amin Dada', *African Affairs* 76 (302): 21–38.

Mazrui, A.A. 1988. 'Is Africa decaying? the view from Uganda', in H.B. Hansen and M. Twaddle (eds), *Uganda Now.* London: James Currey.

Meagher, K. 1990. 'The hidden economy: informal and parallel trade in Northwestern Uganda', *Review of African Political Economy* 47: 64–83.

Middleton, J.F.M. 1953. 'The social organisation of the Lugbara of Uganda.' D.Phil Thesis, University of Oxford.

Middleton, J.F.M. 1954. 'Some social aspects of Lugbara myth', *Africa* 24 (3): 189–99.

Middleton, J.F.M. 1955a. 'Notes on the political organisation of the Madi of Uganda', *African Studies* 14 (1): 29–36.

Middleton, J.F.M. 1955b. 'The concept of "bewitching" in Lugbara', *Africa* 25 (3): 252–60.

Middleton, J.F.M. 1955c. 'Myth, history and mourning taboos in Lugbara', *Uganda Journal* 19 (2): 194–203.

Middleton, J.F.M. 1958. 'The political system of the Lugbara of the Nile-Congo divide', in J.F.M. Middleton and D. Tait (eds), *Tribes Without Rulers: Studies in African Segementary Systems.* London: Routledge & Kegan Paul.

Middleton, J.F.M. 1960a. *Lugbara Religion: Ritual and Authority Among an East African People.* London: Oxford University Press for the International African Institute.

Middleton, J.F.M. 1960b. 'The Lugbara', in A.I. Richards (ed.), *East African Chiefs.* London: Faber.

Middleton, J.F.M. 1962. 'Trade and markets among the Lugbara of Uganda', in P. Bohannan and G. Dalton (eds), *Markets in Africa.* Chicago: Northwestern University Press.

Middleton, J.F.M. 1963. 'The Yakan or Allah Water Cult among the Lugbara', *JRAI* 93 (1): 80–108.

Middleton J.F.M. 1966. 'The Resolution of Conflict Among the Lugbara of Uganda', in M.J. Swartz, V.W. Turner and A. Tuden (eds), *Political Anthropology,* Chicago: Aldine Publishing.

Middleton, J.F.M. 1969. 'Conflict and variation in Lugbaraland', in M.J. Swartz (ed.), *Local Level Politics: Social and Cultural Perspectives.* London: University of London Press.

Middleton, J.F.M. 1970a. *The Study of the Lugbara: Expectation and Paradox in Anthropological Research.* New York: Holt, Rhinehart and Winston.

Middleton, J.F.M. 1970b. 'Political incorporation among the Lugbara of Uganda', in R. Cohen and J. Middleton (eds), *From Tribe to Nation in Africa: Studies in Incorporation Processes.* Scranton, Pennsylvania: Chandler Publishing.

Middleton, J.F.M. 1971a. 'Prophets and rainmakers; the agents of social change among the Lugbara', in T.O. Beidelman (ed.), *The Translation of Culture: Essays to E.E. Evans-Pritchard,* London: Tavistock Publishers.

Middleton, J.F.M. 1971b. 'Some effects of colonial rule among the Lugbara', in V. Turner (ed.), *Colonialism in Africa 1870–1960*. Cambridge: Cambridge University Press.

Middleton, J.F.M. 1982. 'Lugbara death', in M. Bloch and J. Parry (eds), *Death and the Regeneration of Life*. Cambridge: Cambridge University Press.

Middleton, J.F.M. 1985. 'The dance among the Lugbara of Uganda', in P. Spencer (ed.), *Society and the Dance: the Social Anthropology of Process and Performance*. Cambridge: Cambridge University Press.

Middleton, J.F.M. 1992 [1965]. *The Lugbara of Uganda*, 2nd edn. Fort Worth: Harcourt Brace Jovanovich.

Middleton, J.F.M. and D.J. Greenland 1954. 'Land and population in West Nile District, Uganda', *Geographical Journal* 120 (4): 446–57.

Moore, E.D. 1931. *Ivory, Scourge of Africa*. New York and London, Harper & Brothers.

Moorehead, A. 1960. *The White Nile*. London: Hamish Hamilton.

Morphy, H. and F. Morphy 1984. 'The "myths" of Ngalakan history', *Man* 19: 111–32.

Moyse-Bartlett, H. 1956. *The King's African Rifles: a Study in the Military History of East and Central Africa, 1890–1945*. Aldershot: Gale & Polden Ltd.

Museveni, Y.K. 2000. *What is Africa's Problem?* Minneapolis: University of Minnesota Press.

Mutibwa, P. 1992. *Uganda since Independence: a Story of Unfulfilled Hopes*. London: Hurst and Co.

Nalder, L.F. (ed.) 1937. *A Tribal Survey of Mongalla Province*. London: Oxford University Press for International Institute of African Languages and Culture.

Nzita, R. and Mbaga-Niwampa. 1995. *Peoples and Cultures of Uganda*. Kampala: Fountain Publishers.

Obbo, C. 1988. 'What went wrong in Uganda?' in H.B. Hansen and M. Twaddle (eds), *Uganda Now*. London: James Currey.

O'Connor, A. 1988. 'Uganda: the spatial dimension', in H.B. Hansen and M. Twaddle (eds), *Uganda Now*. London: James Currey.

O'Fahey, R.S. 1973. 'Slavery and the slave trade in Dar Fur', *Journal of African History* 14 (1): 29–43.

O'Fahey, R.S. 2002. '"They are slaves, but yet go free": some reflections on Sudanese history', in Y.F. Hasan and R. Gray (eds), *Religion and Conflict in Sudan*. Nairobi: Paulines Publications Africa.

Okot p'Bitek. 1989. *White Teeth*. Nairobi, Heinemann Kenya.

Oliver, R. and G.N. Sanderson (eds) 1985. *Cambridge History of Africa Vol. 6 (1870–1905)*. Cambridge: Cambridge University Press.

Pain, D. 1975. 'The Nubians, their perceived stratification system and its relation to the Asian issue', in M. Twaddle (ed.), *Expulsion of a Minority*. London: University of London: Athlone Press.

Parkin, D. 1966. 'Urban voluntary associations as institutions of adaptation', *Man* (ns) 1 (1): 90–95.

Payne, L. 1998. *Rebuilding Communities in a Refugee Settlement: a Casebook from Uganda* Oxford: Oxfam UK.

Peel, J.D.Y. 1995. '"For who hath despised the day of small things?" Missionary narratives and historical anthropology', *Comparative Studies in Society and History* 10: 581–607.

Pieres, J.B. 1989. *Nongqawuse and the Great Xhosa Cattle-killing Movement of 1856-7*. Johannesburg: Ravan Press; Bloomington and Indianapolis: Indiana University Press; London, James Currey.

Pinter, H. 1978. *Betrayal*. London: Eyre Methuen.

Pirouet, L. 1988. 'Refugees in and from Uganda in the post-colonial period', in H.B.

Hansen and M. Twaddle (eds), *Uganda Now*, London: James Currey.

Pirouet, L. 1995. *Historical Dictionary of Uganda*. Metuchen, New Jersey and London: Scarecrow Press.

Posnett, R.N. 1951. 'Some notes on West Nile hills and history', *Uganda Journal* 15 (2): 165–76.

Powdermaker, H. 1962. *Copper Town: the Human Situation on the Rhodesian Copperbelt*. New York: Harper & Row.

Powesland, P.G. 1957. *Economic Policy and Labour: a Study in Uganda's Economic History*. Kampala: East African Institute of Social Research.

Pratt, M.L. 1992. *Imperial Eyes: Travel Writing and Transculturation*. London: Routledge.

Prunier, G. 1983. 'Le magendo', *Politique Africaine* 9: 53–62.

Ranger, T.O. 1999. *Voices from the Rocks: Nature, Culture and History in the Matopos Hills of Zimbabwe*. Oxford: James Currey.

Richards, A.I. (ed.) 1954. *Economic development and Tribal Change; a Study of Immigrant Labour in Buganda*. Cambridge: Heffer and Sons for EAISR.

Riches, D. (ed.) 1986. *The Anthropology of Violence*. Oxford: Basil Blackwell.

Ricoeur, P. 1998. *Critique and Conviction*. Cambridge: Polity Press.

Roberts, A.D. (ed.) 1986. *Cambridge History of Africa Vol.7 (1905–1940)*. Cambridge: Cambridge University Press.

Robinson, R. and J. Gallagher with A. Denny 1981. *Africa and the Victorians: the Official Mind of Imperialism*. London: Macmillan.

Roosevelt, T. 1926 [1910]. *African Game Trails: an Account of the African Wanderings of an American Hunter-naturalist*. New York: Charles Scribner & Sons.

Rowe, J.A. 1988. 'Islam under Idi Amin: a case of deja vu?' in H.B. Hansen and M. Twaddle, (eds), *Uganda Now*. London: James Currey.

Rupesinghe, K. (ed.) 1989. *Conflict Resolution in Uganda*. Oslo: International Peace Research Institute; London: James Currey; Athens: Ohio University Press.

Said, E.W. 1997 [1975]. *Beginnings: Intentions and Method*. London: Granta Books.

Sanderson, G.N. 1965. *England, Europe and the Upper Nile, 1882–1899*. Edinburgh: Edinburgh University Press.

Sanderson, G.N. 1971. 'The origins and significance of the Anglo-French confrontation at Fashoda', in P. Gifford and W.R. Louis (eds), *France and Britain in Africa*. New Haven and London: Yale University Press.

Saul, J.S. 1976. 'The unsteady state: Uganda, Obote and General Amin', *Review of African Political Economy* 5: 12–38.

Scott, J.C. 1976. *The Moral Economy of the Peasant: Rebellion and Subsistence in Southeast Asia*. New Haven, Yale University Press.

Seftel, A. 1994. *Uganda: the Rise and Fall of Idi Amin from the Pages of Drum*. Lanseria, South Africa: JRA Bailey Photoarchives.

Shiroya, O.J.E. 1972. 'The Lugbara of Northwestern Uganda: migration and early settlement', *Uganda Journal* 36 (1): 23–34.

Shiroya, O.J.E. 1984. 'The Lugbara states in the eighteenth and nineteenth centuries', in A.I. Salim (ed.), *State Formation in Eastern Africa*. Nairobi: Heinemann Educational Books.

Simpson, D.H. 1960. 'A bibliography of Emin Pasha', *Uganda Journal* 24 (2) 138–65.

Smith, G.I. 1980. *Ghosts of Kampala*. London: Weidenfeld & Nicholson.

Smith, I.R. 1972. *The Emin Pasha Relief Expedition 1886–1890*. Oxford: Clarendon Press.

Soghayroun, I. 1981. *The Sudanese Muslim factor in Uganda*. Khartoum: Khartoun University Press.

Southall, A. 1953. *Alur society: a Study in Processes and Types of Domination*. Cambridge: W.

Heffer & Sons.

Southall, A. 1954a. 'Alur tradition and its historical significance', *Uganda Journal* 18(2) 137–65.

Southall, A. 1954b. 'Alur migrants', in A.I. Richards (ed.), *Economic Development and Tribal Change: A Study of Immigrant Labour in Buganda*. Cambridge: Heffer & Sons for EAISR.

Southall, A. 1975. 'General Amin and the coup: great man or historical inevitability?' *Journal of Modern African Studies* 13 (1) 85–105.

Southall, A. 1977. 'The bankruptcy of the warrior tradition', in A.A. Mazrui (ed.), *The Warrior Tradition in Modern Africa*. Leiden: E.J. Brill.

Southall, A. 1980. 'Social disorganisation in Uganda: before, during and after Amin', *Journal of Modern African Studies* 18 (4): 627–56.

Southall, A. 1988. 'The recent political economy of Uganda', in H.B. Hansen and M. Twaddle (eds), *Uganda Now*. London: James Currey.

Southall, A. 1995. 'History and the discourse of underdevelopment among the Alur of Uganda', in W. James (ed.), *The Pursuit of Certainty: Religious and Cultural Formulations*. London and New York: Routledge.

Spear, T. 2000. '"A town of strangers" or "A modern East African town"? Arusha and the Arusha', in D.M. Anderson and R. Rathbone (eds), *Africa's Urban Past*. Oxford: James Currey.

Spencer, P. (ed.) 1985. *Society and the Dance: the Social Anthropology of Process and Performance*. Cambridge: Cambridge University Press

Stengers, J. and J. Vansina. 1985. 'Western Equatorial Africa, section B. King Leopold's Congo, 1886–1908', in R. Oliver and G.N. Sanderson (eds), *Cambridge History of Africa Vol. 6 (1870–1905)*. Cambridge: Cambridge University Press.

Stewart, P.J. and A. Strathern. 2002. *Violence, Theory and Ethnography*. London and New York: Continuum Books.

Stigand, C.H. 1914. *Administration in Tropical Africa*. London: Constable.

Stigand, C.H. 1923. *Equatoria, the Lado Enclave*. London: Constable.

Sunseri, T. 1997. 'Famine and wild pigs: gender struggles and the outbreak of the Maji-Maji war in Uzaramo (Tanzania)', *Journal of African History* 38: 235–59.

Taban, L.1 [*sic*] 1984. 'How to Maintain Refugees in your Midst for the Love of Humanity While the United Nations High Commissioner for Refugees Looks Over Kyber Pass and Doles Out Goodies to Afghan and Vietnamese Expatriates: A Spirited Diatribe.' Paper presented to University of Oxford Refugee Studies Programme Symposium, *Assistance to Refugees: Alternative Viewpoints*.

Taylor, A.J.P. 1950. 'Prelude to Fashoda: the question of the Upper Nile 1894–5', *English Historical Review* 65 (254): 52–80.

Thomas, H.B. and R. Scott. 1935. *Uganda*. London, New York, Toronto: Oxford University Press.

Thompson, E.P. 1991. *Customs in Common*. London: Penguin.

Tolstoy, L.N. 1957 [1869]. *War and Peace* (trans. R. Edmonds). Harmondsworth: Penguin.

Tucker, A.N. 1940. *The Eastern Sudanic Languages*. Oxford: Clarendon Press.

Turton, D. 1994. 'Mursi political identity and warfare: the survival of an idea', in K. Fukui and J. Markakis (eds), *Ethnicity and Conflict in the Horn of Africa*, London: James Currey.

Twaddle, M. 1972. 'The Amin coup', *Journal of Commonwealth Political Studies* 10 (2): 99–111.

Twaddle, M. 1989. 'Violence and rumours of violence in Uganda during the early 1980s', *Cambridge Anthropology* 13 (2): 28–44.

Twaddle, M. 1993. *Kakungulu and the Creation of Uganda*. London: James Currey; Nairobi, EAEP; Athens: Ohio University Press; Kampala: Fountain Publishers.

Van Gennep, A. 1967 [1911]. *The Semi-scholars* (ed. and trans. R. Needham). London: Routledge & Kegan Paul.

Vansina, J. 1990. *Paths in the Rainforest: Toward a History of Political Tradition in Equatorial Africa*. London: James Currey.

Vico, G. 1984 [1948]. *The New Science of Giambattista Vico*. Unabridged translation of the Third Edition (1744) by T.G. Bergin and M.H. Fisch. Ithaca and London: Cornell University Press.

Virmani, A.M. 1996. 'The resettlement of Ugandan refugees in Southern Sudan, 1979–86', PhD dissertation (field of Political Science), Northwestern University, Evanston, Illinois.

White, H. 1987 [1980]. 'The value of narrativity in the representation of reality', in *The Content of the Form: Narrative Discourse and Historical Representation*. Baltimore and London: Johns Hopkins University Press.

White, L., S.P. Miescher and D.W. Cohen (eds) 2001. *African Words, African Voices: Critical Practices in Oral History*. Bloomington: Indiana University Press.

Wilson, Rev. C.T. and R.W. Felkin. 1882. *Uganda and the Egyptian Soudan*. 2 vols. London: Sampson Low, Marston, Searle & Rivington.

Wilson, T.M. and H. Donnan (eds) 1998. *Border Identities: Nation and State at International Frontiers*. Cambridge: Cambridge University Press.

Woodward, P. 1978. 'Ambiguous Amin', *African Affairs* 77 (307): 153–64.

Woodward, P. 1988. 'Uganda and Southern Sudan', in H.B. Hansen and M. Twaddle (eds), *Uganda Now*. London: James Currey.

Woodward, P. 1991. 'Uganda and Southern Sudan 1986–89: new regimes and peripheral politics', in H.B. Hansen and M. Twaddle (eds), *Changing Uganda*. London: James Currey.

Wright, M. 1995. 'Maji-Maji, prophecy and historiography', in D.M. Anderson and D.J. Johnson (eds), *Revealing Prophets: Prophecy in Eastern African History*. London: James Currey.

Wrigley, C. 1988. 'Four steps towards disaster', in H.B Hansen and M. Twaddle (eds), *Uganda Now*. London: James Currey.

Youngs, T. 1994. *Travellers in Africa: British Travelogues, 1850–1900*. Manchester and New York: Manchester University Press.

Zartman, I.W. (ed.) 2000. *Traditional Cures for Modern Conflicts: African Conflict 'Medicine'*. Boulder and London: Lynne Rienner Publishers.

Index